HAY LIBRARY
WESTERN WYOM

D0467539

RUSS

ESTONIA LATVIA LITH. BELARUS RAINE

RUSSIA

TIC SEA

POLAND

Vistula
Warsaw Krakow

Oder

CZECHO SLOVAKIA

Elbe Berlin Bratislava

GERMANY

Danube Vienna

Linz AUSTRIA

ankfurt Main Nuremberg
Regensburg

Speyer Venice

elle Strasbourg Rhine SWITZ. ITALY Po

Nancy
Toul Milan

Geneva

Rhone

From the collection of
Janette E. Horst
1921 - 2000

Andorra

SPAIN

Through *Europe* at Four Knots

A Tale of Boating Mayhem and Family Adventure

Les Horn

INTERNATIONAL MARINE / McGRAW-HILL
*Camden, Maine • New York • San Francisco • Washington, D.C.
Auckland • Bogotà • Caracas • Lisbon • London • Madrid
Mexico City • Milan• Montreal • New Delhi • San Juan
Singapore • Sydney • Tokyo • Toronto*

International Marine

A Division of The McGraw-Hill Companies

10 9 8 7 6 5 4 3 2 1

Copyright © 2000 International Marine

All rights reserved. The name "International Marine" and the International Marine logo are trademarks of The McGraw-Hill Companies. Printed in the United States of America.

Library of Congress Cataloging-in-Publication Data
Horn, Les.
    Through Europe at four knots : a tale of boating mayhem and family adventure / Les Horn.
        p.   cm.
    ISBN 0-07-136137-5
        1. Boats and boating—Europe. 2. Horn, Despina. 3. Horn, Charles. 4. Horn, Victoria. I. Title

GV776.42.H67 2000
797.1'24'092—dc21   00-026694
[B]

This book is printed on 50 lb. Sebago

Printed by R. R. Donnelley & Sons, Crawfordsville, IN
Design by DeDe Cummings
Endpaper maps by Matt Kania
Production management by Dan Kirchoff
Edited by Jon Eaton and Jennifer Comeau

THIS BOOK IS DEDICATED TO MY CREW:

THE BEST FOR'ARD HANDS A SKIPPER
EVER FATHERED.

AND THE MOST FORGIVING
MATE A MAN EVER LOVED.

There is pleasure in the pathless woods,
There is rapture on the lonely shore,
There is society where none intrudes,
By the deep sea and music in its roar.

-LORD BYRON

ALEA JACTA EST

SPECIFICATIONS

LOA	7.31 m (24 ft.)
Beam	2.60 m (8 ft. 6 in.)
Draught	0.8–2.0 m
	(2 ft. 7 in.–6 ft. 6 in.)
Displacement	2100 kg
Sail Area	21 m² (226 sq. ft.)

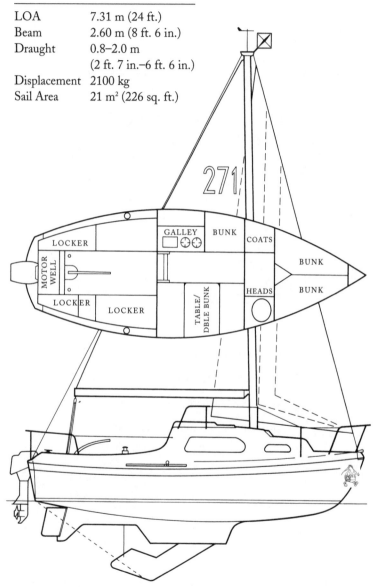

Contents

a thank you

To all family and friends for the support and encouragement they have given during the saga of getting our tale to print, in particular Lewis and Meloni Karai, whose idea it was that I begin to write. And to Graham Townsend, Teresa Horn, Pauline Syrett, and Rowan Emberson, who in spite of their busy lives proofread my first attempts with such diplomacy that I was always keen to try again.

And most important, to the one who made it all possible: my wife, Despina, whose ruthless editing not only kept my feet on the ground, but kept this book to a manageable size.

to the reader

This is an account of a family odyssey through the inland waterways of Europe, an adventure that took us from the River Thames in England to the Aegean, via the Danube and Black Sea. The tale portrays the idyllic bliss of exploring a hidden France and Germany, as well as the infectious desperation of a decayed and collapsed Eastern Bloc.

The threads of our story, the whys and wherefores of how we

came to make such a journey, wove themselves from a long string of coincidence and circumstance. Therefore, by way of introducing the crew, here are a few of the fateful waypoints that led us on the road to Troy, as it were.

I was born in Aberdeen, Scotland, and my wife, Despina, in Alexandroúpolis in northeastern Greece. Having met in London, we started our life together by emigrating to the liberating space of New Zealand. Four years later, our son, Charles, arrived, followed a couple of years after by our daughter, Victoria. The years passed, and although we were happy in our adopted home, Despina and I would often daydream of one day visiting the "old country." Though bound by the same sentiment, we each had our own romantic notions of our return. Whereas her flight of fancy modestly saw her presenting her offspring to their grandparents in Greece, my fantasies took us sailing over the sparkling blue Aegean.

Slowly, these longings jelled to a determined resolve to make our dreams come true. Oddly enough, the first practicality was setting the deadline for the end of the enterprise. We would have to be back and settled in New Zealand in time for Charles to start his secondary school education at the age of thirteen. From there we worked backward, allotting one summer for the Aegean and one summer for Scotland. And as we had previously traveled between the two by road, rail, and air, we decided that this time we would sail, which of course added another summer. So we would need to begin our expedition when Charles was ten and Victoria eight. It is the pleasures and trials of this summer's passage—an uncertain venture at best, since the navigable highway we followed was not even completed until two years after our tranist—that spawned the following yarn.

One
The Offing

HAVE YOU EVER WONDERED why the actual date of Easter keeps changing from year to year? It wasn't until that holy week dovetailed so neatly with our departure plans that I realized the answer: it's fixed according to the phases of the moon—Easter is always after the first full moon following the first day of spring. Of course, this has always been obvious to the intrepid yachties of England's east coast, who use the high spring tides to get afloat and spend their Easter up the proverbial tidal creek.

I say *intrepid* because Essex folklore as professed by "Old Bill," our village neighbor, ordains, "Ye be sure of rain, Easter weekend!" As for us, though we were far from fearless, it was a case of "Rain or shine, *alea jacta est*—the die is cast!". . . And it fell spinning, along with Easter 1990, in a whirlwind of hectic activity in the second week of April.

At the beginning of the enterprise I had made a list of all the things we needed to do. Then, full of self-satisfaction at my efficiency, I ticked off the first few as they were done. But it wasn't long after pressing these start buttons that I, like the sorcerer's apprentice, awoke to find that my dream child was developing a ruthless momentum of its own. If for some reason I couldn't clear an item quickly enough, I felt as though *it* was ticking *me* off.

First we had to complete the boat's winter refit before it was put back in the water or, more to the point, in the mud of low tide, because on the salt marsh creeks of the Thames estuary, Sod's Law dictates, "A vessel settling out of reach in a sea of mud will align itself with the owner's free time."

Up until the final few weeks I had enjoyed every minute of working on her. Making that broken, jammed, loose, missing, torn, and gouged old boat whole again and, above all, making it *our* boat, was deeply satisfying. I even enjoyed the weekend drive to the yard, which never failed to produce a warm glow of anticipated adventure. I felt these were the steps to make a dream come true. But farther down the track I could see that time was running out. Some jobs had to be given greater priority, others just patched up to make do, and yet others set aside.

The most frustrating aspect of the travel arrangements was our dealings with the tottering Eastern Bloc countries. Our applications for permission to pass through what remained of their "people's paradise" seemed, in the spirit of the times, to have gone west.

Repeated telephone calls to the various embassies either remained unanswered or were immediately cut off. Undaunted, I eventually got through to the Bulgarian embassy, where a cautious voice whispered through the phone to inform me, "Strange things are 'appening in my country" and "Zee rules are being changed every day," which we found out later was true, and not always for the better. The voice advised me to leave everything until we reached Vienna or Belgrade and "bother" the embassy staff there. I decided the same would do for the others, and gave up.

Throughout this first testing brush with the Big Brothers of the East, there was one glimmer of light. Ironically (in view of more recent history), it was Yugoslavia. They replied promptly, with our stamped, self-addressed envelope cleverly taped to a larger parcel containing lots of information on cruising the Adriatic, although it was their stretch of the River Danube we had asked to sail down. They saw no objections to our passage as long as we reported to the local police station every night. And with British passports, we wouldn't even need a visa.

The last terrible bane, and in many ways the most unsettling for us as a family, was throwing off the shackles of modern urban living. The children finished the school term and said good-bye to their friends, a sad business that Victoria found impossible to do without a flood of tears. Then came the part that brought the tears to my eyes: the struggle to clear all our accumulated furniture and household junk from the two-bedroom house we had rented in the Essex village of Wickford for the past seven months.

Before leaving New Zealand we had boarded up all our furniture in one bedroom, sold or lent anything that didn't fit, and rented the house. The same golden rule applied now: "If it can't go in, it goes out." Only this time our tiny, 7-meter sailing boat set the limit.

Our rental house was now an empty shell that echoed every sound. Despina and I spent our last night on our camper-van squabs (long seat cushions) on the lounge floor, but I was too excited to sleep and lay awake all night. Although my body was exhausted, my mind raced on. I was deliriously happy and couldn't stop thinking about the journey before us. I reviewed all our preparations and made mental notes of things I had to do the next morning. Then, in the early dawn hours, I experienced a most profound change of mood, brought on perhaps by the starkness of the room in the dim twilight. Doubts crept in and I began to torture myself with thoughts of what I might be letting my family in for.

There were so many unknowns about the route we had chosen. Would we be able to handle the currents on the Rhine and Upper Danube? Were the Main–Danube and Constantsa canals even open? Would we be allowed to pass down the full length of the Danube and Black Sea coast? How difficult would it be to get supplies in Eastern Europe? Would there be more violent revolution or civil war? Could we and our boat endure if things went seriously wrong?

Feebly I tried to rationalize: sure, there were risks, and inevitably we would find ourselves in tight spots. But I would be careful, as I had always been, to minimize them; Despina would make doubly sure of that. And life is just as fragile no matter where or how one chooses to live it. I burrowed my head deeper in the philosophic sands, but it didn't pacify my fears and I sank farther into depression.

In a cold sweat, I watched through closed eyes a terrifying preview of some of the most dreadful boating accidents imaginable. Soon frightened half to death, I had to make a conscious effort to pull myself together. I spent the rest of the slow daybreak patching up my shattered nerves and trying to convince myself of the positive aspects of the trip. Our children had been brought up in a sheltered paradise, and this experience was sure to broaden their horizons and nourish their cultural roots.

Turning to the more pleasant things in life, I became aware of Despina deep in uproarious slumber, as if rehearsing a chain-saw solo in an empty Carnegie Hall. Now here lay another unknown: Despina, my long-suffering mate, had done a tremendous amount of work on the boat. In spite of her misgivings about the trip, she was committed to giving it her best shot. However, I knew there was a limit to how many "boating problems" she was prepared to take. She had jumped ship twice already during my checkered sailing career.

The more memorable of these was in our early courting days and on the auspicious occasion of my first command under sail, when in mutinous indignation she clambered ashore and marched back to the Serpentine boat-hire kiosk to await my somewhat erratic return from my first solo voyage. Poor Despina, she was to have much cause to rue waiting that fateful day. On the other hand, it was painfully evident she wasn't losing sleep over any imaginary trials ahead.

Despite the early morning chill, it was light enough to get up. I had done a good job of counseling myself and was again eager to get going, for this was the day I had been waiting for.

Everyone was to have a bath, because we suspected it might be some time before we could enjoy that luxury again. Little did we know that it would be all of twenty months, and that in the interim I would have ample occasion to ponder the significance of my last conventional bath.

As I lay quietly soaking my already bruised body, a section of five ceramic tiles quite mysteriously dislodged themselves from the wall and collapsed into the bath, striking me with shocking carnal accuracy. After I recovered my composure, the Viking in my blood warned that this was an ill omen on such a day. But the canny Scot that pulses there, too, urged that there was no time for such superstitious nonsense. The landlord was coming at 9:30 A.M., and if I wanted the deposit refunded I would need to repair the wall quickly.

Fortunately, owing to their soft landing, none of the tiles had broken, but now it was urgent to get bathing over with so the cement would have time to set.

Finally, attended by a satisfied landlord and a small gathering of well-wishing neighbors, we piled into our much-beloved camper-van, Rolo, for the last time and drove it and the last of our furniture to their new owners. To compound our sense of loss, we now had to hail a taxi to take us to the Wat Tyler Maritime Park.

The chatty cab driver, keen to engage in polite conversation, asked Despina what her plans for the day were. Not wanting to go into great explanations, she replied evasively, "It's a nice day for a walk." This seemed to do the trick, for being familiar with the Canvey Island walkways, he kept this general topic going until he pulled up at the park. Before allowing the taxi to move off, Despina cast about in a bit of a panic, asking, "Who has taken the coat hangers?" (She had found them during the last-minute check of our camper-van.) The driver, finding them under the front seat, said, "Here, luv, are these what you're looking for?" Despina exclaimed in relief, "Ah, yes! I mustn't forget those." Looking searchingly at her, the driver replied, "No luv, that really *would* spoil your walk, like!"

Returning to us in fits of laughter, Despina remarked, "He would have thought me completely nuts if I had told him I was off to sail through Europe to Istanbul, instead of just potty for taking coat hangers for a walk."

All the problems of the past weeks seemed suddenly to lift from our shoulders as we walked through the park to the waterfront. But beyond the warm, intimate shelter of the trees, a chill southwest wind swept in across the vast open marshlands of the Thames estuary. It had a cooling effect on my emotions, too. I became aware of a surrounding void. We had well and truly burned our bridges, and with the van gone I felt our world drawing in around the limiting space of our boat.

Like our feelings, Holehaven Creek is an area of marked contrasts, not everyone's idea of a stunning landscape, but I liked it. To my eyes, even the encroaching industrial display of petrochemical refineries and trooping power pylons intensified the stark, timeless beauty of the drying creeks and marshes. The incoming tide snakes its way northwestward from the Thames, allowing the local fleet of some thirty colorful craft to float for about two hours every high spring tide.

We picked our way down a narrow pontoon and over a wide motor launch to our boat, a Vivacity 24. A mountain of supplies, hurriedly unloaded the day before, had to be stowed. As Despina packed things away, Victoria meticulously recorded each item and thus became our enthusiastic quartermaster. In the months to come we only needed to ask where something was for her to rush off and consult her files.

So engrossed was she in her task that she never felt the slight giddiness beneath us as the boat began to settle in the mud. Charles, on the other hand, sat alert and shot worried glances at us to see if we were alarmed every time the boat sank a little more. In a very short time she bedded down firmly and evenly.

By evening, with the kerosene lamp lit, our immediate surroundings positively glowed. We quite forgot we were sitting in a hole of liquid mud on the edge of a dark and lonely marsh.

Unfortunately, our departure was to be delayed the following morning as the weather deteriorated. Cold, showery westerlies made our plastic-covered boom tent gasp and crackle in the sudden blustery assaults. Charles and Victoria busied themselves decorating their forward cabin: Peter Rabbit and Victoria Plum to starboard and heraldic shields and Doctor Who to port.

We considered picking up a swinging mooring farther down the creek, but our present berth was both comfortable and convenient, with a freshwater faucet by the pontoon, a clean toilet block not too far away, and a handy boat chandler where I bought some last-minute spares, although I hadn't been a very good customer in the past. In a bid to cut costs, most of our gear was secondhand or adapted from less durable alternatives I had found in local hardware stores.

We could also let the children loose in the park between showers to burn off their plentiful excess energy. This had been their playground during the months I had worked in the boatyard, and they had had many weekends to explore the enchanting forest paths and learn the history of the area. One tidbit they brought back was that the park was named after Wat Tyler, a local man who led the Peasants Revolt of 1377. After marching on London the protesters successfully put a stop to the dreaded Poll Tax. We were all familiar with the issue because our stay in Britain had coincided with widespread protests at the reintroduction of the tax.

Eventually, our departure was hastened by the intervention of two individuals. One was the park warden, who with an urgent harassed air voiced his concern that we might miss the spring tides and end up marooned and squatting for two weeks in his marina. Apparently a council by-law prohibited boat owners from staying overnight on their vessels.

It was late at night when I came face to face with the second individual. Before settling down to our illicit slumber, I poked my head round the end of the boom tent to check our mooring lines. There, stretching up on its hind legs from the adjacent motor launch, was a large, inquisitive rat. Thankfully, it got as big a fright as I did. Yes, we would definitely be leaving the next day.

Departure day dawned with a strong southwest wind and the odd drizzle patch. All that was required was the tide to jack us free from the mud that threatened to keep us hostage. Unfortunately, a customs officer with hostage-taking in mind arrived just before high tide. He meticulously checked the boat papers and had us in a panic when repeated radio checks failed to confirm us as a local vessel. But eventually he let us be, and we later heard that a large drug haul was made on a yacht returning here after an Easter smuggling trip to the Netherlands.

A rising tide is the time for action on the East coast salt marshes. Several boat owners appeared, and I was soon involved in hauling off a cabin cruiser that was blown aground near us with engine trouble. Then, with the brave crew standing by, ready for anything, it was our turn to perform.

On the third pull our 10-horsepower outboard motor roared into life and then settled down to a steady purr. Despina released the mooring lines for Charles and Victoria to gather in, while I asked the skipper of the yacht that was boxing us in to take our stern line, to help spring us round him into the teeth of the strengthening wind.

All seemed set, but when I tried to back up, the motor kept jumping out of the reverse-lock, throwing the propeller out of the water with a dreadful scream. A little vexed after four attempts, I pressed the bucking motor down with all my weight and steered back around the stern of the small yacht.

We pivoted into the channel on the taut spring line, and as it slackened I shouted to the attentive skipper to release his end. He began to fumble and tug at the three or four granny knots he had tied around the cleat. I desperately worked the motor to try to maintain our position, but the boat was blown swiftly sideways and landed back on the mud, broadside on, and stuck fast.

What an appalling start! I watched the flustered skipper as he finally tugged our stern line free and tossed it overboard in a climactic flourish as if it were a venomous snake. Within minutes the warden appeared with a press-gang of six strong fellows to the rescue. A line was passed from our bow, and with the crowd all pulling from the end of the pontoon, we were soon dragged round to point out to the channel. With all hands standing on the port gunwale, I gunned the motor forward, and amidst a muddy swirl and hearty cheers from ashore we were free.

Recovering from the embarrassing shame of our inglorious start, Despina went below to winch down the centerplate, the metal centerboard that would allow us to navigate shallower waters. Somewhat tersely I was given the news that the "unmentionable" centerplate was jammed in the up position. To my dismay, it seemed all her predictions about the boat were coming true right from the start. While looking for a suitable boat, Despina had fallen in love with a more spacious MacWester 26. Although the sale eventually fell through, it somewhat colored her appreciation of the many advantages the Vivacity possessed over the heavier Mac-Wester with its fixed bilge-keels. I was condemned like a latter-day Macbeth with the prophecy, "With an outboard motor and an 'unmentionable' centerplate, all we will have on this trip will be trouble!" (In the event we would have trouble enough, but it would be these two much-maligned attributes that would get us out of it.)

With the wind blowing 20 to 25 knots I decided to test the steerage and the power of the motor by turning a few times into the wind. The maneuvers cheered me up by proving that I could rely on the cast-iron stub keel, which encased the centerplate, to reduce leeway to a great extent by itself. We followed the creek as it turned south and prepared to lower the mast for our next trial, a

Thames flood barrier. This looks like a bridge, with a huge concrete gate suspended above the channel that can be lowered in an emergency.

After a brief struggle, Despina released the stainless steel pin that secured the forestay at the bow. This allowed a long aluminum scaffolding tube, attached to the foot of the mast, to act as a lever that I could work by means of a block and tackle from my position at the tiller. We shot under the barrier with meters to spare.

A quick reversal of the operation had the mast up again, and back in the cockpit Despina beamed with triumph at something going right for a change.

The creek broadened and twisted to the east as we neared the oil refineries at Coryton. Just before the junction with the Thames, we picked up a vacant mooring—after the fourth tilt. The wind was howling, and an attempt to put up the boom-tent had to be abandoned for fear of damaging it.

But the humbling first day of our maiden voyage was not over yet. Just as we climbed into bed, our cozy little ship touched down on the mud, and an hour later it began to tip precariously to port. I lay half awake, tentatively pressing myself against the squabs that formed our double bunk on the converted Formica-topped dining table. Then suddenly Despina, sound asleep as usual, turned over, causing both us and the squabs to slither off the slippery table and land in a heap in the narrow gangway. There, jammed in like a set of wooden blocks in a parquet floor, we spent the rest of the night waiting for the tide under the flickering light of a nearby refinery flare-stack.

Out of this nocturnal upset came the happy discovery that, with the tiller lashed over in the strong ebb, the boat actually steered itself off the shore. Of course, when the tide turned, the boat did the opposite and gently nudged against the mud bank, but we never felt it and always remained afloat and upright.

Easter Sunday produced a good supply of hidden chocolate eggs as well as vicious hail storms, which left icy white drifts in all the corners of the cockpit.

Between showers I worked on the motor and discovered a broken rubber suspension mount, the probable reason for the reverse-lock misbehaving the previous day. I wired it up temporarily and drilled the tilt bracket to accommodate a locking pin (an adapted 100 mm nail), which would ensure we could use reverse gear at maximum power.

During the squalls, I would sit in the cabin and dictate my log to one of my young scribes, who reluctantly shared the duty on alternate days as part of their "boat-school-work." They would scribble and rub away, while keeping a sharp weather eye out. As soon as the squall passed, they would encouragingly announce, "Oh, look—it's stopped raining!"

Our plan was to take a shake-down cruise up the River Thames before heading across the English Channel on the next neap tide, so we were in no hurry to stir farther in the freezing cold. Moreover, there were still plenty of outfitting jobs to do. One was adapting a box I had already made to double as a workbench and raised seat for the helmsman. It was now required to function as a toilet step for the shorter members of the crew, who were having difficulty climbing aboard the thunder box.

When we bought the boat, the previous owner had recently installed a brand-new porcelain sea toilet. To my horror, while I was cleaning the hull for painting, the fiberglass patch over the old toilet exit just came away in my hand. On the delivery trip, Charles and I had sailed up the Thames with a 50 mm diameter hole through the bottom of the boat, covered by a square of loose fabric held in place by only a few barnacles.

The regulations for the nontidal stretch of the Thames require all craft to be equipped with chemical toilets. Therefore, when I repaired the old exit properly, I disconnected the sea toilet and adapted the same porcelain bowl to fit tightly over a plastic bucket. Using the standard chemicals, it served the purpose and was only a little "high" in purely the lofty sense, which was now remedied by the versatile "poo-dium."

Another refinement I tried to introduce for our sanitary requirements was the use of the bailer bucket (dubbed the pee-bailer for P.R. purposes). This was in a bid to reduce the number of times we had to empty the loo, but it met with universal disapproval. By setting an example, I thought I would soon coax my prudish crew around to seeing the practical side of my suggestion. But that afternoon my subtle campaign of crew education took an unfortunate turn.

I had been delayed reinstalling the depth-sounder because I had misplaced the brown paper bag containing the plug fittings. At last it came to light, and I prepared to do the needful in the cockpit. But before starting the fiddly job in the cold, I decided to satisfy another need.

Thus engaged with the bailer in the stern, I happened to turn my head just in time to see the open paper bag, with my fittings, being sucked up from the cockpit floor and carried overboard by a spiraling wind eddy. I stood incredulous (and immobile) as it gently alit on the surface of the water. It seemed to hover there like a buoyant Welsh coracle, tantalizingly near the side of the boat.

Galvanized into desperate action, I shuffled forward to the rescue. As quickly as I could, I set down the bailer and, snatching up a boathook, lunged at the bag. Though stretched right over the cockpit coaming, I barely managed to touch the balloon-shaped bag, before—with spinnaker set—it sailed away out of reach. Exasperated, I stepped back and got stung to the heart when my left foot didn't quite fit inside the versatile bailer. I collapsed, a broken man, to suffer the howls of derision from my delighted crew.

Refusing to give up, I launched the inflatable dinghy and, with a following westerly, set off to salvage the paper bag. It had run aground on the far side of the creek, but I was hopeful that the fittings were still inside, because the bag's gaping mouth still floated above the waterline. Carried swiftly across the creek I hardly had time to row before I was alongside the muddy bank and peering sadly into the empty, soggy void. Stoically accepting defeat, I pushed off to return to the fold, but my torments were not yet over. As seems always the case with boating problems, they have a spiteful habit of conspiring with others.

This was the first time I had used the inflatable. Pressing against the strong wind, I found that each time I pulled hard on the oars, they would pop out of the rowlocks. This was aggravated in part by the port side apparently wilting due to loss of air. By the time I had reset the oars, the dinghy would be blown back on shore. It was no use. A pair of closed-eye rowlocks joined the new depth-sounder plug on my shopping list.

By tying the oars to the rowlocks with the painter, I was able to shape a slanting course across the creek, which took me about 100 meters downstream of the boat. I was only able to make up this ground by hopping from the lee of one moored vessel to the next. On the last sprint Despina, who was waiting anxiously on deck, threw me a line and fished me in, bless her heart. Deciding not to tempt providence any further, I retired below to regain my composure in readiness for the start of our expedition up the Thames on the next day's flood tide.

Two
The Thames: "But Isn't France the Other Way?"

18 APRIL

THANKFUL TO SEE THE LAST OF THE CREEK, we all smiled under our woolen hats when the boat's bow dipped purposefully as it breasted the stronger motion of the flowing Thames.

Drawing only 0.8 meter, I had resolved to keep to the shallow water, well outside the shipping channel on the downbound side. Like a pedestrian on a busy road, I preferred to face the oncoming traffic instead of risking them coming too close from behind.

Once Despina had sorted out which rope was which, she hoisted both mainsail and working jib and we savored the blissful moment of reverberating peace when the motor was cut. Thus settled with a fair wind and tide, we pressed on up a river that once was plowed by Celt, Roman, and Viking prows.

And so it was time for "history lessons"—and Native Americans were at the top of the list for today. My two pupils scanned the riverbank for Gravesend, where according to their book the legendary Pocahontas died in 1617.

Despina, on the other hand, was not impressed with the barricaded waterfront and disappeared below looking for trouble: "The 'unmentionable' centerplate is still jammed," she interrupted, "and the paddle log doesn't work!" After all the wallowing in the mud we had done, it was no surprise the log had seized up, but I had promised Despina that the motion of the boat would cause the troublesome centerplate to drop.

There was motion enough as we learned to cope with gushing millrace-like tides and the raking wash of passing ships. We had a rude awakening next morning when we and our "bedroom" did a monstrous "Fosbury flop." I had packed away all loose gear for just such an eventuality but had overlooked the wooden chopping board, stowed alongside the cookstove. It flew out across the cabin and with a loud *whack* chopped a bit of fiberglass out of the wall just inches above Despina's head.

Under a heavily overcast sky, we again rode the flood up through the bowels of London. Lying at either side of the river at Beckton and Crossness are the two largest sewage farms in Europe, where over 1 trillion liters of sewage are treated every day. Charles and Victoria looked suitably impressed when I boasted that I had contributed to this great achievement some twenty years earlier: as a young draftsman, I worked on enlarging the macerating station at the works.

The parklike spaces in this stretch of the river provide a sanctuary for a variety of bird life. Our two young ship's ornithologists were given the task of identifying them from their wildlife reference books.

Then it was time for the ship's radio ham to contact the Thames Flood Barrier Control with the VHF radio. As it was the first time I had used my new, phonetic call sign, I started off by mixing up my Golfs with my Foxtrots. This was instantly swooped on by the two young ship's mistake hawks, who simultaneously tried to prompt me as to the correct sequence—until I didn't know if it was a Foxtrot or a Tango I was doing. Eventually, after threats of making "contact" with them, I was granted peace to stutter through the procedure and gave the controller our estimated time of arrival.

Like the heads of gigantic knights in armor, the row of flood-barrier piers reared up out of the gray horizon. It certainly fired the children's imagination, and after they consulted the ship's library their parents became proficient in both the mechanics of the barrier and the statistics of the floods prior to its construction.

Sweeping north, we entered London's decaying docklands. Suddenly, in that eerie canyon of hollow buildings, we were shocked rigid by an explosion of harsh roaring noise. Then, like a wild bull entering an arena, a large hovercraft, enveloped in spray, shot out from around the hidden bend at Bow Creek. It skidded broadside on, as if out of control. When it was only 15 meters away its stern swung past in a scything sweep as it slithered to a quivering halt. It happened so quickly that all I managed was to instinctively shut the throttle, which just added the "sauce" to the sitting duck.

A little unnerved, Charles pointed to a sign that proclaimed this forsaken corner to be the London hoverport. Its seeming attempt at a body-slam on us turned out to be the standard docking procedure after the tight bend—executed, of course, with the usual ferry-pilot panache.

Rounding the side of the Isle of Dogs we entered Greenwich Reach. On the skyline stretched the rigging-draped masts of the *Cutty Sark*, the famous Scottish-built tea clipper, now a dry-docked tourist attraction. In front of the landing stages was a confused melee of large tourist ferries. Like predatory fish, they jostled for positions alongside to spawn another wave of tourists ashore. After our recent fright, we had no desire to join such a bullying free-for-all. The weather also was beginning to look dreary, so we decided to leave the visit until our return passage.

North round Limehouse Reach we passed through the kind of landscape one could imagine left after a nuclear holocaust. Abandoned, and in varying stages of demolition, lay Surrey docks. Slowly they were being smashed apart to make way for the trendy tower block developments we could see rising up from the surrounding industrial devastation. Turning west into the Lower Pool we saw the narrow entrance to the Regent's Canal, which passes north through London and joins a waterway system that could have led us to the north of England if our boat had been only a hand's width narrower. Then in short succession we came across two more engineering marvels: first the Brunels' Thames tunnel, the first ever to be driven under a river, then the first of the Thames bridges, a symbol of London itself—Tower Bridge.

The ship's researchers were at work again, gathering information on the succession of bridges that have spanned the river since Roman times.

We had to wait an hour, by an isolated pontoon, for the lock gates of St. Katharine's Yacht Haven to open. Once inside our first-ever lock, Despina and I were forced to stand in the rain while manning the shortening ropes as we rose up to the level of the inner dock. Standing on the streaming deck, I could feel the cold rainwater trickle back up my arms. I wasn't cheered any when told that it was going to cost us £20 to sleep in our own boat that night. As another icy drop leapt inside my armpit, I began to muse that it must be situations like this that give the cynics the view of boating as "standing under a cold shower ripping up bank-notes."— ". . . while being ripped off" seems more to fit the bill these days!

At the far end of the lock, a crimson miniature version of the Tower Bridge mechanism slowly lifted, causing an instant traffic jam along the quayside road. The inner lock gates opened for us to move out and, like huge jaws, the two bloodred halves of the bridge dropped impatiently, just missing our mast. We made a mental note to beware of the teenage lockkeeper on the way out.

The rain stopped as abruptly as it had started, leaving us to glide over the millpond surface of the small inner haven. Tall, overbearing buildings enclosed the deep pool and dimmed the natural light. From every high ledge draining rainwater still cascaded down, giving us the impression of entering a peaceful subterranean grotto. We slipped into our designated berth under the towering concrete and glass facade of the ritzy Tower Hotel.

Our young sailors insisted that we explore Tower Bridge by night. Its massive floodlit towers and their pointed Gothic architecture transported them to fairyland. The ghostly white glow of the Bloody Tower's castle walls, on the other hand, set the scene for all sorts of horror stories about prisoners and executions.

When your immediate living space is surrounded by brackish water and is confined to a 7-meter boat, you develop a genuine appreciation for good shower and laundry facilities—or even just running hot water. At St. Katharine's we indulged and spoiled ourselves until 11:30 the following morning, the earliest that the lock could operate.

Once through the lock we moored back at the pontoon to unstep our mast. Typically, there was a lot more wash-making traffic rushing about us, just when such a tricky job needed to be done. There were a few close calls in which wrenches and rigging screws had to be pounced on before they rattled off into Davy Jones's toolbox.

We cast off into the impetuous flood tide late in the afternoon. Pressed by a cool following wind, we surged between the massive stone piers of the bridge, and in a brief, mouth-gaping second the tall towers went spinning past overhead. To our right, Traitor's Gate slipped by as we entered the City itself, dominated by the great leaden dome of St. Paul's. London Bridge crept past, followed by a dark forest of other bridge canopies, all ringing to the weird calls of Charles and Victoria as they tested the echo. Apart from the odd tourist ferry we had the river to ourselves.

Sweeping round King's Reach to the south, we approached Waterloo Bridge. The black hull and tall masts of Captain Scott's Polar Expedition ship, H.M.S. *Discovery*, stood out from the row of other old-timers ranged alongside the tree-lined embankment. This sight reminded us of our happy New Zealand dinghy-sailing days on Lyttelton Harbour and our favorite picnic spot on Quail Island where, in a beautiful pine-fringed cove, one can still see the animal quarantine huts that Scott had built to house his doomed ponies.

Under the bridge leading into Charing Cross Station, we all ducked with fright as the thunderous rumble of a train passed over our heads. Then it was the graceful vaults of Westminster Bridge, with the glorious statue of Queen Boudicca (also known as Boadicea) and her daughters on their bronze war chariot. Fired up by their heroic pose, Despina climbed up on the cabintop, armed with not a spear but a camera, to snap the crew as we made a triumphant sortie past the Houses of Parliament.

As if summing up the wonderful kaleidoscope we had just passed through, we ducked under the statue-bedecked Vauxhall Bridge, sculptured to depict all the classical virtues of London.

After seeing so many of London's enduring landmarks, we were amazed to find one in the haggard throes of demolition: the last word in pollution until Chernobyl, Battersea Power Station—

a gigantic brick box with huge smokestacks at each corner. We could still remember, from living here seventeen years ago, the burning taste of sulfur from the monster's persistent attempts to choke us and the other residents of Putney. I have to admit, I was well pleased to see that old dragon getting its comeuppance.

Finding a berth for the night started to present quite a problem in the tidal river. A deep-water jetty would be ideal, but every pier we came across had a large, threatening notice board: "Private Property—Keep Off."

Our problem was solved when we spotted a huge green unattended barge moored in Chiswick Reach. This was used by the Port of London Authority as a garbage skip (dumpster) for flotsam collected on the river.

After a week aboard I was attuned to every noise and motion of the boat, becoming instantly alert to the change in the boat's straining stance at the turn of the incredibly strong tides. This forced me to get up several times during the night to check the mooring lines and their canvas parceling, which were all showing signs of heavy wear.

As everyone else was staying in bed, I killed the time before breakfast with a very rewarding rummage in the skip. The noise of my booty coming aboard soon roused the crew from their bunks. Despina was not amused at her husband's "blatant scavanging!" That is, until Charles piped up, "That's why we call him *skipper*, isn't it?"

These grumblings from below decks were soon quelled by an amazing change in the weather. At long last the sun was shining in a clear blue sky as we traveled up through yet another Constable painting, complete with tree-clad reaches, white swans, and fine old houses fronting the river. At the entrance to the Grand Union Canal a narrow-boat (riverboat) with twining rose motifs brightly painted on every conceivable spot added the final brush strokes.

With the flood still running we scooted through the Richmond weir gates and were at Teddington Lock on the turn of the tide. Here was our first encounter with the most striking quality of the canalized part of the river: the leisurely pace of life. The elderly lockkeeper issued our canal license at the cost of £15, which allowed us to navigate on the river for a maximum of fourteen days; after that we would incur costly registration.

With this formality completed he went on weeding the flower bed by the office while waiting for *Rose*, the painted narrow-boat, to chug up around the bend. Once she was inside, the lockkeeper sent us all up with the press of a button.

Emerging from under Kingston Bridge, we came upon the inviting scene of an English country pub that provided a row of large mooring rings along its river frontage. A large lunchtime crowd spilled out along the embankment wall, so we joined them, our legs dangling above our boat and two handles of English beer at our elbows.

I fell into conversation with two friendly young fellows who were interested in the boat. Responding perhaps to the effects of the beer and the oddly phrased question "Where do you hope to end up?" I replied with almost reckless abandon, "er . . . the French canals!" whereupon they both laughingly asked if I wanted any more crew.

When our handles were empty, it was time to be off. I had moored facing downstream, so with Despina pushing off hard at the bow, I helmed the boat round in a tight arc to head upstream again. Surprised at our maneuver, one of our spirited new friends called over, "But isn't France the other way?" Before waving goodbye, I made an exaggerated display of scrutinizing our chart and then turning it upside-down.

Next, Hampton Court Palace came into view—the little place by the river of that property-grasping megalomaniac Henry VIII, who picked it up for a snip of his executioner's ax.

Hanging all our car tires over the side, we tied up on two trees alongside the river bank and went for a walk around the magnificent grounds. Charles's diary tells only half the story:

> Saw 200 year old vine and got lost in the maze for 41 minutes, enjoyed myself!

We kept vigil by the gate among the throng of other wise parents who knew not to enter the "maze of mazes." Just as the attendant went off to rescue Charles, a loud rasping jet noise was heard in the sky overhead. The word went round like a ripple: "It's the Concorde!" Impulsively I stepped back to see over the foliage and was instantly tripped by a low wire-hooped fence, which sent me sprawling on my back in the flower bed.

I had always been unlucky with the Concorde. Back in the early seventies, I had tried to be one of the first to see it flying and hitchhiked via Paris to Toulouse to see the French prototype being tested. The day before my arrival at Toulouse, it was flown to Paris, to do a few laps of honor around the city.

We arrived at the next lock to find the lockkeeper purposefully putting on his jacket. He shouted apologetically that he had closed up and was going off duty. With our passage thus seemingly blocked, we turned back downriver to find a mooring for the night.

A squat, black police launch passed slowly up the river. It turned around, and when it was some 5 meters from us, its blue strobe light suddenly started to flash. Then, with a wailing shriek of the siren, the whole front of the launch reared up out of the water and leapt forward in a swelter of white foam. In the same instant our boat seemed to drop like a stone from beneath us, to land with a shuddering crash on the riverbed. With my hand clutching the tiller to catch my balance, I felt the vibration of a renting *crack* as something split on the rudder below. Glaring round in disbelief, I saw the two sniggering faces of the policemen glancing back over their shoulders to view their handiwork.

Our boat was left pitching in a vortex of muddy water and foul language. Recovering from the trauma, I tested the rudder. It appeared to function all right, but now the boat would definitely have to be hauled out for damage inspection.

While I was still smoldering, a cabin cruiser came on the scene and headed straight for the lock. To our surprise the skipper began locking himself through. The lockkeeper apparently had assumed we knew that the public are allowed to operate the locks manually outside normal working hours—we live and learn.

The American skipper, who came over to cruise the Thames on a regular basis, showed me the ropes while I helped with the donkeywork at the wheel winches.

With my newly acquired knowledge under my cap, we meandered a further 50 kilometers up the river, reaching our highest point at Maidenhead. We had numerous occasions to stop along high, grassy banks with an array of fine stout trees to tie our mooring lines to. We would let the children romp free in the woods, where Charles would soon be Davy Crockett and Victoria the last of the Mohicans. Time for us to relax and wash down our lunch with a can of McEwan's.

Mooring for the last night outside Skindle's Hotel, we caught up with Chris and John, in-laws who live in the area. Chris had just arrived back from visiting her daughter (married to my cousin) in New Zealand. News from home is always welcome . . . but New Zealand sounded so far away. Were we homesick? No, not yet. A wonderful adventure was ahead of us and we were only just beginning.

Three

Maidenhead: What Goes Up Must Come Down

24 APRIL

MAIDENHEAD WAS AS FAR UP the Thames as our time would allow. Our sights were set in the other direction, where we had a long schedule of appointments with the impatient tides.

On our downstream passage we again sailed past the medieval silhouette of Windsor Castle, somewhat spoiled by an incongruous tower crane sprouting vertically from the battlements. Then it was on to Runnymede, the place where the Magna Carta, that milestone of Western democracy, was signed in 1215.

An educational trip to the rotunda-style monument and the John F. Kennedy Memorial provided classroom material for our children. They were happy to gather information from books and tourist brochures, copy from inscription and information boards, and ask questions to fill in gaps. Neither of us remembered enjoying schoolwork as much.

We hadn't gone far next morning when we were surprised to hear people calling to us from the riverbank. It was John and Julie of the Thames cruiser *Sunfish*, whom we had met while mooring at Staines a few days before. They waved us over to moor at the bottom of their riverside garden, unspoiled by the omnipresent Private Property notice. We spent a very pleasant hour with them, which included a tour of their printery. Our youngsters would spend the next couple of weeks improving printing techniques in their forward cabin.

When I mentioned our need to beach the boat, John told me of an embankment wall the locals used in the tidal basin at Teddington Lock. I intended to inspect the rudder and implement an idea I had for levering down the jammed centerplate. This involved attaching a rope to the bottom of the plate, which could then be threaded up the center of the mast-lowering scaffolding tube. By sliding the tube down the rope, I hoped to exert a downward pull on the plate when levering on the round bilge of the hull.

Before I could get started, I had to deal with a rather difficult lockkeeper, a small, embittered man, self-condemned to a life of dealing with "the public!" He could *tell* I was trouble at first sight but had dealt with my sort before. "No!"—the place was not suitable for yachts. I walked round to check and thought we could manage. "No!"—we could not pick up a vacant mooring in the basin, they were all private property. "No!"—we could not anchor there either, there were "unexploded bombs from the last war lying about the riverbed." "Well," if I was going to be obstinate, he gravely announced, he wouldn't be held responsible. And of course there would be a charge of £2 to dry out against the weir embankment.

At six the following morning, the last of the water drained away from the rudder. Although the bottom corner had been broken off, I was pleased to find no other damage and just filed the jagged edge fair. To my surprise the log paddle wheel rotated freely, indicating that its problems lay inside. Turning my attention to the centerplate, I passed the blade of my handsaw up the inside of the case and couldn't find anything jammed in it.

The trouble, it seemed, was around the pivot area, which I found impossible to get at. Trusting to luck, I shackled my prepared lanyard to an existing hole in the toe of the plate. It was remembering this mysterious drill hole that had led me to the tube-lever idea.

With these jobs done, I got out the paints and touched up our logo and the boat's name on the bows. It was difficult at first to think of the boat by its name. With so many teething problems it had become almost a dirty word within Despina's hearing—used at my peril. We had the name before we got the boat: *Alea Jacta Est,* the die is cast. It had been chosen as a statement of our resolve and commitment to see the project through. The fact that the boat in which we intended to descend the swift Rhine and Danube currents came furnished with only a 10-horsepower outboard made the name seem even more apt. There would be no turning back. Yet in time, even Despina's high-pitched rendering of "this blasted boat" would mellow to *Alea.*

The 7-meter spring tide that floated us off caused quite a bit of flooding downriver. One car that had been left parked on the embankment displayed only its roof above the water level. We decided to ride out this fearsome tidal range, rafted up to another driftwood barge for the night. Our first attempt at going alongside developed into a desperate tug-of-war with the tide. It was no use, the crew was forced to let go of the mooring warps. Leaving Charles and Despina marooned atop the big green barge, we were swept away.

Now it was Victoria's turn to scramble on deck and gather in the trailing lines before they could foul the propeller. On our second go, my new forward hand poised bravely in the bow and heaved the lines to the castaways, who with frantic haste made both bow and stern fast to secure us a safe berth.

A visit to Kew Gardens was on our list for the following day. Kew Pier lies several meters off and parallel to the shore, which made me think we would be able to moor behind it, out of everyone's way. There was only one snag: I hadn't allowed for these spring tides, and we touched bottom. This was disappointing, for with lunch already packed, we were looking forward to stretching our legs in the gardens.

The deserted pier was the only place a boat could moor, but with barbed wire and a chained lock on the gate, it didn't look as if we would be allowed to use it. However, on discovering that the padlock on the gate had not been fastened, we decided to seize the day. Quickly, we moored as close to the end of the pier as possible. Before abandoning ship I dropped the plow anchor down the side in case our lines were drastically interfered with. With 300 acres of garden wonderland to explore, we lost track of time. The newly opened, ultramodern Sir Joseph Banks house pleased us particularly, as our home in New Zealand is close to Banks Peninsula, named after the same botanist, who accompanied Captain Cook on his 1769 voyage. Victoria's diary sums it up:

Saw a video of things made from plants. There was a cotton plant with 'real' cotton hanging off. Went into a room covered with mirrors showing the forests being destructed! Fed a squirrel with some cookies, it liked them. Bought a card for my class. It was a lovely sunny day.

We returned to the pier in the late afternoon to find that *Alea* had company. A large tourist ferry was moored alongside the pier, and its agitated pilot was standing over the interloper—waiting? Deciding that discretion was perhaps the best course, we settled down to wait too—on Kew bridge. Ten minutes later, after a final brandishing glance at his watch, the pilot marched back, locked the gate, cast off, and was soon gone. Charles and I had to scale the barbed defenses to retrieve the boat. The girls crossed the bridge, and we picked them up at the opposite bank.

The next day was Saturday, April 28, and, unbeknownst to us, the day of the Hammersmith Rowing Regatta. We had arranged to rendezvous with two New Zealander friends at Hammersmith Bridge for the ride down through central London. We saw Ivor and Ruth waving from a jetty on the left bank as we ran foul of the many rowing sculls and their megaphone-wielding coaches, practicing for the events. It was no use pointing out that it was they who were on the wrong side of the river, for it only brought more amplified abuse.

Judging my turn across the river to cut in behind a rowing eight that was coming upstream, I was forced to dally halfway across because the oarsmen suddenly started a "stop—go" rowing technique that slowed them down. Now the other end of my original clear slot came charging downstream on us: two racing coxless pairs.

Both pairs had to perform the same braking maneuver to avoid running into us. Unfortunately, one of the girls was so intent on racing that she kept on rowing. This caused their scull to slew round and almost collide with the other coxless pair. Disaster was only averted by the rest of the rowers calling on her to stop. As if awakening from a trance, the dazed "gorgon" exploded in a maniacal tirade of foul language. She may well have been coxless, but she swore like a stoker's mate.

Eventually we pulled alongside the jetty to greet our new shipmates. There they were, cowed in a corner under the onslaught of the "keeper of the quay"—a little, nicotine-stained man who, speaking in rasping asthmatic gasps, asked us whether we could "read the Private Property sign."

It transpired that this cockney living on his wits was trying to extract a £3 embarkation fee. Nevertheless, faced by a united front of ancestral Scottish reticence, he relented and signaled Ivor and Ruth to board—gratis.

Leaving all the "aggro" astern, we made a fast passage downriver on the last of the ebb. Again it was a spectacular game of "I Spy" with the sights of London. This time my attention was caught by the thirty-five-hundred-year-old Egyptian obelisk, Cleopatra's Needle, which cost six seamen their lives on its voyage here.

At Southwark Bridge the low tide had revealed a muddy verge, where several wading searchers with metal detectors worked over the scene of last year's *Marchioness* tragedy, which claimed fifty-one drowned—a sobering reminder that collision on this river is a real danger. Then, thankfully, came a sight to commemorate a voyage with a happier outcome, the Mayflower Pub, built near the place where the famous ship set off for the Americas. Her captain is buried in the nearby riverside churchyard.

At Greenwich we moored at a deserted timber yard and spent the afternoon strolling around the crowded streets and parks. Chichester's *Gipsy Moth IV* is a sad fish out of water, prostituting itself for the tourist dollar.

The *Cutty Sark*, whose namesake was a harlot-witch, sits easier in her trade, excused by that dignity that makes the ship a classic. So with resignation we stood under Meg's tail and said good-bye to Ivor and Ruth, who were preparing for their own adventure through Europe, the hard way—by bicycle.

Back in the familiar waters of Holehaven Creek the next morning, we set about putting the tube-lever theory to the test. Whether or not we could force the centerplate down would decide whether we could carry on. Our only other alternative would be to have the boat lifted out and professionally repaired, which would most probably mean missing the favorable tides. At present they were ideal, working for us at each leg of the trip around the Kent coast and the Channel crossing itself. It would be weeks before they would be so accommodating again.

So, with fingers, legs, and eyes crossed, I lowered the tube down under the keel. Despina unwound the winch a fraction each time I put pressure on the lever. Little by little we managed to get the plate half down, giving us enough for sailing, and I was confident that it would soon slacken some more with the motion of the sea.

Before hauling the mast upright, I bolted the radar reflector to its top in preparation for running the gauntlet of the traffic in the shipping lanes. Soon we were transformed into a sailing boat again and slid away from the mooring at 4:00 P.M., again on the ebb tide.

Close-hauled, *Alea* leaned gently into a light easterly breeze. To the southeast the low-lying marshlands of the Thames estuary, the scene of so many of Charles Dickens's novels, were dominated by the huge concrete smokestack on the Isle of Grain.

Alea was sailing really well, and even when the wind dropped further, we were able to maintain our 4-knot cruising speed by changing the working jib for the larger genoa. Cutting through the Swatchway, we rounded Grain Spit. On our port beam lay the array of yellow marker buoys surrounding the wreck of the *Montgomery*, an American Liberty ship from the last war, still packed full of explosives. The corroded radio masts, careened awash, give a graphic enough warning to keep well clear.

Entering the Medway Approach Channel, I set tilt on a corkscrewing dash across the choppy estuary with the children perched up in the bows. There they whooped and yelled as if on a roller coaster, while their mum harangued them with her own graphic warnings of dangers.

Soon what looked like an impassable barrier of factories, wharves, and mud banks stepped aside, allowing us to pass up the gray alleyway of the Swale.

At Queenborough I tried another boat chandler for a plug for the depth-sounder. It was the same story: they would need to send to the manufacturer for a replacement. Not wanting to wait, I decided to tape the wires on directly. In 2 meters of water, the sounder was adamant there was 7 meters, and there it remained no matter what depth we were in.

The Kingsferry drawbridge stands astride the long narrow channel of the Swale. I saw the bridge start to rise as soon as we dropped the sails. Aiming the bow at the center of the opening I slowly motored forward, watching for the red signal light to change to green. As I drew nearer it became obvious that it wasn't going to change, and I started to turn away to starboard.

Suddenly the bridge-keeper stuck his head out of his control box window above and shouted impatiently: "Get a move on, I can't wait all day!" When I pointed out that the signal was still red he shot back in.

I should have completed the turn. Instead, I impulsively turned back. Caught broadside to the flood tide, which accelerated as it squeezed past the bridge piers, we were swept beam-on toward them. In the same split second, I gunned the motor and gave the tiller an almighty yank toward me. I could feel the mahogany stock bend with the force that pivoted the boat into the opening, missing the stone pier by a prayer. We were under and through in the blink of an eye, swept on but stunned.

The best medicine for a sailor's shattered nerves is the curve of a billowing sail. Under full therapy we surged southeast, on through the flat, reclaimed farmland of Kent. The Swale turns due east at the Lilies, requiring us to beat into the strong easterly wind. But at this point the strait broadens out, allowing longer tacks. With the depth-sounder still recording 7 meters, the exhilarating tacking across the shallow mud flats was too much for Despina's nerves. As she feared a grounding each time we closed with the shore, I was soon relegated to midchannel and the motor.

By dark we were anchored in the lee of low-lying Fowleys Island, and after a fine supper I settled down with the chart to plot the course for the following day's jaunt round the coast to Ramsgate.

Four
Misadventure off the Goodwin Sands

THIN BANKS OF WISPY WHITE MIST hung low over the creek when we got up at 5:00 A.M. on May Day. Despina hauled in the mud-caked anchor chain, exuding a babble of muttered curses that got worse by the meter.

With the "anchorhand-a-whey," I headed *Alea* east in the channel that the pilot book calls South Deep. I hadn't gone 50 meters when the boat slid to a halt and grounded. The price for getting off was for the centerplate to be raised. The protruding plate was our safety margin. As long as we could raise it, a gentle grounding in mud or sand was no great problem.

Afloat once more and with a strong ebb running, the boat needed to be held in one place while we went through the plate-lowering performance. Knowing I was risking trouble, I asked Despina to drop the anchor again. Of course, the mud in the Swale was all my fault.

We slowly eased ourselves round the island, west about, where we knew a channel existed. Just past Faversham Creek, where the channel turns northeast, a blustery 15-knot easterly sprang up, allowing us quickly to cover the 3 nautical miles to the Swale's eastern exit.

Just after passing the exit buoys we were approached from seaward by a man waving and shouting at us from a 4-meter open sailing dinghy. He arrived off our port bow in a dramatic flurry of crackling sailcloth and flaying ropes, and we both hove-to in the moderate short chop. He was a tall elderly man with long white hair plastered about his waxen face, which was framed in stark relief against the huge turned-up collar of an RAF greatcoat. A long multicolored scarf and woolen gloves with the fingertips missing completed his "escaped from Colditz" look.

Suddenly, he sprang up and through cupped hands called, in a pronounced public schoolboy accent, "Hello, where you heading, old boy?" as he himself headed for'ard, to tumble headlong into the bilges of the dinghy. We were thunderstruck and could only watch as he laboriously pushed himself back along the side deck, like a slowly closing concertina.

I called over, "What's the trouble?" To which he replied, "*Trouble?* There's no trouble, old boy, just wondered where you were heading." "He's drunk!" Despina hissed under her breath. Then, as if more proof was needed, he pulled out a half-empty bottle of whiskey and, smiling theatrically, offered to share what was left, if he could join us.

It would have been difficult enough for a sober young person to have made a safe transfer, let alone this pickled "old boy." I managed to persuade him that the best place for him was on land and that there was a warm pub waiting for him at Faversham. With the vision of this new utopia, he scrabbled and pulled at his sheets as the wildly swaying sails took him careering straight down the fairway.

East by Gore Channel, we rounded the North Foreland and noticed a marked improvement in the motion of the sea. It was 11:15 A.M., and the tide had just turned. At this point, it floods south from the North Sea to refill the English Channel.

The coastline from Margate around to Ramsgate is an abrupt broken edge of high, gray chalk cliffs that drop sheer to the rock-scoured shore. It was here that Dickens set the scene of his *Bleak House*, and well he might!

At 12:30 P.M., Despina breathed a great sigh of relief when she found herself safely inside the breakwater and under the lofty, hotel-filled facade of Ramsgate.

The next morning, while waiting for the flood tide to take us round to Dover, I set about patching the leak in the dinghy. Also waiting at the pontoon was a large French yacht bound for Dunkirk. While my glue dried, I went over to chat with the middle-aged skipper and his wife. They were not very forthcoming. I got the impression that either I had interrupted a domestic quarrel or they suspected I wanted to borrow something.

I tried to discuss my plan of turning south after the East Brake buoy and following the inside channel past the Goodwin sands. With a pained expression on his face, the husband replied dismissively, "I also." Getting the message, I returned to my own patch.

At 11:30 A.M., we got clearance to leave the harbor. Following about 200 meters behind the French yacht, we headed out along the dredged channel into a 12- to 15-knot easterly. Despina climbed up on the coach roof and raised the mainsail. Soon after passing the Dike buoy, the French yacht raised both sails, rounded a cardinal buoy to the right of the channel, and sailed off to the south. This maneuver caught me on the wrong foot, as we were sorting out a territorial dispute between the children.

Knowing that the French yacht was going our way, it was so easy to simply follow—a mistake. As *Alea* swept round the buoy, I watched the spectacle of foaming waves beating about its base but failed to check the top mark or question my surprise at the buoy's appearing so soon—a big mistake. Despina raised the jib, while I set *Alea* on course and sheeted in. Somewhat perplexed, I saw the French yacht 50 meters off our port bow—heading back north! A heated argument was going on in the cockpit, with arms being waved in all directions. No warning bells rang, so I dismissed their sudden about-face. Perhaps they had decided to take the shorter route to Dunkirk, around the outside of the Goodwins. I sailed on without checking my position—a bigger mistake.

Alea was bowling along over the turbid green sea on a steady beam reach. Although there was not a cloud in the sky, the eastern horizon was smudged out by a bright haze, and the sea breeze was cool. To the west lay the flat, featureless coast, dominated by the cooling towers of Richborough Power Station.

As the time for my first half-hourly position fix approached, I took a bearing on the cooling towers and the Ramsgate harbor light. But when I went below to check the chart, I was dismayed to find that the cooling towers weren't on it—only a water tower, 5 miles away at Deal. They were, however, marked in the pilot book, so with my dividers and after changing scales, I transferred their position onto the chart. This all took time, but finally I ruled my two position lines across the chart. The first line instantly told me we were in trouble; the second confirmed it. They crossed on the northeast corner of the Brake shoal, 1½ miles west of where we should have been.

I sprinted up the companionway steps, grabbed the tiller from Despina, and pushed it hard to starboard while frantically hauling in the mainsheet. Heeling over steeply, *Alea* careered round to port and immediately ran aground. The deck tipped forward as we came to an abrupt halt, then fell sideways again. We were all thrown sprawling across the cockpit and somehow momentarily held, like pins on a magnet, while the sea leapt about us in a mad frenzy. Suddenly, the hull lifted and lurched forward, galvanizing us into action. Despina rushed below to winch up the centerplate, while I scrambled back and started the motor.

I could feel the pounding and rolling on the keel diminish as the sails dragged us into deeper water. A short burst of the motor and we were free, heading east. We must have just clipped the edge of the shoal. If I hadn't turned when I did, we would have run square onto it. I called to Despina to try lowering the plate again; fortunately, it went down almost to its original position. Carefully, I reset a southeastly course to pick up the channel at the South Brake and West Goodwin buoys.

It was obvious by now that the French skipper and I had left the channel at Ramsgate, at the wrong buoy. But which one? It wasn't on the chart or in the pilot book—or so I thought, until I bent back the sides of the book and found the Quern buoy hiding in the center crease. Of course, this was no excuse.

At Deal the coastline is driven high above the sea again, on vertical white chalk cliffs. Here, we are told, Caesar landed to invade Britain in 55 B.C. Looking from the sea it is hard to believe he would have chosen such a place, especially after you have seen low-lying Pegwell Bay only 8 miles farther up the coast.

Soon after tying up at Dover we were boarded by Customs agents, who there and then cleared us for the next day's departure for France.

As a farewell to Old England we bought fish and chips, carefully budgeted to use up the last of our British currency, and climbed up to Dover's massive Norman castle. Under the stone battlements, with the panorama of the harbor and the strait spread out below us, we broached our heat-baked parcels. There wasn't a breath of wind and the sea lay calm, its vast sweep of blue flecked by the dark outlines of distant ships on the forbidding sea lanes. Far on the southern horizon, the evening mist hid tomorrow's destination.

Five
The Channel Crossing, "Hedgehog" Style

3 MAY

------->>-------------------------------

BEFORE BREAKFAST I WALKED OVER to the seafront to check visibility. The marine forecast had predicted 7-mile visibility, but I could see a veil of gray mist less than 3 miles away. Although it looked marginal at the moment, I felt confident it would improve, once the sun had worked on it a while longer.

As a safety measure I unpacked the dinghy and secured it along the port rail. My biggest fear of the crossing was being run down by a large ship. After our unsatisfactory trials at inflating the dinghy quickly, I decided to travel with one side already inflated so that in the event of a catastrophe it could provide the proverbial straw to clutch at. Despina took out her own insurance against disasters by giving the children half a seasickness tablet each and their life jackets to wear—in bed.

At 6:00 A.M., when the lock gate and bridge opened, we left

the inner dock in the company of another yacht. While it followed a pilot boat out, we moored by the quay to coax the centerplate lower. I was pleased when it moved right down with only a gentle pull. With it now hanging vertical, a second use for the attached lanyard came into play. By leading it forward and making it fast to the bow, I effectively locked the plate down. This was an added safety feature, as it would prevent the centerplate from falling back inside the hull in the event of a knockdown.

Just as I finished, I was startled by a sergeant major–type harbor officer, who shouted at me from the quayside, "Situation please!" It was a bit early in the morning for me to understand his clipped efficiency. When I asked what he meant, he was most put out and wanted to know why I hadn't followed the pilot boat, like the other yacht. Peeved, he explained that he would have to call the pilot back for us, as regulations stated that all vessels must be escorted from the harbor.

When our chaperon arrived, we followed meekly. In the narrow channel between the quays, the pilot launch, for no apparent reason, suddenly turned sharply to starboard and crashed head-on into the stone harbor wall. Passing close by its still-foam-churning stern, we were nonplussed to see the two officers rolling about on their seats in an uncontrollable fit of laughter. Not knowing what to make of their antics, we headed on out to sea, our nervousness forgotten in the puzzling hilarity of the moment. There was only a light 5- to 10-knot easterly and a nasty short chop slopping about. Despina, who was at the tiller, called me on deck to deal with our first collision course: a 12-meter yacht was drifting down on us as the lone skipper struggled to raise his sails. I slowed and went astern of him. It seemed typical for the only two boats on square miles of sea to be heading straight for each other.

Looking back at Dover a short time later, I was surprised that all I could see of it was the smudged outline of the western breakwater. I hurriedly took its bearing as it dissolved into the mist that was rolling in behind us. Using this and the only other visible landmark, a tall radio mast west of Dover, I got a good position fix. A quarter hour later, at 7:30 A.M., the radio mast had also disappeared. However, by dead reckoning, I judged we had reached the edge of the westbound shipping lane.

Because of the heavy traffic and the many collisions, the center of the Channel has been divided into two lanes that separate the traffic going in opposite directions, like a motorway. Ships traveling west use the lane nearest England, and traffic going east takes the one nearest France. Boats crossing the lanes must head across at 90° to the traffic flow, irrespective of tidal set. This regulation supposedly is policed with radar and spotter aircraft, and some offenders are prosecuted.

Mindful of this and a hundred other things, I twisted the compass ring to 135° and set tilt for France. As the wind was light, we motor-sailed at about 5 knots. If I had guesstimated correctly, as we pressed ahead, the ebb tide would carry us sideways to Calais.

The mist now completely surrounded us. Like the smoke from a damp scrub fire, it hung low, with the odd teased-out white wisp reaching up to the clear blue sky. We were traveling in the middle of a large arena of bright visibility that was miraculously staying with us as we moved forward.

Charles and Victoria joined us in the cockpit. Everyone looked plump and cheery, trussed up in their life jackets, prepared to follow the motion of the waves and enjoy the ride. It was the first time we had ever been completely out of sight of land. This gave us mixed feelings of immense freedom and uneasy isolation. Looking about her fog-encircled world, Despina remarked, with a brave smile, how solid *Alea*'s decks now seemed in the absence of terra firma. Left with only the "hope" of seeing land again, she was beginning to trust "this blasted boat" more than she had while it lay in the mud at Holehaven.

A dark shadow appeared in the murk off to port and quickly materialized into a large tanker. I held on course and thankfully watched its bulky image move across in front of us. Then another came into view, then another. Glancing over, I judged each one's position in relation to a point on *Alea*'s lifelines, then watched carefully. If the ships appeared to progress along the wire, I knew we were safe.

The second ship plowed on round, but the hazy form of the third one sat under the wire, a little behind our cabintop, growing clearer and bigger. Unless one of us altered course or speed, we were destined to collide.

It was a very one-sided game of chicken, and it was about egg-laying time. Throttling down, I disengaged forward gear and let the sails press us on at a more sedate pace. The merchant ship began to edge ahead, its rust-stained superstructure rearing up over our cabintop.

I switched off the motor several times to listen to the Varne foghorn lowing deeply in the mist to the west. I got a rough idea of our progress as the direction of its mournful groan passed farther astern.

The mist closed in to about 1 mile as we entered the eastbound lane. I had dabbled at the game of chicken in the first thoroughfare, but we were about to play nerve-racking hedgehog in the second.

It seemed we had struck the rush hour. Spread about on a broad front, a stark array of ships advanced on us from the west. Here the mist was a blessing in disguise, although I don't know what we would have done had it closed in on us completely. Conversely, had the visibility allowed us to see the full extent of the traffic, we would have no doubt turned back. As it was, the situation just developed about us and I was forced to make the best of it.

The memory of it is just a jumble of impressed images. A steady stream of huge ships passing in front as well as behind us. Letting fly the sails for the umpteenth time to lie hove-to in the churning slop. The sinister spectacle of a rusting steel-plated cliff face sliding relentlessly past less than 40 meters away. The mute presence of Despina, her knuckles white as she gripped the seat coaming beside me. And the most vivid of all, the unconcerned trust of our children as they played below with their toys.

Just as I thought I had passed being frightened half an hour before, we were assailed by the dreadful noise of an approaching hovercraft. Although hedgehogs don't lay eggs, the one I was playing nearly did. The amplified roar came up from the south and thundered on through the mist to our left. Thankfully we were not in its path. In fact, it never showed itself, but as I followed the direction of the sound, a blurred shadow caught the corner of my eye just astern of us. Turning round, I was confronted by a huge ferry overtaking us 100 meters off our starboard quarter.

Recovering from the initial shock, I realized that the sea-lane traffic was holding back to let the ferry pass. I'd never thought I would be thankful for being close to a ferry. Hurriedly, I increased speed to prolong the shielding effect it was providing us. The ferry pilot, who apparently had his own ideas about crossing the shipping lanes at 90°, was angling over toward Boulogne, which in fact helped shelter us a bit longer.

We returned a friendly wave to the ferry passengers and made our final dash for the "line." As if to make up for all the tensions of the crossing, out of the mist on our port bow materialized the entrance buoys to Calais harbor. The sense of euphoria was incredible. It was 11:15 A.M., and I felt as if we had just crossed the Atlantic.

With the French tricolor flying from our mast, we left the motion of the sea, not to feel it again for another six months. In the sleepy atmosphere of Calais harbor we picked up a vacant mooring to await a visit from Customs.

This was not only the day of my first Channel crossing, it was also my birthday. Clandestine preparations had already taken place, behind "closed washboards," for the double celebration. When all was revealed I was presented with a beautifully iced cake and a succession of gifts—it was magic!

We were somewhat disappointed that Customs didn't come to the party when their invitation, the requisite yellow flag, was flying so nicely from *Alea*'s crosstree. Tired of waiting, Charles inflated the dinghy so we could all go ashore to look for them. Entering an official-looking office on the quay, we found a round, agitated little man furtively shuffling the papers on his desk. Despina spoke to him in French, but ignoring her, he spat back at me in heavily accented English, "Why! Do you 'ave something to declare?" Taken aback, I had to admit that I didn't. Showing instant Gallic amazement, he jeered, "Well, why do you want the Customs, then?" In the face of such Voltairean logic, we could only beat a hasty retreat from our impatient mentor, tut-tutting either at his unruly papers or at us foolish foreigners. Somehow it was official, then—we had made it to France!

A peculiar sultry tranquillity hung about Calais, and something in the style of the buildings gave the air of moldering grandeur from some bygone era. We thought we had lots of time to sightsee, until I discovered that my watch needed to be put forward one hour to catch up with French time.

Back aboard *Alea*, we lowered the mast and stowed it on deck in double-quick time. At 7:00 we motored over to tackle our first French lock. Finding the first set of gates open, we nosed into the empty lock chamber and scanned about the top of the wall for a bollard to tie up to—there was none! We maneuvered close to a rusty ladder, and Despina nervously climbed up the 4-meter wall with our mooring ropes. The bollards she found there were too far away to be of any use to us, so retrieving the ropes, I looped them round a rung of the ladder. *Alea* was secure, but Despina, still atop the wall, felt far from it.

She feigned approaches from all angles in an attempt to come down the ladder before deciding I could pick her up somewhere farther along the canal. Not knowing quite what to expect in a French lock, I chided her to climb down. Against her better judgment she relented and, with an ill grace, allowed me to "talk her down." I told her to sit on the edge of the wall and let her legs dangle beside the ladder. She was then to turn round onto her tummy, but unfortunately she flipped over to the wrong side, away from the ladder. To her great distress, she found herself like a stranded whale, floundering half over the edge of the wall.

Needless to say, it was instant death—for me! Never was a husband or sailor lashed so mercilessly—thankfully, from the electrified air above. I encouraged her to try again, and she flopped over nearer to the ladder while I guided her feet onto the rungs.

Just as Despina stepped back on deck, a crowded English yacht came into the lock. The skipper appeared to have all his in-laws crewing for him and, surprisingly, he still had his mast stepped. They all seemed oblivious to the fact that there was a low, fixed bridge at the far end of the lock, so I mentioned it to their bow hand. Amid hoots of laughter the news was relayed back to the skipper, who shamefacedly had to back out of the lock.

When the end set of gates finally opened, the first set remained open too, because the tide had risen to the level of the canal. If only I had waited at the mooring, we could have just motored through the open lock and saved the temper of my birthday.

We ventured no farther but found a spot for the night under Calais's tower clock, France's equivalent of Big Ben. Presumably its clanging chimes went on all night, but we never heard anything after our heads hit the pillow.

Six
France Ahoy

THERE WAS NOT ANOTHER BOAT in sight as we headed inland. We had the Canal du Calais all to ourselves. I sat up on the podium, placed on the port cockpit seat, and steered *Alea* over the glassy, calm water.

After an hour, the combination of my improvised chair not having a backrest and the tiller not having an extension began to make me uncomfortable. I saved my leaden arm by tying a boathook to the end of the tiller. Soon this extension led to the solution to my back problem. Directing the end of the boathook forward, I climbed onto the cabintop. With my legs dangling inside the companionway hatch and my back cushioned against the handrail, I had found the perfect steering-*cum*-lookout post. Then came the ultimate in steering evolution: the autopilot. Placing the podium next to the tiller, Victoria, the keenest helmsman in the crew, could stand on it to see where she was going.

Exploring the French countryside, we turned up a narrow side canal to the village of Audruicq. Just inside the junction stood a bevy of anglers who immediately waved us back. "Impossible!" they cried, indicating how incredibly shallow the water was.

Smiling and nodding gratefully, we nosed slowly on through a delightful cacophony of French curses as they retrieved their lines. Of course we never touched bottom, and so learned to ignore similar advice volunteered by other fishing enthusiasts throughout the trip.

The turbid water of the canals teems with fish. The whole length of the canal system is dotted with the floating carnage exacted by the churning, barge propellers, yet despite these kills, *Alea's* hull often resounded with a loud *thwack* as a leaping fish bounced off.

After spending a peaceful night almost hidden in a tall reed bed, we headed on to join the River Aa. Stopping just before the town of Watten, we trooped off in search of Hitler's secret weapon. The Blockhaus, a V2 rocket site, had been recommended to us as "not to be missed." Despina asked directions from a tall middle-aged man sunbathing in his garden. Following three very athletic attempts to explain the route to himself as well as us, he decided it was easier to drive us there.

At breakneck speed he drove us through winding forest back roads, until suddenly we came to a skidding halt by a clearing. "Voilà!" he triumphantly announced, and there in front of us were the barbed-wire-laced gates of what looked like a run-down POW camp. Charles and Victoria ventured a "Merci beaucoup" before our good-natured chauffeur sped off in a cloud of dust.

We wandered over to an unconvincing replica of a German guard-post marked *billet* and paid our entrance fee. Before the ticket hatch was curtly guillotined closed, a woman's voice hissed from the dark interior that the tour couldn't begin for an hour. We didn't catch the reason for this but decided to have our picnic lunch in what looked like the reception area of Stalag Thirteen.

It turned out that the establishment was waiting for a busload of elderly French tourists to arrive. Once they all had their tickets, a quaking trumpet fanfare sounded over an ancient loudspeaker system. The tourist group fell silent and came to attention as a scratchy military tune started up. Apparently it was being played on a windup gramophone, for every time a young man tried to leave the kiosk, the record would begin to die. Wincing, Charles indignantly asked, "What's that?" When I whispered that I thought it was the Turkish national anthem, a dapper-looking gentleman in front of us turned and proudly announced in broken English, "Noaw! It iz zee March of zee Résistance." Suitably chastened, we stood at attention and behaved until the sound was abruptly cut off—the tour was ready to begin.

Our tour guide beckoned everyone to follow him into the forest. He was carrying a thick overcoat, which looked very odd in the sweltering heat. We laughed at this as just another feature of the loony organization that had monopolized this tourist attraction.

A short way along the track he stopped, and when we had all gathered round, he began a lecture on the site's history. After some prodding, Despina began to translate for us, but she was quickly shushed by a matron dressed in black. We stopped three more times but could see no significance in the chosen shady spots. The only thing I understood was his liberal repetition of "le Bum de Tall-Boy"—the code name for the heavy-penetration bomb designed by Barnes-Wallis of "Dam Buster" fame.

Then, growing regrets at having been sucked in by this amateur peep-show were dramatically expelled. Suddenly, the forest opened out and there, in a dazzling expanse of light and sky, towered the awesome spectacle of the Blockhaus. Like some featureless medieval castle, the gigantic block of weathered and bomb-damaged concrete stood surrounded by a weed-clogged moat. As we walked round the edifice in cowed silence, the imprint of the original timber molds seemed to bewail the tragedy of the slave labor that had placed them there.

Down in the bowels of the cold, dank labyrinth, our now "sensibly dressed" guide ran a flickering film of Von Braun's infamous start of the space age. Even the rash of goose pimples and chattering teeth couldn't detract from the amazing apocalyptic atmosphere of the place.

The other great climax of the tour was reemerging into the luxurious hot sun. The subdued procession of awed pilgrims spontaneously broke out in a gabble of noise as we all stamped and rubbed the heat back into our limbs. As well as making us feel like liberated captives, our subterranean chilling made us enjoy all the more the cross-country hike back to *Alea*.

Through the following week we seemed to lurch from one domestic crisis to the next. Despina jumped ashore into some long grass and got her legs badly stung with nettles. A day later—

crash!—she fell over in a lock and skinned her ankles. Then—*crack!*—she broke a tooth while eating crusty bread. Although only one suffered the physical pain, it led the rest of us to discover another facet to the saying "All in the same boat."

The week it took to cover the 240 kilometers to Compiègne was also a testing time in coming to terms with the French locks. On the Thames, the highest lift had been just over 2 meters, whereas here they were all around 4 meters, with one monster at Saint-Omer raising us over 13 meters. We soon discovered that they were not designed for small pleasure craft, with the vertical rows of bollards spaced 30 to 40 meters apart to serve the long barges. Fortunately, a metal ladder was nearly always provided, and we could secure *Alea* to the ladder and one bollard.

Although in time we were to pass locks twice its height, the lock at Saint-Omer was quite an experience. In addition to the unaccustomed height, the normal leaf gates were replaced by one lifting guillotine type. We were uneasy enough just entering the dark, slimy lock shaft, let alone passing underneath the shower of unwholesome canal water dripping from the raised gate.

Saint-Omer was one of the rare occasions we shared a lock with a French pleasure boat. Prior to this we had concluded that the only pleasures the French got from their canals were fishing and dumping garbage in them—but here was a family out for a Sunday jaunt. While the turbulent water flowed into the deep, echoing chamber, the skipper screamed and harangued his hapless teenage son manning their bow line. In the momentary lulls, the beautifully sweet voice of the mother would come to the boy's defense, only to be blasted by another earsplitting tirade. The incident stayed with us for the next few weeks, during which time we were careful not to outperform the French family scene.

A little north of the town of Béthune, I assembled our fold-in-half bicycle. Early next morning I set off in search of bread, petrol, and a collection point to dump our "household" rubbish. It was too early for the shops to be open, so I just cycled for miles through the cool, tree-lined country lanes.

The baker proved the hardest to find. Armed with my phrase book, I asked directions from an old man. Although French, he insisted on speaking to me in Dutch. Inevitably, he sent me the wrong way. Then I tackled a tradesman painting a house; to my dismay, he was Italian. All he was interested in was *balla*. He repeated the names of Italian towns and mimed a bit of nifty soccer footwork. I gathered he was asking which soccer team I supported. To humor him I said, "Aberdeen." Incredibly, he exploded with delight, as if he had just scored a goal, and shouted, "Dennis Law! Dennis Law!"—the name of an Aberdeen center-forward from thirty years before.

My quest ended when I approached an elderly woman sweeping the doorstep of what looked like a typical village house. Her daughter had to be called out to unravel the mystery of what I was after. To my astonishment, they both burst out laughing, linked arms, and did a little dance. Then, taking me by the hand, the jovial pair led me into the building. Voilà!—their family business: a bakery!

We turned off the Grand Gabarit into the Canal du Nord and came to grief in the lock at Moeuvres. At each side of *Alea* I had slung one of our two pile-mooring planks. This helped to protect the hull and seemed a convenient way to carry them. Soon after we entered the lock, the water began to swirl and tumble as it rushed in from the underwater sluices. As *Alea* rose, Despina and I quickly began to take it in turns to move our mooring lines up the ladder rungs. Suddenly, we felt the boat begin to tip toward the lock wall. My heart leapt when I looked down and saw the starboard plank caught in the lock ladder. Despina frantically called to the lockkeeper to stop, while I tried to kick the plank free. It was jammed solid and quickly disappeared below the rising water.

I scrambled to the companionway to get a knife and roughly brushed poor Charles off the cookstove, which he was clutching in order to pull himself up to the high side of the boat, now listing 40 degrees. Snatching up the bread knife, I bolted outside again. Despina was sprawled across the foredeck, desperately trying to claw herself over the rising port gunwale. The rope attaching the plank to the boat was so taut that it seemed I just touched it with the knife and it flew apart. With the sudden release of pressure, the boat shot upright, catapulting me back over the lifelines to land in a heap on the cockpit floor. Glancing up at the control tower, I saw the lockkeeper turn from the window and push his way through a press of people craning over each other for a better view of the show. Only now did he think of stopping the influx of water.

Reminded of my own duty by plaintive cries from the bow, I made my way forward, where I found the bottom half of my mate fighting desperately to keep from following her top half overboard.

After this incident I got rid of one plank and carried the other well inboard like the "old hands" do. There was still a lot to learn about life on the canals.

Our next lesson was to negotiate our first tunnel: a 4-kilometer-long rock-hewn gallery at Ruyaulcourt. We got the green light and entered the narrow cavern. At the beginning, with the closeness of the tunnel walls zipping by, it appeared that we were traveling dangerously fast, but after we eventually saw the pinpoint of daylight at the other end, it seemed to take an eternity to reach it. Despina stayed up at the bow with a boathook and fended off the unusual amount of flotsam trapped in the tunnel.

As the small, arched portal slowly crept closer in the dim cellar light, a blurred shadow of a barge appeared to flutter by the opening. Then to our horror the black silhouette filled the exit and slowly blotted out the light as it entered the tunnel. I switched on our searchlight and reduced speed, and we anxiously watched the thin halo of light around the barge. Thankfully, the barge began to retreat, putting the diabolical eclipse into reverse. As the halo brightened, relief quickly turned to exultation: we had a barge on the run! Sensing blood, I accelerated, sending little *Alea* charging on. For all the bargee knew, the bright searchlight bearing down on him was that of the *Titanic* itself.

The bargee looked menacingly rueful when we emerged into the warm sun. I tried to make up by giving him a subdued *merci* wave. Somehow, I doubt there was any "mercy" shown to the next tourist vessel he happened to get the drop on.

As we headed on through the flooded forest swamps of the Somme, Charles and I had great fun zigzagging across the river to head off the canal-crossing *coypu*. These beaver-sized rats showed great single-minded determination once committed on their paddling swim. It was impossible to get them to turn back; they would only submerge with a loud *plop* if we got within a boat-length of them.

The fact that all French locks close for the night suited our lifestyle immensely—after 7:30 P.M., you know your mooring is not going to be disturbed by another vessel's wash until morning. On one such occasion, just before the Epénancourt lock, we moored behind a strong-looking wooden yacht flying the American "star spangled banner." Scotty and Marguerite of the *Robin* invited us over for a chat. Friendly and the picture of health, they had cruised the Mediterranean and were heading up to northern waters after wintering in Paris. An interesting conversation developed when we told Scotty about the Blockhaus; he had been involved in the American space program and had actually worked with Von Braun and his team.

When the sky became overcast for the first time in three weeks and a cool southwest wind blew, the children went below decks to work on their scrapbooks. Meanwhile our sunshade worked equally well in sheltering us from the odd shower, and so rigged we left the wooded deltas of the Somme and entered the Canal Latéral à l'Oise.

Near Ribecourt we came upon a rash of Private Property signs, the curious *Privé*. These appeared very much out of character, for we hadn't seen them anywhere else. They were nailed on houses, fences, and even on the trees—in fact, everywhere except on the little huts at the bottom of their gardens. These unexpected signs were explained when we met an Englishman being taken "walkies" by his dog. Before he was yanked away he managed to tell us that lots of English people had bought property in the area because it was so cheap compared to England.

Seven

Citizens of
Compiègne

I I   M A Y

ON FRIDAY, MAY II, we arrived at Compiègne, a picturesque market town that sits astride the canalized River Oise. It was here that Joan of Arc was captured in 1430 and thus became the city patron. We decided to make a quick visit to the Museum of Lead Soldiers. Looking at the impressive layout of the Battle of Waterloo, Charles noticed that the Gordon Highlanders were labeled as English. This offended his Scottish heritage, and a correcting entry had to be made in the visitors book: *Ecossais!*

The lock at Compiègne was less than a kilometer downstream from where we had moored. I remember looking downriver from the bridge and noting which side the gates were on, blissfully ignorant of the fact it would be almost three weeks before we would pass through them.

By the time we got back aboard, the level of the river had dropped, possibly due to the draw-off for the lock. I could feel that *Alea* was sitting on something submerged in the river—something that must have snagged the keel itself, for raising the centerplate fully didn't help. After a lot of pushing and pulling and heavy revving with the motor, we finally managed to reverse off. We had just got out into the stream when the motor stalled. As so often happens, we had hardly seen a barge all day, but at that moment *four* were bearing down on us. I pulled and pulled on the motor's starting cord—nothing! Beginning to feel the urgency of the moment, I screwed open the throttle fully and voilà, it roared into life—but when I throttled down to engage gear it died again. We were sitting directly in the path of an oncoming barge only 20 meters away, and another one was coming up in the opposite direction. In desperation I started the motor again in the same way, but instead of throttling down, I slammed it into reverse. *Alea* shot back as the barge sliced by not 3 meters from our bow, then the motor stalled again.

The wash from the barge struck our starboard bow, sending *Alea* into a hobbyhorsing spin to port. As the rest of the barge swished past, I looked up at the sullen face of the young bargee in the wheelhouse and realized we had come very close to "making his day." He hadn't deviated from his course or slowed one bit. *Alea* pivoted right round and, facing the other way, began to drift slowly downstream, beam on.

Just then, Charles gave out a terrible shriek of pain and distress. Victoria had thrown a book at him and the corner of it had gone into his eye. This was all we needed! The culprit was summarily dragged out into the cockpit and punished. Amid the howling wreckage of family mayhem, Despina and I looked at each other, completely bewildered by the sudden turn of events. As two more barges hauled by on either side of us, we became aware of another refinement to the general misery of our situation—it was starting to rain.

I started the motor again at full throttle. Engaging forward gear with a wincing *crash!*, I headed *Alea* down to the lock at full speed. As soon as I throttled down the motor stalled, but we had enough way on to reach the lock quay. By hauling *Alea* round into the mouth of a nearby side canal, we were able to get out of everybody's way.

Here I tried fixing the motor by progressively renewing the plugs, the petrol, the carburetor needle, and the points, all to no avail. Next morning, suspecting the problem lay in the carburetor, I stripped it and boiled it in a tin can. It still refused to work.

I was religiously following the "mechanics by numbers" sequences of the workshop manual for the outboard. Now the little arrows led me to look deeper into the electrical systems for the fault. With my little ohmmeter I couldn't get a reading from the condenser, and the ignition coil's readings were completely different from what the manual said they should be. I decided to replace both units. We found a helpful chandler nearby, but his prices were daylight robbery—for these two units he wanted 800 francs. We were over a barrel and had to accept. After that, there was nothing more I could do until the spares arrived from Paris.

On the outskirts of Compiègne sits a grand royal palace, once the home of Marie Antoinette and then the Napoleons. After passing through the formal palace gardens, one can walk for miles in one of the largest forests in France. We found our way to the Armistice Clearing to visit the replica of the railway carriage where Marshal Foch and the German generals signed the 1918 armistice. Twenty-one years later, Hitler had the original carriage brought here from a Paris museum so that he could receive the French surrender in it. True to character, he had the carriage blown up in 1944 to prevent a future encore.

At long last the spare parts arrived. Before installing the ignition coil (*le bobbin* to the French) I tested it and found it had the same WRONG resistance reading as the old one. With everything in place, the motor still wouldn't work! I took the *bobbin* back to the chandler, who phoned the manufacturer in Paris. They explained that the test described in the manual needed to be done with parts of the factory sealed unit removed. This explained why this *impossible* test was the only sequence in the manual illustrated by an artist's impression, while the others all had actual photographs. I was very peeved that they refused to take their *bobbin* back. Instead of going and boiling my head as they implied, I went back and boiled the carburetor again—and got about as much joy!

The manual now enticed me into the pistons. This required me to take apart the whole motor, for which I needed a flywheel puller. I was able to make one from my store of scrap metal, but the center bolt sheared off first go. I took the broken parts to a nearby garage to get a larger bolt threaded in. Using my parts as a template, the generous owner welded up a complete new one for me and refused any payment. *Vive la France!*

The pistons and rings all appeared good, but I discovered a blown gasket, which could have allowed exhaust gases back into the carburetor. By the time I was ready to order more spares, we had run into the weekend and an incredible series of local and national holidays.

Well, there was no real hardship, for we all thought Compiègne was a delightful spot to be held hostage. We were moored on the isolated tip of a narrow island that formed part of the construction of the lock. The town put on a wonderful parade in honor of Joan of Arc, and for a few hours we were transported to medieval times, as knights in full armor rode through the main streets. Art lessons, kite flying, boat renovations, and struggling to read *Tintin au Congo* in French filled our days.

Finally the French went back to work and our spares arrived. Half an hour later I had them in the motor, but I still had to shake my head in despair.

Everything pointed to the carburetor, but I couldn't find what was wrong! In roaring exasperation, I resolved to force petrol through every gallery in the carburetor, to convince myself there wasn't a blockage. Filling a plastic syringe with petrol, I managed to squirt one hole before the whole syringe melted in my hand. Fortunately, I had one more syringe, so after saying, "Oh bother!" (in French of course), I changed to using methylated spirits. Forcing the nozzle down the air-bleed hole, I squeezed, and out popped the shriveled remains of an insect. This kind of blocking was to occur several times again. However, it would only take me nineteen minutes to clear—instead of nineteen days!

With the motor purring diligently on the transom, we eagerly cast off our bonds from the Ile des Rats and felt *Alea* free again beneath us. Near 5:00 P.M. on Wednesday, May 30, we finally passed through the Compiègne lock.

After three weeks in dock, all our hard-earned experience of the locks was thrown to the wind. In one rash moment of excitement, we entered the lock chamber at Verberie in too great a hurry and woefully ill prepared. The lock's water level was just below the top of the quay, because we were to be lowered down.

Despina jumped ashore and made fast with the bow line while I fluffed about moving the stern line from the starboard cleat to port. As *Alea* was tethered only at the front, the stern began to slew across the lock and threatened to collide with the double barge occupying three-quarters of the lock.

Despina started pulling us back with a rope Charles had thrown to her. We almost had the situation under control when the lockkeeper pulled the plug on us. The water level and the back end of *Alea* suddenly dropped incredibly fast, leaving the bow to tip up in the air, as the overhanging end of the stowed mast had caught on the edge of the quayside. We desperately tried to throw off the mast, but the weight of the boat was pressing it into the ground. Just as the lockkeeper reversed the process, *Alea* toppled sideways against the wall and crushed the port navigation light. Slowly the water level rose, and as the pressure came off the front, we were able to sort ourselves out. Some weeks later I was able to do a cheap repair job on the port light by using the bottom corner of a red plastic tomato sauce bottle.

In our travels through the lush green countryside, we were not alone. First there were the French barges, carrying mainly gravel from A to B and for all we could tell from B to A as well. Then there were the pleasure craft: the Dutch in their steel motor launches, the Germans, and of course the Brits in their yachts, all out to enjoy the idyllic aspect of canal life. But none had the wherewithal to match the grand style of the Parisians.

At Pontoise, the last lock on the River Oise before it joins the Seine, we watched the fairy-tale spectacle of a brightly lit Mississippi-type paddle-steamer locking through at night. Contrasting with the dark, ghostly quiet of a short time before, the lock now reverberated to the buzz of people, the clinking of wine glasses, and the throbbing beat of music. The jet set of Paris, decked out in elegant evening dress, thronged the steamer's saloons and lounged at the rails. Not bad as a preview of Paris, our next port of call.

Eight
To Paris and Back

I JUNE

FOR THE LAST 15 KILOMETERS of the River Oise, we snaked along a continuous green avenue of draping willows and shining rhododendrons. At Conflans-Sainte-Honorine, we found a veritable floating town of barges. There was even a barge painted white to serve as a church. Moored up six, sometimes ten abreast, most looked deserted. The sad notion that they were laid up awaiting work that would never come made them reminiscent of the grim harvest at a whaling station.

Ahead of us lay the steel-gray T junction with the Seine. I had to keep my wits about me while we nipped across to the far side of the wider and busier Seine. Here we came across the largest barge-tow yet—four barges plus the pusher—and then stared in amazement at two huge, double-decked monsters transporting motor cars, six abreast by fifteen nose to tail.

Although the overall appearance of the river was grand enough, the water was the filthiest we had seen. As the ocean sailor knows he is nearing land by the appearance of birds, the river traveler knows he is downstream of a city by the floating cavalcade of condoms that drifts past. By the profusion of this particular trail, we could tell there was some basis to the reputation of the city that lay at its inception.

We had to negotiate two locks on the 69-kilometer leg to Paris, and both were enormous. A daunting 180 meters in length, they were so jam-packed with barges we couldn't moor at the side and had to secure alongside a friendly barge. Passing under several motorway overpasses choked to a standstill at rush hour, I felt the languishing stares of the weary motorists, who sat surrounded by a cloud of exhaust fumes while we forged past in an almost indecent glut of air and space.

Still in the outer suburbs and with the sky turning a very threatening black, we decided to moor by the entrance to the Saint-Denis Canal. Soon the rain was lashing down and the children and I huddled in our tartan plaids to watch a stupendous thunderstorm through the open end of the boom-tent. We had great fun reeling with exaggerated shrieks at every blinding flash.

When that show passed, we peeked at another seemingly natural phenomenon through an open porthole in a nearby barge. A singing bargee set about cooking supper. She must have shopped at a supermarket, because a succession of plastic grocery bags, wrapping film, and Styrofoam trays came flying out the porthole. Busily she sang, chopped, and chucked, not even having to look up to score a bull's-eye every time. In no time at all, a long bobbing flotilla of garbage stretched off into the night on its voyage to the sea.

Because the River Seine takes such a sweeping turn to the west of Paris, we entered the city from the southwest. Near the inner suburbs, we came upon a vast car factory crammed on an island in the middle of the river. In an open concrete recess in the island's embankment, a desperate soul had made his home; the only access was by shinnying down a drainpipe. This was a desirable property with easy access compared to the next abode we chanced upon nearer the city center: on a narrow ledge under an ornately sculptured bridge lay a coffin-sized cardboard box with bedding inside. On a coat hanger beside it hung a neatly pressed pair of trousers.

These were contrasts indeed to the luxury apartment blocks and houseboats that lined the banks. Probably because the Seine is nontidal, many more pleasure craft moor along the riverfront here than on the Thames in London. They come in every shape and size, ranging from medieval galleon–type restaurant ships to the eccentric's concrete submarine houseboat. Falling somewhere in between were the many work barges converted to houseboats. We came across one that was the namesake of our own *Alea Jacta Est* and wondered what momentous decision had inspired that one.

The first famous Paris landmark to reveal itself to us was the Eiffel Tower. A few brief tantalizing glimpses between buildings set us off on an exciting game of "peekaboo" for a time. Then, plugging round another sweeping bend, we caught its delicate frame standing in miniature, clearly in our sights near the distant end of the long, open fairway. It slowly seemed to grow, until its graceful and intimidating bulk towered over the left bank.

The river was congested with sight-seeing ferries. These huge glass-covered boats take visitors down the river as far as the miniature version of the Statue of Liberty standing on the tip of an isolated island. A moment's pause by the verdigris bronze colossus allows the cameras to click, then the ferry heads back for the next load.

Bridge after elegant bridge swept overhead. Grand architecture blossomed on every side, each passing structure outdoing the last. Spacious boulevards branched off the tree-lined river promenades like great tributaries of the Seine itself.

Passing the regal facade of the Louvre, we got the green light to wind our way round the delightful Ile de la Cité. After a plethora of old stone bridges, we got a remarkable back view of the buttressed apse of Notre-Dame.

There was one more lock to pass through before we came to rest in the fashionable Paris marina, which is formed in what used to be the moat of the Bastille. It was Saturday, June 2, and we had the dubious honor of being the first to pay the new high-season fee of 77 francs per night—still less than half of London's St. Katharine's off-season rate.

With our delay at Compiègne, we had arrived in Paris on the last day traffic was to be allowed into the Paris end of the Marne-au-Rhin Canal to travel east. Each year the Canal Authority closed off selected sections of the canal system for maintenance. We were not prepared to hurry through and miss the sights of Paris, so we resolved to forgo that canal and instead partially retrace our path back north and join the River Marne farther along.

During our five days in Paris, we felt as if we were walking inside a living montage of every painting we had ever admired of the place. Even the wafting aroma of exotic perfumes the glamorous Parisians seem to shower in can be breathtaking. Sadly, these are made all the more appealing as a relief from the fetor of urine, which seems to linger at every corner for the want of public toilets.

We strolled along miles of cobbled streets, from the Champs-Elysées to the fascinating backstreets of Saint-Germain. There we read the many memorial plaques for the Parisian Liberation Fighters, gunned down at the exposed junctions. These poignant shrines gave the street corner a tragic air, especially when the plaque read *identité inconnue*, "identity unknown."

It was while reading one of these that we had cause to worry that we might follow the 1944 martyrs. Suddenly squads of machine-gun-wielding police burst out of two vans that screeched to a halt on either side of us. Instinctively, we grabbed the children, then froze. As soon as we realized it was the bank behind us they were storming, we crossed the street very smartly and ducked down a side alley. The kids and I wanted to watch the action from around the corner but got dragged off by our own "gendarme," who didn't feel safe until she was three blocks away.

In the Louvre, I gazed on the *Venus de Milo* and in bravado took a photograph of the crew by the *Victory of Samothrace* as a pledge that was to lead us to high adventure in her home port in Greece the following year.

There was nothing of bravado about the two halves of breast armor we gaped at in Les Invalides. Worn by a young cavalryman on his last charge at Waterloo, it displays the macabre but irrefutable proof of his duty done. Two jagged, fist-sized holes trace the path of the fatal shot that had swept him from his mount.

Here too is the sad spectacle of another veteran of that fateful day, Napoleon's stuffed white horse, Vizier, once the subject of many an illustrious painting but now an emaciated and moth-eaten omen to both mortal man and beast.

To the relief of our aching feet and thigh muscles, it was time to say *adieu* to Paris. After locking back into the Seine, we waited at the side for a barge to chaperon us through the predatory ferries. Tucking in behind a likely "minder," we glided down the Seine for a grand encore.

Turning back into the River Oise, we stopped at Jouy-le-Moutier. Our mooring was at the foot of a large ornamental garden on the grounds of the local estate. The empty manor house appeared to be in public trust and was housing an exhibition on water conservation. The children got a great deal of enjoyment out of it, with pamphlets for their scrapbooks and a day spent watching various videos on the theme. The two staff members were very pleased to see us, as it seemed we were their only visitors. Still tired from our Paris marathon, Despina and I spent the day dozing in the sun-baked cockpit while the children ran wild in the garden.

That evening, Despina got out the Chinese wok and conjured up an Englishman. Twice before we had noticed that when eggs were on the menu, some English-speaking gentleman would come along the canal path and stop for a chat. Although it never happened again, that night it did seem as though she could pull an Englishman out of the air by mixing eight eggs into a pan of stir-fried vegetables. To commemorate her wizardry, we had a competition to name the dish. Victoria won with "Pommy Pie." And on this impressive occasion its magic brought a solicitor who worked in Paris and was considering buying a quaint farmhouse in this area.

We headed back up the Oise, where we encountered for the first time a few water-skiers, who came zipping by uncomfortably close. We had no problems with the locks this time but had our first tense encounter of a different kind at a railway bridge.

Rounding a bend we came upon the bridge, which had three archways. Upstream traffic like ourselves passed under the arch on the far right, while downstream traffic used the far left, marked on our side of the bridge with a NO ENTRY sign above the exit. Massed on the parapet above our archway was a gang of five small boys pelting stones at one of the pier marker-buoys. When they saw us there was great excitement and a mad scramble to collect armfuls of ammunition. The marker-buoys got a respite as they intently awaited us bigger fry.

As luck would have it, while we were still some 50 meters away and frantically wondering how to handle this situation, they all dashed over to the exit side of the archway, obviously thinking there was more sport in catching us coming out the other side.

This meant that just as we reached the bridge, the parapet would hide us from their view. When *Alea* entered this blind spot, I pushed the tiller hard over and turned sharp left. We ran along parallel to the bridge past the middle archway and turned sharp right, through the downstream-traffic archway. When we emerged, the bombardiers had run back to the other side to check on why we were taking so long, giving us even more time to escape. The ruse worked so well that only two optimists bothered to let loose at us, but we were well out of range.

Next day we tried to moor at Compiègne to buy a gas refill but touched bottom again. Not wishing to tempt providence, we decided to forget about the gas and get out of the place as quickly as possible.

A little north of the town we turned due east into the River Aisne. We were covering new ground again. Winding its way between two great forests, the Aisne was, we judged, the nicest untouched river scenery yet.

By the village of Attichy, the recently built landing-stage provided solely for pleasure craft invited us to moor. There was even a toilet block under construction. We were to benefit from many of these newly supplied facilities throughout eastern France. Most were still free of charge, but the more established ones had introduced fees. Even the locks were being adapted to cater to tourist vessels, with new bollards being inserted midway between those set for the standard barge length. With all these sprouting amenities and the decline of the barge industry, it was clear this free canalling utopia could not last. We really felt grateful to all the waterway authorities for being able to use such a marvelous travel network toll free. Tolls on the hundreds of locks we used would have amounted to a sizable bill.

We tied up next to a French launch and took advantage of the low landing-stage to get Charles and Victoria to give *Alea*'s hull a scrub. When one side was completed, *Alea* needed to be turned round. We thought we would combine this maneuver with a trip back out of the village to bury the chemical toilet. Despina and I set off on our own while the children played ashore. Our French neighbors got quite alarmed and called to us—"Les enfants?" Despina had to explain to them that we were not abandoning our children, merely turning the boat. Their broad grins and knowing nods on our return indicated that they obviously had their own explanation as to why we had disappeared around the bend for twenty minutes.

The weather over the next few days turned cool and gray. We continued east and left the Aisne by way of our first "staircase" lock, two lifts one after the other. That evening the children went to play in a nearby gravel pit and amid great excitement began to find fossils of small marine creatures. The best find was a complete shark's tooth uncovered by Charles.

A day later "boat school" lessons took a dramatic swing forward from the age of the dinosaurs with our next archaeological finds. At the quiet hamlet of Loivre, on the Canal Aisne à la Marne, we noticed a sign pointing to a First World War German cemetery. Intrigued by the idea of land being set aside to lay the invader to rest, I resolved to cycle to the cemetery. Charles wanted to come too, so with his legs hanging askew and a cushion for padding he rode pillion.

The neatly maintained cemetery contained nearly forty-five hundred dead. Most had been killed in the last year of the war, and it was interesting to see that several headstones displayed both the Jewish Star of David as well as the Iron Cross.

There must have been a pretty intense battle, for the area was littered with pieces of shrapnel and other war debris. As we fossicked along the side of the fields I was summoned over by the umpteenth, "Hey, Dad, look what I've found!" When I looked over, I was horrified to see Charles standing over a huge unexploded artillery shell. Just as I was telling him to get away from it, a farmer drove up in a small van. Quickly I flagged him down and pointed out the danger we had unearthed. The jovial farmer just laughed and told us to have a look by the signpost, where we would find a pile of "Not so 'eavy ones!"

To prove that this was not a laughing matter, I later emptied out the charges from several .303 bullets we had found. After seventy years in the ground, the cordite still flared up fiercely when a match was put to it.

That afternoon we reached the city of Reims and moored at the council marina, directly across from a very busy motorway where huge articulated trucks with trailers thundered past every few seconds. In a world where time is money, it was difficult to see how any barge haulage could compete with such a brutally swift and mobile system. In spite of my having to caulk my ears with cotton wool in order to sleep, we stayed two nights. It cost 35 francs per night, and a 100-franc deposit got us a little plastic card that opened the toilet and shower block.

Reims is a sad shadow of its former self. The tourist brochures hail it as the "martyred city," and most postcards show it as it once was. After the horrendous devastation of the last two wars, the place has been patched back together. There is a depressing air about what appears to have been a half-hearted repair, as if a stopgap until the next holocaust struck. However, looking at photographs showing the extent of the destruction suffered—seven houses left standing out of the original fourteen thousand—it's hard to blame them.

With such a history it seems almost prophetic that the building to have survived all, even the wrath of Attila the Hun, should be the Porte de Mars, the gate of the God of War, a two-thousand-year-old Roman triumphal arch whose impressive bulk stands doggedly at a central city intersection. Time and again the scourge of war has swept in through its high portals, although the last time Mars used this particular gate it was to quit, for instead of to a railway carriage in an isolated forest, it was to a classroom in Reims that the German generals came to surrender in 1945.

As is so often the case, the more stark the seeming reality, the more lavish the hidden depths can be. This is literally the case at Reims, for deep below the city is the rabbit warren of world-famous champagne cellars. Some of these have almost 20 kilometers of galleries burrowed out of the dry chalk. We went on a guided tour of Mumm's and found it fascinating. Our guide was an English girl, who, in her explanation of how the wine is made, mentioned the grapes being transported by lorry. At the end of the lecture, she asked if there were any questions. One puzzled tourist, an American chap, wanted to know what a lorry was. "Oh, a *truck*! Gee, I thought it was some weird French word."

Alea felt pretty high tech leaving Reims, for we could finally tell how fast (or slow) we were really going, with the precision of one decimal place. With the help of the elderly "young skipper" of the *Bell of Bell Quay*, I had managed to solder a loose connection in the log console that had defied all my attempts with a heated screwdriver. This left only the echo sounder to be repaired for *Alea*'s "winter refit" to be complete.

The waterway began to weave around steep bluffs and hills, the south-facing sides of which were lined with row upon row of green vines. As the land rose about us, so too did the number of locks we had to negotiate. Most were unmanned automatic locks, which were great when they worked properly, because we could lock through at our own pace. Inevitably with the cocktail of electronics and water, our pace often became static as we blundered through minefields of malfunction.

The first thing that could fail was the piece of gadgetry that let the lock know we were approaching. I think they may have been conducting trials, for there were many different systems, all recently installed. The most reliable was a vertical plastic tube suspended like a bellpull over the center of the canal. Despina, positioned in the bow, would pull and twist on it as we passed; if she missed, I got a chance at it. The worst were the radars and electronic eyes, which failed to see our fiberglass boat because they were designed to detect metal barges. We couldn't tell they hadn't detected us until we had reached the lock and found it refusing to cooperate, at which point we would have to go back and wave our Chinese wok some more at the sodden little box.

The next temperamental hurdle was the infrared sensor at the bottom of the gates, which stopped them from accidentally closing on a vessel still in the entrance. Unlike the other devices, they would often be hypersensitive to our presence and refuse to let the gates close even though we were safely moored inside. I would then have to climb down and pass my foot across the light beam. If these remedies didn't work, Despina telephoned the area lockkeeper, who would come speeding to our rescue on his standard-issue moped.

Just before reaching the River Marne, we almost came to grief on another piece of electronic wizardry at the entrance to a 2-kilometer-long tunnel. This was a horizontal steel scaffolding tube that activated the signal lights when a passing barge presumably brushed against it. Because it stuck out some 2 meters from the side and barely above water level, it could have done severe damage to *Alea*'s hull had we brushed it. After steering round the end of it, I needed all my strength to get it to budge with the boathook.

When we emerged from the tunnel, we went directly into a flight of seven locks. Finally, at the end of this climactic labor, we turned southeast into the River Marne. It was Sunday, July 17, and after our 300-kilometer detour, we were back on course again. However, we were now four weeks behind our estimated schedule—a delay that was to raise the specter of winter storms on the latter stages of the trip. Yet at the moment the only regret was that we had incurred over twice as many locks by going round by the River Aisne. There was still a lot to be thankful for. The detour had taken us through some of the most beautiful and poignant parts of France we had experienced, and really, the number of locks was nothing compared to what was to follow.

Nine

Odd Fish in the
Haul to Nancy

IT WAS LATE AFTERNOON when we arrived at the town of
Châlons-sur-Marne. This is where Attila and his Huns got their
comeuppance at the battle of Châlons in 451 A.D.

Near the town's center was yet one more lock to negotiate before we could join the festival taking place in an adjacent riverside
park. This turned out to be a get-together put on by the sizable
Portuguese community of Châlons. To the accompaniment of
dancers in national costumes and a lively Portuguese band, we
demonstrated to the happy crowd how to run aground and get off
again, all to the beat of a samba.

From our meager ship's library, Charles was able to glean that
in this far-flung foreign field we had crossed the path of our old
friend Henry VIII again. It was here that young Henry launched
the lasting tradition of the English soccer hooligan abroad. After
a controversial result in a "friendly" jousting tournament, he and
his fans started taking the place—and their French hosts—apart.

History records this misunderstanding of match rules as the "Little Battle of Châlons."

We didn't resume our own "little battle" with the automatic locks until noon the next day due to heavy rain in the morning. Then, showing a great deal of dash, we charged down on our second lock at Saint-Germain. But it obviously knew we were coming, for we ran straight into an ambush. For every type of lock we had encountered, we had quickly devised an efficient operating routine. However, each time we reached proficiency, some variation of the lock design or its operation would catch us off guard and cause havoc. In spite of this, one thing we had grown to trust was the standard vertical metal bar that ran up the side of the lock wall. When this was lifted the lock would start to either fill or empty. These bars were so heavy and robust that we would moor the bow to them. Despina was getting so worn out lifting them that we had to change the routine so that after securing the stern, I ran forward and yanked it up.

On this occasion, the instant I touched it, the water started gushing in with such force that it blew *Alea* away from the side. The snatch on the fixed stern rope was so great that it sheared off the stern cleat. At the same moment Despina lost hold of the bow line. All we could do while the water boiled about us was frantically rush about fending off the slimy walls as we spun from one side of the empty chamber to the other. Eventually the onslaught ceased as the water level equalized. We made our escape showing considerably less flair than when we had entered.

I needed to fix the cleat right away, so I decided to tackle it while we wound our way through a steep, rocky gorge. All along the high crest of one cliff were massed thousands of agitated squawking crows. They were under attack from about thirty hawks that were wheeling and diving on them. Each time a hawk made a hurtling swoop, a section of the black fringe would, at the very last moment, make what looked like a mass suicidal jump vertically down the rock face. The instant the outwitted hawk shot past, the wily crows would pop back up again, as if on elastic.

Amidst this spectacular and distracting show my running repair of the broken cleat took an inevitable turn. I had great difficulty removing the remains of one of the bolts, and when I finally did, it fell overboard—with my counterclockwise bolt remover still attached.

After all our disgruntled trials and tribulations with the high-tech automatic locks, it seemed as if someone on high had decreed it was time we had a lesson in gratitude. On entering the Marne-au-Rhin Canal, we came upon a long series of manual locks. Instead of a lockkeeper stationed at every lock, one assistant would conduct us through five or six locks. At the end of his patch, he would hand us over to another moped-mounted chaperon. With a lock nearly every kilometer, progress became slow and arduous. Charles and Victoria ran around ashore quite freely, and every now and again they would race us to the next lock.

After four days of personal lockkeepers we grew accustomed to the quiet company of the weather-beaten country chaps dressed in their dark workaday clothes. Then out of the blue came a complete enigma: a very distinguished and refined lockkeeper who looked like a yuppie hill-walker in his bright designer clothes.

He chatted with us in excellent English, and although his questions were general enough, I later wondered if he might have been from some police agency. Ridiculous as that idea may seem, we did have an absurd little skeleton in our "locker." We had two sets of passports, British and New Zealand, which we alternated between all through the trip so as to avoid paying for visas. In France, due to the dispute over the *Rainbow Warrior* bombing, "Kiwis" now needed visas. If such petty restrictions could be introduced overnight, we considered it in our interests not to mention "The Land of the Long White Cloud." Despite our notions of skulduggery, no one ever asked to see our passports in France, and only twice did I have to show the boat papers.

At the end of his lockkeeping stint, our cultured friend held open the last lock gate for us. With a broad grin he announced, as if reciting some immortal lines from *The Three Musketeers*, "Now I must 'and you over to zee most 'andsome lockkeeper in all of France." It appeared a very odd twist of comic fate that this sophisticated yet outlandish person should be the one to introduce the next outrageous extreme.

Waiting for us at the next lock was a stooped giant of a man—the Quasimodo of the canal world. Immensely strong, he would wind the sluices open effortlessly with one hand, while I needed both hands and all my stamina to keep the handle grinding round. There was always a few minutes' rest while we waited for the lock to fill, before the gates could be wound open. Each time, he would take out a small snuffbox and carefully tap out two parallel "gunpowder trails" along the back of his hand—one for each nostril. Then, with an almost frenzied darting of his head, he would noisily "vacuum up." It must have been powerful stuff, for it had about the same effect as if a wasp had just shot up his nose. First, he would blink as if suddenly struck blind, then he would start to reel and stamp about, trumpeting and sneezing into a huge florid rag.

It had been no problem before to arrange stopping times with the lockkeepers for lunch and the like, but with "Sneezimodo" it was different. Before riding off on his protesting moped, he pointed to the next lock and rasped out the word *manger*, eat. When we arrived at the lock, he was busy opening the gates. Thinking we would have lunch after locking through, we entered the lock. To our dismay he disappeared, leaving us to have our break at the bottom of what can only be described as a dripping cesspit. Just as we were about to eat, he reappeared, chewing on the last of his lunch, and started locking us through. He couldn't have had ten minutes to *manger*, while we missed out altogether.

After two swing bridges and twenty-one locks, we had advanced a grand total of 20 kilometers along and 56 meters up. At 5:00 P.M., we were glad to stop for the night near the well-kept farming village of Longeaux. Where we moored, tall trees lined the fields on either side of the canal. Unfortunately, it turned out to be the local meeting place for the district's owls, who hooted and moaned all night. Stalking out in my pajamas, I tried sending a few stones crashing through the branches but only got a chorus of unruffled but disparaging *ooowh*s for my trouble. There was nothing else for it but to break out the cotton wool.

The following afternoon we reached the village of Demange-aux-Eaux, which sits at the mouth of the 5-kilometer-long Mauvages tunnel. Because there is no ventilation system to remove motor exhaust fumes, an electric barge is employed to tow vessels through. The lockkeeper–*cum*–tow pilot–*cum*–local grocer collected the only fee we ever had to pay on the French canals, and this, he emphasized, was for the compulsory tow. There were only two scheduled tows per day. We decided to linger awhile and made an appointment for the following afternoon.

The canal water was the cleanest we had seen so far, so I gave in and let Charles and Victoria go for a swim. We took the opportunity to test their life jackets, which kept them amused until the sun went down.

After dark we followed the local villagers to a nearby field. There we found quite a large crowd gathered to commemorate the martyrdom of Joan of Arc, whose birthplace was only 19 kilometers away at Domrémy-la-Pucelle. Curiously, there was no effigy. Instead, the bonfire was built in the form of a well-made log cabin packed with brushwood. This made a spectacular blaze, and after the roof and walls had caved in, we were treated to a wonderful fireworks display as a grand finale.

At 1:20 P.M. the next day, we motored down to the mouth of the tunnel and moored in behind the two other vessels making the passage—a barge and a recently arrived hire launch, chartered by a party of Germans. The lockkeeper had given us a leaflet in English setting out the instructions and rules on how we were to form a convoy. It expressly said that motors were not to be used and vessels had to supply their own towropes. I got ours ready and waited for the lockkeeper to give his instructions. He came down the quay and said something to the skipper on the launch in front of us, then turned and walked back the way he had come. I called after him, and to my astonishment he started to run. I yelled at the top of my voice, which brought the startled crew of the launch out on deck; even the bargee left his wheelhouse to stare back at me. But the lockkeeper, without a backward glance, jumped aboard the tug and immediately set off with only the barge in tow.

Then the German skipper told his crew to cast off and followed the barge into the tunnel. I was flabbergasted but felt I had no alternative but to follow. In hindsight, we should have stayed, for we set off on what turned out to be a two-hour nightmare.

We caught up with the launch a short distance into the tunnel. Traveling unnecessarily slowly, the skipper was having great difficulty steering straight and repeatedly crashed into the sides. Even with the throttle closed, *Alea* kept gaining on him, requiring me to engage reverse frequently to prevent a collision. The fumes from their diesel began to choke us. I shut everyone in the cabin, but the children still felt sick. Forced to steer from the open cockpit, I tied a scarf around my face, but very soon my head was throbbing. I decided to stop and try backing out. Reversing along the dimly lit channel was difficult enough, but no sooner had I begun than the tunnel lights, which must have been on some sort of relay, started switching off. It was no use. We had to go on—ahead.

Thinking there might be a wider section halfway through for passing, we tried to attract the launch's attention to see if we could signal them to let us go in front. Despina went up to the bow and sounded the foghorn repeatedly. This brought a face to peer briefly through the glass, but they never slackened their ricocheting snail's pace. Even banging their stern with the boathook couldn't rouse them. There was no escape, we just had to stick it out.

Nor was there any escape for the currish lockkeeper when we finally emerged at the other end. How frustrating it is to berate and curse a sod who you know doesn't understand the finer points of what you're yelling. Poor Despina suffered as much flak, acting as my unwilling interpreter and pacifier. We couldn't get any explanation from him for not towing us through; perhaps it was because we hadn't bought any supplies from his shop? All we could do was to take his name and tell him we would complain to his district office in Nancy. Of course by the time we got there, tempers had calmed and we found better things to do.

However, our troubles didn't end with the tunnel. Feeling miserable, we decided to take a break for tea. The kettle had just boiled when another lockkeeper pulled up in a van. He told us that we had to keep up with the charter launch for twelve more locks because the electronic monitoring gear had been preset. (That's progress for you.)

We found the launch's crew waiting to help us moor in the first lock. While I nosed *Alea* alongside, a rather top-heavy, muscular woman clapped her hands at Despina and barked in that endearing Teutonic way: "Give me zee rope!" Despina obeyed immediately and threw her the bow line. All in the same movement, the woman caught the rope and swooped it down on the nearest bollard, as if roping a struggling wild steer at a rodeo. I screamed "No!," but it was too late. *Alea* still with some way on, abruptly came to the end of her tether, and slew round into the lock wall with a jarring *crash*.

I'm afraid Despina copped another spattering of "French" as I "explained" why she shouldn't have handed over her mooring rope to people we had recently seen bouncing off the walls of the tunnel.

At the next lock, the crew of the launch activated the exit gates to close on us. Fortunately, the lockkeeper quickly lifted the emergency stop bar just in time to save *Alea* from being pinched in the doors. To minimize any further mishaps, the lockkeeper moved us up to the front position so that we entered and left the locks first. This certainly turned the tables, for now we watched them get into some of the same pickles we had experienced, while learning the ropes.

The climax of their folly came when we had to wait outside the last lock for a barge to lock through from the other side. The charter boat, coming up from behind to moor, made a long approach run, skimming close along the side of the embankment. The same woman who had "hankered us down" in the lock, now—as if still at the rodeo—leapt ashore with the bow line. Having misjudged the speed, she went pelting forward along the towpath, desperately flailing her arms to keep her balance. At the same instant that she made her valiant leap, the launch, for no apparent reason, turned sharply away to head out into midstream again.

No way could anyone criticize this "cow wrangler" for ever giving up her mooring rope, for she seemed spliced to it. With her body still a-wobble from her wild, pounding stride, she was suddenly *pinged* sideways. And at dogged full stretch, she hit the water like a surface-launched torpedo.

At first I thought she couldn't swim and ran back to the rescue. She was having a frantic struggle near the bank, but it was only to get her footing on the sloping and slippery side. Eventually I got an arm to her and helped her up the embankment. Apart from a show of agonizing embarrassment at her sudden transformation from a flying Valkyrie to a waterlogged Rhine maiden, aptly named U-na was all right.

As soon as we cleared the lock, we moored for the night, thankful to put an end to a somewhat trying day.

The following morning, after we had strolled through the hushed tranquillity of a nearby pine forest, the traumas of the previous day were all forgotten. Thus revitalized, we ventured on, in a better frame of mind to appreciate the landscape on this side of the divide. The waterway now felt quite elevated as it skirted the edge of a range of high hills. By midday the sun was hot and the water looked inviting. As the children wanted to swim, we decided to linger awhile and absorb the panoramic views of the far-off farmland and forests below.

No vessels passed us during our rest, and by the time we were ready to set off, the canal water had become so clear that we could see the sandy bottom. To my horror I saw a snake almost a meter long, quite at home swimming below, where the children had been less than an hour before.

After dropping down another series of fourteen automatic locks, we reached the town of Toul. Here we found the largest and best-appointed of all the newly provided council marinas, completely free of charge. We joined the friendly company of three other yachts: an elderly English couple from Southampton doing a circuit of the canals, a Swedish couple returning home after a year in the Ionian, and a very adventurous Dutch couple heading off on a three-year trip to their dream destinations of the Nile and the Amazon. They had built their superb steel ketch, *Lelie*, themselves.

Next day was very hot, which made the 2-kilometer walk to a recommended supermarket very tiring—especially the trek back, as we were all loaded down with bags of groceries. Noticing that the others had fallen behind, I stopped by the wayside to wait for them. A tree growing in a garden facing the street cast an inviting pool of shade nearby. Stepping into its coolness, I laid down my bags and leaned against the metal railings of the garden fence.

Almost immediately, I felt a terrific *thump!* in the small of my back and a sharp stabbing pain. I was propelled forward with such force that I stumbled and fell. Somehow, the momentum carried me on through an instinctive rolling turn that set me back on my feet again to face my attackers. Only then did I see and hear the two frenzied Alsatian dogs whose snapping jaws pressed between the bars of the fence. When I saw the bloody tear where I had been bitten, I went berserk. All I wanted was to strike back. Frantically searching the ground, all I could find was one measly pebble. Throwing it as hard as I could, I missed the brute. By this time Despina, with more presence of mind, had flagged down a passing motorcyclist. This considerate young chap not only drove me directly to the hospital but came in to explain that I had been bitten by a *chien*.

After waiting three-quarters of an hour with two other patients, I went into a rest room and bathed the wound with providentially very hot tap water. It appeared that the impact of the dog's muzzle had knocked me away before its jaws could close properly. Only one canine tooth had torn the skin about 25 millimeters while the rest had caused only superficial scratches surrounded by bruising. Eventually a doctor dressed the wound and gave me a nasty injection in the stomach, of all places. Then I waited another "un moment" (a half-hour one) until a doctor who spoke English could be found to explain the bad news: I had to go back and get the dogs' registration papers from the owners so the hospital could check whether the dogs had been inoculated for rabies. If not, I would have to stay in the hospital for eleven days to undergo a preventive treatment against the disease. In addition to the odious task of contacting the dogs' owners, I had to go to a chemist in town to buy another drug that was to be injected into my arm on my return. Thankful that it wasn't my leg the dog had gone for, I made my way back to *Alea* to collect my interpreter so I could complete the errands.

By a great stroke of luck, when we returned with the serum, one of the hospital staff recognized the address where the incident had happened and in fact knew the owner. It was quickly arranged over the telephone that the owner would bring in the necessary papers. With that part of the problem solved, they gave me my jab and told me to return in the evening, by which time they would know whether or not the dogs were free of rabies.

It was odd that beasts I so vehemently wanted to send to hell in the morning now evoked all my best wishes as to their well-being.

Happily I got the "all clear." Then, when we produced our British National Health "blue form," the doctor tore up the hospital bill in fine French style because she did not have time to fill in the form.

After Toul, we locked into the River Moselle. This broad, spacious river with its far fewer locks was a welcome change. In some places it was so wide that there were buoys marking the channel for the deeper-drafted vessels that came up from the Rhine.

In the afternoon, the heat became sultry and the sky darkened with heavy black clouds. Just as we moored in the lock at the village of Pompey, the storm struck. Suddenly a cold, violent wind came tearing down on us from astern. While descending the 3-meter drop into the shelter of the lock chamber, we had time to ponder the strength of the lock gates. Waves whipped up by the now screaming wind were crashing over the gates and collapsing into the chamber with the most unnerving roar. When the doors at the other end finally opened, we shot through as if they were the starting gates at the Grand National. Raindrops as big as glass marbles started to splatter about us. It was time to run for cover, so we headed for a nearby pontoon. By the time we finished securing our lines, the drumming tempo had increased to a lashing torrent.

By evening the storm had cleared, allowing us to have a stroll around the deserted and run-down streets of the village. Although it was a dreary scene, our visit was enlivened by a police car chase that squealed and shrieked around the block we were on. As we were accustomed to the sedate pace of the waterways, their hurtling speed was quite frightening. Each time they screeched into our street we took shelter in the nearest doorway. They finally tore off into the distance to finish the senseless drama somewhere else. It seemed to us then, so soon after the Toul incident, that we ran more risks when we ventured ashore than stumbling through the temperamental locks.

In the morning we headed to Nancy—surely one of the most elegant towns in France. The apparent absence of war damage gave us a glimpse of what the other provincial towns we had visited probably looked like before the wars. Tall, ornate, terraced houses sat on either side of spacious, tree-lined, cobbled streets. Elegant palaces, statues, and fountains formed a magnificent fairy-tale town square.

When we returned to *Alea*, we found her being admired by a very sprightly and distinguished-looking octogenarian who positively glowed with the aid of his young lady friend, hanging attentively on his arm. He was certainly a character and spoke very good English, which he had picked up as a seaman in his youth. He was very proud of his town, saying it was the only place that could keep him from the sea. Later that night we were able to appreciate his good taste when, on his recommendation, we visited the central park's rose garden. All the flower beds were individually floodlit, which produced a wonderful visual effect. This glowing extravaganza in the sweet-scented night had other effects as well, best illustrated by an extract from Charles's diary:

Had a lovely ice-cream in the "romantic" rose garden (I use the word "romantic" because there were so many people kissing!— Yuk!).

Because we did not have a refrigerator, we very rarely had white wine, living instead on the delicious reds we could buy for less than 10 francs a bottle. This night we had champagne, a souvenir from Reims, which was chilled at the bottom of the canal on the end of a lanyard. But it wasn't the heady effects of the "bubbly" that conjured up the curious sight we observed during our meal: not 4 meters from our cabin window, a young man, dressed as if on a date and clutching a large brown paper bag, sat down on a park bench. From the bag he took out a brand-new desk lamp and proceeded to calmly and systematically destroy it. After whacking and stomping it on the ground, he carefully gathered all the pieces into the bag and left. With the sudden disappearance of our center of focus, we all looked around at each other and spontaneously gave a communal shrug of our shoulders. In a flash of inspiration, Victoria piped up: "That's why the French shrug so much—it's all these wacky people that are going about here."

Ten

The Hike to Strasbourg

AFTER NANCY WE FOUND a great improvement in the automatic lock system. A flashing light now indicated whether or not the monitoring device had spotted us. This made life a lot easier, although we still managed to be in the wrong places when fuses decided to go. On one occasion we were held in a sort of "half lock" for an hour, with the water flowing in as fast as it drained out. We were compensated this time with the several kilos of cherries we picked from the derelict garden of the now obsolete lockkeeper's house.

In the main the locks had become a wearisome chore, so it was with great relief that we finally reached the highest point on the northern tip of the Vosges Mountains. The divide to the Rhine Valley is a 30-kilometer-long lock-free plateau. This beautiful, lake-strewn tableland is covered in lush forest, where we saw several herds of deer grazing with their young. Curiously, the canal embankment carried on across the lakes, forming a narrow earthen causeway on either side of the channel.

Ever since we had left Toul, the weather had been very changeable. Hot, sunny periods were quickly replaced by violent thunderstorms sweeping in from the west. As soon as we saw them coming, we would moor by the bank, often having just enough time to put out an extra line to a tree before the gale and deluge struck. Half an hour later we would be on our way again, under brilliant sunshine and with little wind.

Luckily, it was during one of these sunny spells that we reached Arzviller, where the plateau and the canal come to a spectacular end in a 45-meter drop. In the old days this difference in height was negotiated by a staircase of seventeen locks. Now the Arzviller *plan incliné* boat lift allows vessels to glide to the bottom inside a contraption that looks like a massive steel bathtub, which is lowered down a great ramp by cable car. *Alea*, moored diagonally across the tub, was sandwiched between two tourist launches. Not knowing what to expect, we were concerned about securing the boat properly, but the descent was so gentle she hardly moved within the tank. We stood on a sort of balcony at the side of the tank and looked down at the concrete pit where our moving tank and its load came to rest. All too soon the gates opened into the lower part of the canal.

Through another series of automatic locks, we continued to wind our way down a steep, forested valley. Soon we arrived at the neat, almost Alpine-looking village of Lutzelbourg. For the first time we noticed a strong German influence in the style of the houses. In fact, with the ruins of a castle perched on the rocky heights above the village, the whole scene looked like a miniature Rhine Gorge. We were now just on the border between the provinces of Alsace and Lorraine, which were held as part of the German Empire from 1871 until 1919. In the evening we found the most poignant symbol of the area's difficult past: the village war memorial. It looked much the same as the ones that stand in every French village square, but here, with a list of French- and German-sounding names, the usual references to the side and ideals they had died for were diplomatically omitted.

Over the next few days progress was slow—the automatic locks kept malfunctioning, and traffic was heavier due to an increased number of charter boats. We were further delayed by a heavy rainstorm that stopped us just north of the city of Strasbourg over July

4 and 5. With the hills of Germany in sight, our excitement and tension about the next phase of the trip began to mount. The thought of the swift-flowing Rhine was scary enough, but we grew even more apprehensive by speculating as to the effect all this rain was having on it.

Despina kept the children busy with schoolwork. They also caught up on scrapbooks and diaries before we all sat down around the tape player for our first lesson in German. We were all basically starting at the same level this time. French had been no problem, because Despina had been able to speak it since her school days. After two months in the land, Charles had reached the top of the class, while Victoria and I could survive—just. Although we carried phrase books for most of the countries we visited and made an effort to learn, we would invariably meet or get handed over to people who spoke English better than we spoke their language. They all seemed to know the joke: the person who speaks two languages is called "bilingual" and the person who speaks only one is called "British."

An overcast sky greeted us the next morning, but the deluge that had continued unabated all night had stopped. After I winkled the mate out of her bed, we got under way and headed into Strasbourg. We had started our sojourn in France on the strangely named River Aa, and now we were ending it on the Rivers Aare and Ill, which flow through the city. Turning up the fast-flowing Ill from the calm of the canal was quite a shock for our little motor. Not only did we have to plug against the 2- to 3-knot rain-swollen current, but I had to remove our wind indicator from above the slung mast so *Alea* could squeeze under the reduced headroom of the bridges. Thankfully, after listening to the disquieting high-pitched whine of the motor for more than a kilometer, we reached the city center.

Strasbourg looked an impressive mixture of French style and German old world practicality. Petite France, the island on which the central city is built, wears a vibrant mantle of the sixteenth century, like a page from a picture storybook. Its steep, red-tiled roofs form a patchwork canopy that is encrusted with rows of tiny dormer windows. These are a legacy of the tanners' drying attics, from when leather work was the town's main industry. We wanted to circumnavigate the island but got stopped by the lockkeeper at the city lock: this was now a privilege reserved only for local tour vessels. We were, of course, welcome to join the bus-loads of tourists queuing at the jetties for a *bateau-mouche* to do the circuit. With the whole city so geared for tourism, it was evident that the descendants of the Strasbourg tanners had found easier meat to skin.

Maneuvering round in our bid to turn back, we ran aground under the inscrutable gaze of several balconies full of lunchtime diners. They watched our antics intently as we all stood out on the gunwale trying to extricate ourselves from what appeared to be their restaurant's foyer.

Returning back downriver, we spotted a likely mooring almost opposite the exit of the other branch of the Ill. Although I helmed *Alea* smartly round to head into the swift stream, we still made a surprisingly long sweeping skid before steadying to drive forward. I felt quite grateful for this relatively gentle current practice before tackling "old man Rhine."

After mooring alongside a stone quay, we settled down to have lunch. Halfway through we all had to turn out on deck to fend off a kamikaze charter boat that apparently wanted to moor on top of us. All the time we were there, we had to fend off these tubs, which are built for livability, not maneuverability. One charter boat came in to "land" behind us; after two aborted buzzes, it was swept some 30 meters farther downstream, where it hit a stone bridge pier square amidships and, judging by the terrific crash that came from inside, broke every piece of crockery and glass aboard. Charles and I went to lend a hand, but the skipper had had enough and decided to moor where they had ended up—under the bridge supports.

Our first task in Strasbourg was to find the port captain's office to collect our mail and motor spares. Strasbourg was the last forwarding address we used on the trip, because at this point, if for some reason we decided not to go on the Rhine, we had the option of heading over to the Mediterranean via the River Rhone.

One of the most beautiful spectacles of Strasbourg is the flood-lit display of the colossal Gothic cathedral. Every so often the subdued lighting would explode into a dynamic Christmas-tree extravaganza of colored lights that would illuminate every niche across the facade, where hundreds of carved biblical figures stood.

In keeping with the popular image of a busy sixteenth-century city, Strasbourg was full of street entertainers who, dressed in period costumes, wandered among the crowds from square to square. The most spectacular was a fire-eater, who came at night to demonstrate how to create a breathing space in a crowd. Vagrants were everywhere too, making us uneasy about leaving the boat unattended.

Security was always a concern, primarily due to the inconvenience of losing a vital piece of equipment needed for the trip, which almost everything we carried was. When leaving *Alea* unattended, we took some basic precautions that apparently worked for us. First, we hid away within the boat such things as the ship's compass and important documents. Then, after closing the curtains to veil temptation, we locked up the cabin using small padlocks that we hoped would break before the fiberglass if forced. To suggest that there was nothing worth stealing on board, we would leave an old pair of wrecked sneakers and trousers sitting out on the cockpit seat. Only in Romania, where even such rags were coveted possessions, did we have to stop leaving *Alea* protected only by these "passive guards."

The only item we thought was of any value to a casual thief was a radio–cassette player that had come fitted with the boat. Just in the past few days we had been hearing radio news reports of the amazing turn of events in eastern Germany concerning the speeding up of unification.

Some East Germans were certainly quick to exercise their newfound freedom by taking a holiday in the West. During an open-air concert we attended, the master of ceremonies began asking members of the audience where they were from. When he hit on a young East German couple who replied, "Leipzig," everyone cheered and began to applaud wildly. The embarrassed couple felt obliged to stand up and thank the friendly crowd. After nodding and smiling all about them, they happened to turn to each other at the same moment. Suddenly, unsure whether to laugh or cry, they flew into each other's arms, to the uproarious delight of the whole gathering.

It seemed everything was going Germany's way that weekend, for they also played Argentina in the World Cup final and won. Charles and I watched a German telecast of the game in a café among a group of bilingual Alsatian soccer enthusiasts, and joined in the celebrations after.

On Monday, fully watered and provisioned, we swept back down the somewhat calmer Ill. Turning along the canal frontage of the impressive Palace of Europe, we headed into the seedy dock basins of Strasbourg harbor. We moored near the north commercial lock so I could have my first look at the Rhine.

Being very apprehensive as to how fierce the river might be, I thought it best to check it out initially on my own. I didn't want Despina to dismiss the prospect out of hand, just because it had rained for the past week. We could just as easily wait a week for conditions to improve.

While walking round the deserted quay, I felt the approaching presence of the river, as if it were a villain lying in wait. Slowly it came into view past the harbor mole, a brown, moving mass of water. I could see the ruffled demarcation line between the glassy calm of the harbor pool and the relentless, conveyor belt–like movement of the river as it rushed past the entrance. Surprisingly, a tidemark of dried mud 3 meters above the surface showed the river to be quite low.

Out on the water a long, black barge with a white bow wave splashing along its side slowly and stubbornly pressed against the current. In marked contrast, two others seemed to glide effortlessly past it in the opposite direction, as if skating on ice. Germany looked remote behind the far bank, which somehow helped to put the river's vigor in a less intimidating perspective. It wasn't flowing as fast as I expected, perhaps as little as 3 to 4 knots. Although the surface showed the odd swirling eddy, it didn't look bad at all! All that was needed for the crew to see it in the same light was brighter weather.

With the Rhine route now more or less decided upon, our next job was to get a chart. Strangely enough, the only river I had a chart of was the River Po in Northern Italy. This was a gift from Emanuele Pastori, the director of the Italian powerboat magazine *Il Fuoribordo*, who sent it in response to my inquiries as to the feasibility of traveling down the Po to the Adriatic. We like to think that his generosity entitles us to refer to him as our only corporate sponsor.

We headed up to the Bassin d'Austerlitz and the Bureau of Navigation to buy our "Carte du Rhin." There happened to be two charts on sale: an international one covering the river from its source to the sea, which cost 590 francs, and a wholly French one at 140 francs, which stopped at the German border and thus left off 145 kilometers of the route we had planned for the German Rhine. Despina scored a diplomatic coup by telling the assistant that she liked the French one best, but it was a pity it didn't go a little bit farther. With a twinkle in his Gaulish eye the assistant replied, "Per'aps I might stretch it a little with zee photocopier." For a third of the price we came away with a pieced-together chart of all we needed for the Rhine.

By the time we made our way round to the south Rhine lock the next day, the last cloud had finally lifted. The lock was huge, with massive horizontal sliding doors that made *Alea* look like a toy in a bath. In view of its potential to raise us some 10 meters, we were surprised when after only 1 meter the steel door rumbled open to let us out.

Before us lay a wide, sheltered fairway lined with trees. At the far end, the millpond surface of this backwater was abruptly shorn off by the thin, coursing flow of the Rhine. Leaving the lock, we felt like intrepid space explorers taking our first tentative steps on an alien planet. Then, to our amazement, a small inflatable dinghy with an outboard motor came zigzagging in from the river. With only a few centimeters of freeboard from its load of two very round and oversize Germans, it made its erratic way toward us. "Hello!—Englander—var izt ze nearest bar? Ve hav comin to France fur a glass ov vine, ja!" It was clear they had had a fair few across the Rhine already. Their complete lack of concern, and their obvious survival in that flimsy, overloaded craft, was really just what we needed to see. If they could do it with that, we would surely manage in *Alea*.

On a second look, the river appeared slower and calmer than it had the day before. Despina, too, was pleasantly surprised. Like me, she had built up in her mind a vision of the Rhine as almost a raging torrent, which made the reality a great relief. She even remarked that she had seen the tidal flow on the Thames looking worse.

Now that the giant was confronted and cut down to a manageable size, we were keen to give it a go.

Eleven
Rhine Madness

AFTER SPENDING OUR LAST NIGHT in France, we awoke to a bright sunny morning. Prior to departure I checked the motor and repacked the bicycle in the locker. Since assembling the bicycle we had carried it laid flat on the foredeck, but that area now had to be kept clear in case of emergency. With misfortune in mind, I decided not to raise the mast. I felt the only alternative to the motor on a fast-flowing river was the anchors. Thus I flaked out the bow and stern anchors, readying them to go over the side instantly if the need arose.

Then it was time to call the children. They were playing happily ashore, quite unconcerned. To them, going off down the Rhine was the same as all the other departures: just when they started having fun, it was time to go.

With everyone wearing their life jackets, we cast off and slipped out onto the Rhine. At first I headed upstream to test the motor against the current. Incredibly, *Alea* plowed steadily on, for the current was no more than 2 knots in the middle. Feeling relieved as well as a little foolish at my initial nervousness, I helmed *Alea* round. She turned downstream in an easy glide, immediately feeling lighter as the hindrance of the current switched to our aid. It was like stepping on an escalator.

We were soon overtaken by the first of a steady succession of barges that ply the busy waterway. There were distinct advantages in having professionals going our way. By following the first barge, we were safely guided past the massive piers of the Strasbourg–Kehl road and railway bridges. I was most grateful for this help, because the two bridges, built only 140 meters apart, appear quite an impenetrable barrier from upriver. The presence of the barges also encouraged the traffic coming up from the opposite direction to keep to their own side.

Because of the fear of flooding in the surrounding low-lying land, places of habitation are situated well back from the river, leaving its spacious tree-bound reaches looking, I imagined, as they had for thousands of years. But where once Roman galleys patrolled the frontier of their empire, low, black barges now hurried on in purposeful procession.

When several of these happened to pass us at the same moment, waves as high as a meter would slap repeatedly into *Alea* from all directions. But we got used to the movement and even felt brave enough to cross to the left bank, to anchor in the open bay at Port de Fort–Louis II for a swim.

We arrived at the French-operated lock at Gambsheim just as the last barge was maneuvering into the chamber. Over a loudspeaker the lockkeeper urged us to follow "vite!," quickly. Everyone seemed to be in a hurry on the Rhine. At the German-operated Iffezheim lock, the last in the series that have semicanalized the upper reaches of the Rhine, *schnell!* was the operative word. Thank heavens we never had engine trouble while in such a lock. They were massive and packed full. When the barges revved up to leave the chamber, the back thrust from their propellers was so strong I had to put an extra turn round the bollard to stop *Alea* from being blasted away from the side in the savage vortex.

After being lowered some 8 meters in total, we slipped back onto the main body of the river that flows over the lock weir. Without warning, the Rhine changed. From a wide, assisting escalator, it became a narrow, snaking helter-skelter that got more venomous by the minute. The speed and turbulence of the water suddenly picked up. From here on the 5- to 6-knot tumbling river is channeled in a weaving course between the submerged ranks of flanking groins. These baffle walls are designed to slow the flow of the river but, paradoxically, at first they greatly increase the flow in the navigable channel. Laterally spaced at an average of 70 meters apart, the longest encroach out into the river as far as 130 meters. They are unmarked apart from a buoyed gate every half mile at the alternating bends of the weaving channel. I had no idea how deep below the surface these groins were, but knowing that the river level was lower than usual, I regarded them as a very real and sinister threat to *Alea*'s keel.

The marine "rule of the road" is to keep to the right, so vessels expect to pass on their port side. A vessel can signal an exception to this rule by flying a blue flag on the starboard side. On this stretch of water, nearly every second or third barge, rather than follow the bends, pushed its way upriver in a straight line while displaying a blue flag. So we were not only zigzagging from side to side as the channel does but also weaving in and out through the opposing traffic. We had to keep a sharp lookout for these signals, as well as judge the correct moment to cut across the front of a very lethal-looking barge, for it seemed that if we didn't cross over, we would be squeezed onto the phantom groins.

Due to the locking sequence at Iffezheim, there is a large gap between each successive batch of downriver vessels. This free space is used by the upriver traffic to jockey for position before reaching the lock.

As the last of our downriver colleagues pulled away, leaving us on our own, we were subjected to a chaotic free-for-all in which the oncoming traffic didn't even bother to signal us. When they came across to our side of the channel, we were left to get out of the way however we could. Barges that were overtaking one vessel were being overtaken in turn by faster and lighter ships, creating up to three "lanes" of upriver traffic.

I was astounded to see one barge cut inside the gate marker buoys to overtake a rival on the inside—over the top of the groins! It was a lifesaver, for if he could do that, *Alea* could certainly afford to risk it. With this realization, I gladly withdrew from the madness and, keeping to the right, took my chances with the lesser of the Rhine evils.

The German border checkpoint is set back from the river in a tree-shrouded inlet, which makes it difficult to spot. Just as we approached, the Customs patrol vessel passed us, lashed alongside a barge. It was lending its powerful engines to help drive the heavily laden vessel against the current. In that moment's distraction, we swept past the opening to the inlet.

I immediately helmed *Alea* round to port and twisted the throttle full. We turned in a sliding, slow-motion spin, then just seemed to hang there, facing back upriver, 30 meters below the entrance, with the outboard screaming at a dreadful pitch. Ever so slowly we started to move forward, building up momentum as I worked closer to the side, where the current is weakest.

We edged our way into the inlet against a strong outflow. Thankfully I was able to ease the throttle off as we began to forge ahead into some slack water. I was amazed the motor could take such punishment without flying to pieces. It was obvious from today's run that there was certainly no going back the way we had come—the die was truly cast.

After such a battle to get to the Customs post, I found the building deserted, a veritable *Mary Celeste*. In the empty foyer I called out, "Hello!" Cocking my ear, I heard the muffled voice of a man shouting from the far end of a side corridor. Following the direction of the sound, I traced it to a closed toilet door. I explained to the occupant behind the door that I couldn't speak German and that I wanted passport control. After a moment's silence, the door was opened just enough for a receptive hand to appear, and the German voice snapped, "Pazzkontrolle!" In no time at all, the business was done. As if from a talking slot machine, our checked passports popped back out through the chink in the door, each one accompanied by a hearty rendering of "Nein problem!" At the fourth pluck it was official: we were in Germany.

With an overwhelming sense of relief at having got off the river, we tied up at the Oberheim Yacht Club jetty for the night. Among the good wishes of the local members we sampled German beer and contemplated our next brush with disaster: running back out onto the Rhine.

The trees blocked any hope of checking to see whether the way was clear of approaching traffic, and because of this "blue flagging" business, barges could pass close in either direction. Our chance came after an engine-racing barge slowly and doggedly, as if drilling concrete, pressed itself past the opening. Despina kept a lookout, but in the strong currents, there wasn't much hope of holding back once in the mouth of the inlet.

Luckily the coast was clear. We shot out into the racing flood and sped off downstream at 8 knots. A strong northeasterly, blowing against the flow of the river, added to the considerable turbulence set up by the busy traffic, but we ducked down the right side, out of everyone's way, and avoided the worst of it.

Our only real gauge of progress was the series of kilometer signs set up along the embankment. The signs step out the length of the Rhine from its source in Switzerland, unlike other rivers, which are usually measured from where they end.

The first German town to risk its buildings on the banks of the Rhine is Speyer, a place we were looking forward to visiting. It was then, when we needed the accurate position of the harbor entrance, that we discovered our chart photocopies were fading in the sun. Of course, the first area to "white out" was the river frontage of Speyer.

The river makes a sweeping S bend at the town, which is built on the left bank. By keeping a careful count of the kilometer posts, we were able to judge when to cross to the other side. *Alea* seemed to cross in a long diagonal glide before bobbing across the threshold into the harbor calm.

The harbor pool was filthy and crowded. Despina didn't mind, but I remembered that our bleaching chart had shown a smaller *Boot-hafen* farther downriver. Against Despina's better judgment, I discarded our "bird in the hand" and headed back out.

I was right: about half a mile downriver we came to another small harbor, which was empty apart from a low timber pontoon moored in front of a rowing club. As soon as we went alongside, the "Club Commandant" swooped down upon us. "Nein, nein!" it was "verboten!," even for "eins Minuten!" He was adamant about giving us the "boot" from the "haven," assuring us that we would find a yacht club 4 miles farther on.

I didn't quite believe him, so I tried going back upriver to the first harbor. The motor didn't seem as strong as yesterday, and although we were gaining ground slowly, to continue such a flogging was just asking for trouble. Throttling down, we surrendered—

Alea to the relentless current, and I to an equally unrelenting torrent: "If you had listened to me . . . !"

With a little less zeal, Despina ticked off the miles as we swept on under the spectacular Speyer single-tower suspension bridge to reach our next port of call. At the designated point we turned into a long, narrow, tree-lined inlet that opened up to a blue lake surrounded by lush green forest. It was here, while trying to get directions to a mooring, that we discovered the German love for nudism. It seemed every person we hailed rose up from their cockpit in the buff.

We had entered an old loop of the Rhine, left over from the nineteenth-century engineering efforts to straighten the river's course for shipping. One negative effect of this was the increase in speed of the current, hence the need for groins. However, these redundant loops at either side of the realigned cuts provide a natural habitat for wildlife, as well as beautiful recreation areas. As a conservation measure, it was *verboten* for any vessel to spend the night other than on a registered mooring. These were only at the yacht clubs, which of course got quickly booked.

We did eventually find a berth at the Speyer Motor Boat Club, which occupies an idyllic spot on the north shore and has every amenity. The clubhouse was an old Rhine steamer set up on chokes at the head of a manicured lawn, well above the shoreline.

It was time for a conventional hot shower, our first since Paris. Despina also got the chance to do laundry, and as usual, nothing was spared in the blitz—even clothes issued only the day before were shanghaied.

After this universal cleansing we set off to the village, whose name, Otterstadt, recalls the bygone days when otters played by the Rhine. We had plans of visiting Speyer, but the bus stop was next to the village bakery. Flush now with the mighty deutsche mark, we couldn't resist. Speyer was foregone for *Apfelstrudel* and a monumental chunk of *Schwarzwalder Kirschtorte* (Black Forest cake).

Back at the club, the children couldn't wait to go for a swim. They splashed and played, reveling in the luxury of unrestricted space.

This halcyon day was further enhanced when a skipper of a large launch came over and introduced himself in flawless English.

Egon was a well-built man with a small, clipped beard. He had the healthy, alert air of a lion hunter on safari. Friendship was pledged with a dram—a toast—which Egon ratified with a bottle of white wine straight from his fridge: "As bees flew home with ladles of treasure, the minutes winged their way with pleasure." Then it was all aboard Egon's car for a tour of regal Speyer. The town appeared in high spirits too, with bright flags and banners proclaiming that this was the two thousandth year since its founding.

The following day aboard *Elmar*, Egon's new launch, we hurtled up and down the Rhine at a cruising speed of 22 knots. Charles and Victoria loved it, but due to the excesses of the previous night, I was glad when we got back to the tranquillity of the *Altrhein*, the old Rhine. With a speed limit of 3 knots and waterskiing *verboten*, it was more my cup of tea.

After two days' rest, it was time to move on again, to our next port of call—Worms. Egon recommended we stay at the Worm's Motor Boat Club. He also warned me about its notorious entrance, saying that it was very narrow and the current there so strong that *Elmar* always needed full power to enter. He also expressed some doubts about *Alea* managing with what he termed "your ten horses." Somehow, I was picking up Egon's warnings all wrong, taking them to mean that there was a strong outflow through the club harbor entrance, as we had experienced entering other inlets. As he spoke, the idea of making a run at the entrance took seed. In hindsight, I wish I had discussed this kamikaze strategy with Egon before embarking on it.

I assured Egon that if we didn't manage we would just stop someplace farther down. Casting off we said our final "auf Wiedersehen," and when Egon and *Elmar* were just a speck in the distance we turned onto the Rhine again.

We rode the current for three hours in brilliant sunshine to the town of Worms. By now I felt fairly confident that I had perfected the turning technique that got us into harbors. I would push the tiller over when we were about 200 meters upstream from the opening. *Alea* would slowly turn beam-on as if in a prolonged sideways skid, and by the time we got to the mouth of the harbor we would be pointing upriver and ready to cross the threshold. Unfortunately, we arrived at the boat club entrance just as a line of three barges approached from downstream. I tried to slow down and hold back to let them clear, but the current swept us on. Judging to cross just astern of the second barge and about 100 meters in front of the third one, I set tilt at the tiny dark opening in the embankment.

Traveling faster than on previous entrances, *Alea* held a far straighter course. I foolishly thought that what *Alea* lacked in power we could make up with momentum. It was all going so well. We passed close astern of the barge, its wake instantly swallowed by the Rhine. This left a clear 25 meters to the entrance. I could see that several car tires hung like funeral wreaths about its scraped and gouged concrete sides, in memory of past mishaps at this port. At 5 to 6 knots, we were about to cross the bar like a well-aimed dart.

Then, incredibly, *Alea* and the body of water she was on suddenly slid sideways—not downstream with the current, as one would expect, but upstream! I could do nothing and barely had time to call a warning to everyone to hold on. *Alea* struck the side, just forward of her port beam, with a terrific *crash*. I heard wood splitting down below as I was pitched forward by the impact. I was sure we had been holed! Fearing we would sink, I gunned the motor forward, narrowly avoiding another pileup as I made the tight turn into the inner harbor and made a beeline for the nearest vacant berth.

There was no hole, although the gel coat was ripped back to the matting in several places. We were amazed and gratified that the hull could withstand such an impact (clear of all fenders of course) and suffer only superficial damage. What I had heard breaking down below was Charles's bookshelf being thrown from the flexing hull wall. Apart from being badly shaken by the experience, we were quite relieved at having got off so lightly from my blunder. After so many incidents in the canals, I had again fallen foul of the turbulence caused by the propellers of laboring barges. Coupled with my foolhardy approach in combating a nonexistent outflow, it had contributed to the disaster.

The club president, Herr Nagel, helped us move to a berth reserved for guests. He was obviously a fellow romantic, for when he took hold of our bow line, he became enthralled and exclaimed, "Ahh! You have come from zee sea, I can feel zee saltz on your rope!"

It was still early afternoon, so after washing down *Alea*'s wounds in preparation for repair, we set off for a walk around the ancient streets of Worms. Most people remember the ghoulish phrase "diet of worms" as the only highlight of the school history lesson on Martin Luther, instigator of the Protestant Reformation. We enjoyed an ice cream while contemplating the magnificent bronze monument that commemorates his confrontation with the Diet—the church council—here in 1521.

Although he stood for high principle, the tragedy is that more than ten million people were to die in the ensuing wave of religious intolerance that literally tore Germany apart. Of course we could see no obvious memorial to them, or the millions of victims since—that is, until we walked from the spacious landscaped *Lutherplatz* into the narrow and sterile streets of the old Jewish ghetto. Here the eerie ghosts of intolerance and persecution still linger at the deserted doorways, a poignant cenotaph to all the victims of man's latent insanity.

As it was Sunday, we were surprised to find the cathedral doors locked. After admiring its lofty splendor from the outside, we followed the city's fortified wall to the riverfront. It would appear that Worms has been the setting for human tragedy since its earliest days, for here is Germany's equivalent of Camelot in the sagas of their folk hero Siegfried, a Lancelot type. Near the water's edge we came upon the statue of his desperate king, Hagan, throwing the Nibelungs' treasure (a can of worms, if ever there was one!) into the Rhine. Legend has it that he did this in order to put an end to his subjects' killing each other over its possession.

Later in the evening, after troweling fiberglass filler onto *Alea*'s side, we joined Herr Nagel and his friends on the clubhouse balcony, which overlooked the inner harbor and caught the warm evening sun. They showed great interest in our trip, especially when we mentioned the Danube. Going down the Danube apparently was every German boatie's dream.

Unfortunately, this was the cue for the club's nightmare merchant to launch into a disquieting tale. Throughout the planning stages and the trip itself we were haunted by such people, who seem to get some sort of perverse pleasure in frightening impressionable crews with their boating horror stories. Sure enough, boating disasters make good yarns, but they are uneasy bedfellows with family sailing. Herr Nagel, acting as our interpreter, kindly spared us the gory details and said only, "He thinks you vill not make it—your motor izt so . . . einer kleiner" (too small).

I got up early the next morning and sanded off the fiberglass filler to return *Alea*'s flank to new. After breakfast we cast off and managed to nip out onto the Rhine without mishap. It was another hot sunny day that brought out a sprinkling of nude bodies along the banks. The river was becoming a lot calmer with the current reduced to about 3 to 4 knots. Although there was still a steady stream of barges to "sidestep," the number of river groins was decreasing.

At lunchtime we turned into the Erfelder Altrhein, another beautiful, tree-bound, redundant loop. I dropped the stern anchor and ran *Alea* into the shore, touching bottom about 4 meters from a sandy beach. Charles volunteered to take the bow line ashore but needed a helping nudge for the initial jump. Victoria soon followed, and there they stayed for hours, totally absorbed in their play. Only when it was time to go and we asked our two naked cherubs to release the bow line and come aboard did they remember that they hadn't eaten their lunch.

With the Rhine in less of a bustling hurry, the remaining 15 miles to the confluence of the River Main offered us a very pleasant ride. The surrounding countryside appeared more populated, with farmland and village roads reducing the flanking forests to broken thickets.

As we entered the outskirts of Mainz, it was time to get ready for the turnoff into the River Main. My biggest concern was the barge traffic that might be maneuvering at the junction of the two waterways. A railway bridge with its many piers hid everything from view. The exact shape of the river mouth had also vanished from our photocopy chart, in spite of our having guarded the page from the light as if it were some Masonic secret. All I could tell was that the entrance was directly after the bridge, and no matter what we might find, I had to be ready for a quick turnoff.

When we suddenly emerged on the other side of the bridge, I quickly surveyed the scene. On our right was a narrow, sandy spit, sparsely covered with low scrub. This barrier turned the course of the Main sharply to the northwest, so that it merged with the

Rhine some 300 meters farther on. Rearing up on the other side of the spit was the huge gray bulk of a seagoing merchant ship that seemed to take up the whole river as it awkwardly edged itself round this tight bend. Our luck was in, for this was the only vessel in the vicinity and it was going our way—up the Main. At the end of the spit, I pulled the tiller over. *Alea* spun quickly round, performing that familiar sideways glide for the last time on this powerful river. Like a giant hand the Rhine current swept us effortlessly aside and into our next course: the River Main.

Twelve
In the Main: An Easy and Relaxed Affair

16 JULY

AFTER HAVING GROWN accustomed to traveling at 7 to 8 knots, it felt as though we were standing still when *Alea* began plugging up the Main against a 1- to 1½-knot current. A short distance up from the mouth, in a safe mooring, we raised a glass to our success at having survived the traumas of the Rhine. Charles and Victoria found a more practical way of finishing with the Rhine by scrubbing its grime from *Alea*'s decks. Every now and then they would take it into their heads that swabbing the decks was fun, and *Alea* would get "spring cleaned" for free—although this time it cost me the deck brush, which, according to the "witnesses," just threw itself overboard.

Our first priority now was to obtain *eine Fluß Karter*, a chart of the river. The chandler we chanced upon had only a river guidebook, which had very basic sketch diagrams of the locks and

92

selected stretches of the river's 450-kilometer length. More disappointing was the fact that it was all in German. There was obviously a wealth of information on boat clubs and places of interest, but this was all lost on us. Albeit a case of Hobson's choice, the diagrams proved adequate and, as it turned out, a lot better than what we were to use for the rest of the trip.

Just before the Kostheim lock we tucked in behind a large merchant ship and followed it into the chamber. As we were about to moor, a harsh voice over the loudspeaker system bellowed something about *shportz-Boots* being *verboten*. We were ordered out and directed over to the other side of the weir, where we found a small manual lock especially for *shportz-Booters*. Although it was back to grinding wheels again, we were glad to forgo sharing the locks with those intimidating canal leviathans.

There were two more "private" locks before we reached Frankfurt. We passed through the city's suburbs, screened from the river by extensive harbor installations, to emerge suddenly on a long, majestic, tree-lined city reach. When the tall spire of the cathedral appeared to be only a few blocks away, we judged we were as near to the city center as we could get and so moored alongside a set of steps in a vast, empty stretch of stone embankment.

About 100 meters from our mooring we found the Romer, the central square of the old city. A crush of tall, sixteenth-century timber-framed and stucco houses looked to be straight from the pages of a Grimm Brothers' fairy tale.

Just as France is haunted by the specter of the First World War, so too is Germany by the memories of the Second. A photographic exhibition of Jewish life in prewar Frankfurt was engrossing. We peered at old Frankfurt's nightmare, caught in stark monochrome clarity. Somehow the Romer didn't appear so quaint when seen as a swastika-draped backdrop to a Nazi rally. Aerial views and cleverly made dioramas displayed the eventual price the city paid for hosting such extremism. From a landscape of destruction, we could pick out the stone steps where *Alea* was moored. The same steel lattice footbridge that spans the river there today was severed and tipped skyward on its piers.

In the light of such devastation, the extent and quality of the city's restoration is astonishing. Every bullet pockmark has been neatly cut out of the stonework and replaced, giving a credible impression of the city's former luster.

As Frankfurt was the birthplace of Anne Frank, her famous diary was on sale, even in English, which made a popular addition to our ship's library.

When we returned to our mooring we found a huge river cruise-liner, known in the trade as a *Kreuz-fahrt-schiff*, moored almost on top of *Alea*. Fortunately, before leaving in the morning we had remoored a boat-length from the steps to discourage anyone from boarding. This allowed us to move back to the steps and a more comfortable distance from the *fahrt-schiff*'s stern.

No one said anything about our mooring there until we sat down to breakfast next morning. A police launch arrived alongside and hailed us: "Es ist verboten!" Pointing to our set table, I called back, "Frühstück!" (which in actual fact means "breakfast"). The astute policeman, with equal brevity, raised one finger and barked out an emphatic, "Eine Stunden!" (one hour). Within the deadline we finished our *Frühstück*, refilled our freshwater containers, and set off.

Farther up the river at Obernau, we discovered that from there on the width of the manually operated locks was reduced from 4 meters to 2.5 meters. As *Alea*'s beam was 2.6 meters, we had to go back to sharing the main chamber with the commercial traffic. Apparently the Rhine–Main–Danube canal has been so long in the making that when these earlier locks were constructed, 2.5 meters seemed ample.

We passed through some very pleasant countryside but were disappointed to find that every stopping place had the dreaded "verboten" sign on guard. In the evening, finding an "un-verboten" place to stop proved so difficult that it started to get dark. This required the use of *Alea*'s navigation lights for the first time. We finally reached the Wassershportz-Club-hafen at Erlenbacher. The colored disco lights that blinked from the club rooms looked inviting, but the small harbor was so choked with pleasure craft we couldn't get in. Fortunately, just across from it was a Canal Works harbor. These are normally most definitely *verboten*, but at ten o'clock on a Friday night we were getting decidedly less law-abiding.

The distant music from the Wassershportz-Club was an inspiration to our own junior ensemble, who got out their recorders for a moonlight recital. When "Hey Joe" by Jimi Hendrix came drifting across, I rashly took this as my lead-in to a recital of my only claim to musical fame: "Jimi Hendrix died in the next bed to mine." (This was back in my London days, when I lay in a ward of St. Mary Abbots Hospital with a punctured lung.) Having painted myself into a corner, I managed to sidestep any controversial questions from my impressionable crew by describing the "confidence-inspiring" sneakers that the doctor wore while attending to him. Incongruously, they had more holes in them than *Alea*'s security guards.

As no one was about the following morning to evict us, Despina took the opportunity to give everybody a haircut. A large bollard on the quayside was judged to be an ideal barber's chair, for it allowed the barber to stand in one place and prod the customers around in any direction.

Setting off late, we found the scenery enchanting. Thick pine-forested hills rose away from the river, and numerous castles from every age faithfully held sway over their small corners of the landscape. The lofty stone ramparts of Miltenburg Castle took our fancy, so we nosed into a vacant berth in a tiny yacht-club harbor, which cost 10 deutsche marks per night, plus 1 for a shower.

Miltenburg was a beautiful place and obviously a popular local holiday spot. The camping ground was filled with the last word in caravan-trailer design and luxury. Sleek Mercedes and BMWs sat in attendance, an opulent tribute to the wealth and expertise of West Germany. They were made all the more conspicuous by "a caravan from the east" in their midst. A small caravan, reminiscent of homemade versions of the 1950s, that sat beside its matching Trabi, the East German two-stroke "worker's car."

From one man's caravan to another's castle.... After a pleasant, zigzagging forest trek, we found that the intended object of our stop had been converted into a private home and access was *verboten*. We had better luck the following day when we assailed the Henneburg Castle, 19 kilometers farther upriver. The caretaker had apparently fled, leaving us in sole charge. We had great fun hunting each other through secret passageways and winding staircases. The high towers gave superb views of the curving Main Valley and little *Alea* anchored far below.

We discovered that the locks on the Main close at 2:00 P.M. on Sundays, and finding the local boat harbor full, we had to anchor out on the river. I decided to hang out my much-loved kerosene lamp to ward off any night voyagers who might otherwise have blundered into us. While I was stretching out to tie the glowing beacon to the end of the mast, it slipped from my fingers and sank like a stone.

For me, nothing symbolizes the pleasure of the outdoor life more than the functional beauty of a hurricane lamp. Having to fall back on battery power, it was a sad skipper who turned in aboard *Alea* that night. However, inspiration came with sleep, and at 5:00 A.M., I was up putting a salvage plan to the test. With the whisker pole and the two boathooks lashed together, I searched the murky depths and managed to retrieve my trusty friend with its glass still intact.

That afternoon, while passing through wooded countryside, we were suddenly startled by a man running along the riverbank bellowing curses at us. We don't know how we upset him, but it looked as if he had been fishing there. Judging by the passion of the oaths, *Alea* may have inadvertently snatched away "his" equivalent of my hurricane lamp.

Half an hour later we felt the potency of the angler's curses. There was a loud *clunk* from our centerplate, and instantly the rudder went rigid and our motor stopped dead. I tried to tilt the motor up but found it jammed in the down position. The lanyard I had used to lever down the centerplate was wrapped tightly round the propeller. Whatever we had hit had thrown the centerplate back, allowing enough slack in the lanyard for it to reach the rudder and propeller.

Just then a 7-meter yacht called *Liberty* pulled alongside and offered us a tow to a yacht club 2 miles farther upriver. While *Alea* was lugged along, I got to work freeing the motor. By removing the plugs and engaging reverse gear I was able to turn the flywheel and unwind the lanyard from the propeller. Within a quarter hour we were under our own steam again, and thanks to the skipper and mate of *Liberty*, we had hardly lost any time.

This sort of situation was where the outboard motor was a great advantage. Any fouling of the propeller was easily cleared. We picked up numerous plastic bags along the way, which stopped the motor dead. In most cases I could tilt the motor up and clear the obstruction while *Alea* glided on.

The rest of that week was spent flitting from one Germanic beauty spot to the next under the same perpetual sunshine and easy river routine. We found numerous secluded reed ponds tucked off to the side, which made idyllic night anchorages. As the water was noticeably cleaner in these spots, the children went swimming at every opportunity, often enticing in their mother. I was still invalided out of such frolicking due to the slow healing of my Toul dog bite.

We were shocked from our dreamy tranquillity by an inexplicable incident at the picturesque walled village of Karlstadt. As we crossed to nose slowly in behind an unattended motor-launch at a tiny pontoon on the right bank, we were startled by a terrific accelerating roar of a heavy diesel engine. Looking up ahead I saw a barge about 40 meters away, emerging from under a bridge. I could hardly believe the speed at which that barge accelerated from almost a standstill—to make a deliberate charge at us.

As if rolling up a huge carpet, his bow rose up to push before it a growing, tumbling wave. Seeing what he intended, I immediately engaged reverse and raced to get as far from the pontoon as possible. While trying not to move out into his path, I had to keep my distance from the shallow water near the bank. Because of the motor-launch sitting out from the pontoon, he was unable to steer as close to us as he would have liked. When he was almost upon us, I slammed the motor into forward gear and managed to get some steerage way before the splashing bow wave struck.

Calling for everyone to hold tight, I drove *Alea* up and through the now meter-high wash, within 3 meters of the barge's side. Glancing up at the wheelhouse I saw the bargee. He was erect as if on tiptoes and staring back at the barge's stern. Just as it was about to clear the motor-launch, now crashing wildly against the pontoon, he began to spin his helm over. The maniac was trying to sideswipe us!

His stern came sliding in, but *Alea* was now too near the pontoon and out of reach. As it swept by, I pulled the tiller hard over to miss the corner of the pontoon and cut across his deeply furrowed, head-jarring wake. By the time I had circled round he was well downriver. We were completely stunned by this sudden and unprovoked attack.

Alea had come through without even touching bottom, but the motor-launch hadn't fared so well. The mahogany bar of his stern cleat lay splintered in pieces, and deep, ragged gouges peppered the side of the hull. All we could do was resecure its mooring lines before setting off on our sightseeing tour.

On this leg of our trip, locks continued to provide us with plenty of excitement, and we were not the only ones who fouled up by losing hold of our mooring points. At Erlsbrunn the barge in front of us came adrift. As he began to fall back on us, I threw off my stern line and scrambled up onto the quay. Despina was just able to keep pace with the advancing barge by letting out the slack on her bow line. It was as if she were giving the bargee a lesson on rope handling. In a trice of coming to the bitter end, she had it gathered in and thrown to me. It was only just in time, for when the barge's engine roared into life, *Alea* was blasted back by the thrust of the propellers. I was barely able to prevent *Alea* from going back into the closed lock gates.

The next great attraction on our route was Würzburg, the capital of Franconian wine. A magnificent castle sits high above the river, its steep slopes covered in drilled vineyards. We wandered up through the steep streets of the old town, which curve round behind the castle. To our surprise our path ended at the blank sheer face of the castle wall. Detouring along the wall we came upon a small unlocked solitary door that gave access to a steep, narrow stone staircase. Feeling our way up in semidarkness, we made a startling entrance into the crowded castle grounds, where a flower and garden festival was in progress. Later on, we boldly sallied out past the long queues of would-be visitors who were patiently besieging the ticket kiosk at the main gate.

That night we found hospitality at the Nuremberg Sailing Club. Although the spot is some 170 kilometers from Nuremberg by river, the club's members travel the 80 kilometers as the crow flies to spend a relaxing weekend in their secluded river bay. We were invited to join a jolly bunch of yachties for coffee and *Kuchen*—cake—under a shady tree.

It was only then that we learned for sure that the Rhine–Main–Danube canal wasn't open. It had been an elusive piece of information. With the canal having so many revised completion dates, not even a lockkeeper we asked on the Main was sure whether it was open. This meant that *Alea* would definitely have to be transported overland to the Danube.

We came close to having this problem solved the instant it arose, for it transpired that two of our new friends had converted a truck especially for transporting their 9-meter boats on holiday. One, the club president, was leaving the very next day for three weeks on the Adriatic. Although we had just missed out on the loan of their truck, they gave us lots of helpful information. This included not only the name of a Nuremberg boat haulage contractor, Herr Pheninger, but also where we might find him holidaying on the River Main.

During the course of this very pleasant get-together, I had noticed several of our hosts abruptly jump to their feet as if pinched on the bum. After making a hasty adjustment to their chairs, they would carefully sit down again. This appeared all the more curious since no one took any notice of this seemingly reflex action, which hardly interrupted their conversation. Then, with shocking suddenness, I was initiated into the mystery: one moment I was sitting talking, the next I was lying flat on my back in the grass. The back legs of my tubular chair had suddenly sunk about 20 millimeters into the ground. Apart from hysterics from my own family, everyone else was politely reserved in their mirth and apologized for not warning us. Apparently, a small earth-burrowing rodent was responsible for the unseatings. After a few less spectacular tumbles, I too acquired the lightning reflex the instant I sensed that "sinking feeling."

It was here we discovered that whereas the French have their beautiful *bon voyage*, the Germans have their earthier *gute Fahrt* to express the same sentiment. Our first well-wisher, a distinguished-looking lady with a charming smile, didn't appear to notice the desperate struggle we were having to keep a straight face. We were to be farewelled with *gute Fahrt* on many occasions, although I was tempted to use it only once myself.

For a few more idyllic days, we traced the winding river up round another huge north-about loop. On either side the hilly countryside was combed and racked with vast legions of well-cared-for vines. Each day the waiting time at the locks grew progressively longer as commercial traffic to lock through with dwindled. I never grudged this waiting, for it was always a convenient time to catch up on some small maintenance job. If a barge didn't turn up within an hour, we were usually let through on our own, with an embarrassing waste of water.

Although barges were getting scarce, we got a lot of unwanted attention from water-skiers. It appeared that most of them thought that the uncomfortably close buzz they invariably gave us was akin to a friendly welcome.

In spite of these reckless salutes, we could hardly complain about our time on the River Main. Compared to the previous legs it had been, in the main (so to speak), a very easy and relaxed affair. We had passed through a landscape of fairy-tale beauty, where time itself seemed almost to lose relevance in the eternal rhythm of life on the river. Of course this illusion had to end, for even Mother Nature must keep in step with Old Man Time. Almost as if on cue, we noticed the first autumn leaves falling just before reaching the turnoff for the Main–Danube Canal. Nature's warning that time was running out brought us back to the reality of having to be in Greece before the onset of winter. Our estimated schedule still stood at four weeks behind. Although thankful we hadn't added to it on this leg, I had an uneasy suspicion about the next. The prospect of organizing the portage across the divide from Nuremberg seemed daunting as we left the bliss of the Main.

Thirteen
Overland to Regensburg

2 AUGUST

ON THURSDAY, AUGUST 2, we reached a tree-lined fork in the River Main. The only clue that we were leaving the Main was a larger than usual kilometer signboard that proclaimed, "Main 384 km—Main–Danube Canal 0 km." At kilometer 3, we moored in the deserted industrial harbor of Bamberg.

While ashore foraging for water, Charles befriended a river policeman, who offered us the facilities at the floating police station. He also recommended places to visit in his "vunderbar" Bamberg.

Though we greatly appreciated the sights of the medieval city, the most memorable spectacle of that day was seeing the bold newspaper headline—BLITZKRIEG—above the photograph of a burning tank. It was on every newsstand. Had we encountered a time warp and landed back in the Bamberg of the 1940s, or was this the start of World War III? *Nein*: Saddam Hussein had just invaded Kuwait, an event that was to have repercussions on the rest of our trip. At the moment, however, fuel supplies didn't enter our minds as we escaped the world's troubles in the cobbled backstreets of Bamberg.

Next day we arrived at the Forchheim Yacht Club, reputedly the weekend retreat of Herr Pheninger, the haulage contractor from Nuremberg. The club moorings were situated just off the canal in a tree-shaded arm of the River Regnitz. A middle-aged man on the pontoon waved us over. He introduced himself in German as the *Hafen-Meister*, then, on seeing our flag, changed his title to "Harbor Sheriff." There was no doubting the influence of the American forces that have been stationed in this area since 1945. The "sheriff" directed us into berth 25, and we were pleasantly surprised to see that the one next door had Herr Pheninger's nameplate on it. If he turned up, we were sure to see him.

Meanwhile, we were happy to explore the picturesque village of Forchheim, which was built in and through a huge complex of eighteenth-century fortifications. It was impossible to get an overall view of these walls and towers because of the extensive groves of large trees that turned it all into a beautiful country park.

On Sunday we learned that our Herr Pheninger was not about this weekend, but as luck would have it, his apparently wayward son was—a stocky young man, going to fat, it would seem, on the easy pickings from people like us. He ambled down to the jetty and, sizing up the skipper more than *Alea*, quoted "off the top of his head" the ridiculous sum of 1,150 deutsche marks. He wanted 1,000 deutsche marks for the 100-kilometer portage from Nuremberg to Regensburg, plus 150 deutsche marks for craning into the Danube. I thanked "Junior" for his time but "*Nein*—thank you very much!"

When we left Forchheim, we found the canal water a vivid green as if there had been a gigantic paint spillage. It continued for kilometers, making us think we had stumbled into some great pollution disaster. We found out later that the culprit was a river weed whose pollination process had been triggered by the thunderstorm the night before.

This last section of the canal system, with its one 12-meter and two 18-meter lifts, was the end of the trail—a trail that showed its newness with clean white concrete that curved between a flanking balm of young saplings, planted to heal the landscape's recent wound. In many places the canal was built up above the surrounding land like a causeway, giving marvelous elevated views of the rolling wooded countryside. This aspect was cleverly utilized by the construction of cycleways on either embankment.

As we entered Nuremberg our water highway passed alongside a huge American army base. Although motorists on the nearby autobahn had their view censored by a high screen barrier, canal users were given a free "spy." Stretched out below us was a vast airfield type of area covered with row upon row of army vehicles, many of them hidden under camouflage nets. The obvious protrusions of the gun barrels and the complete absence of a living soul made the place look quite menacing.

Still in the outskirts at kilometer 65.3, we turned into the isolated little harbor of the Motor-Yacht-Club Nuremberg. The helpful caretaker, after hearing about our encounter with "Junior," invited me over to his house and enthusiastically set about organizing *Alea*'s overland haul to the Danube. While Herr Beigler phoned around, his dear wife chatted to me intently—in German, of which I understood almost nothing. Each single-word reply I hesitantly made was readily accepted as if I were the neighbor across the fence. I must have said all the right things, for when I got up to leave, she thoughtfully presented me with a bouquet of flowers "für meine Frau" and two jam tarts "für meine Kinder."

Herr Beigler had found someone who was prepared to tow us over for 850 deutsche marks. Thankfully, he wasn't available until the following week, which gave us more time to shop around. By great good fortune, on that very same day I said "Hello" to Peter Steinhauser, a tall, swarthy yachtie working on his wooden sailing boat. Being one of the few club members who prefers sailing to motoring, he was instinctively sympathetic toward us and offered to help. Over a cup of coffee we discovered his natural English was due to a fourteen-year company appointment in Canada. Now his business thrust was into the former East Germany, where he saw great potential.

Next morning Peter made a theatrical appearance aboard *Alea*. Obviously having been the butt of many a "German Officer" joke in his time, he humorously announced: "I have zome good news and zome bad news; vitch do you vont to hear first?" As tradition dictates, we chose the good news. This was that he had found a boat chandler who would transport *Alea* to Regensburg for 400 deutsche marks. The bad news was that the earliest he could do it was in six days' time, and even then only after working hours. Under the circumstances we jumped at the offer. Peter kindly volunteered to finalize the details with our moonlighting haulage man, aptly named Herr Push.

Dominated by the craggy heights of the Kaiserburg castle, the restored medieval central city of Nuremberg is enclosed by an impressive outer castle wall and moat. The drained moat has been laid out in shrubs and trees to make a very pleasant circular walk. Bright canopied stalls and numerous street performers make it easy to glimpse the Nuremberg of the Middle Ages.

Many of the quaint cobblestoned squares contained richly decorated fountains. One, entitled "The Marriage Carousel," displayed large bronze sculptures depicting the maturing stages of wedlock. Starting with attentive young lovers, it progressed round to a hideous old hag throttling her geriatric husband upon a scaly monster. Coincidentally, this day happened to be our own wedding anniversary, for which Charles and Victoria had presented us that morning with chocolates and "boat-made" cards. Mischievously, Despina insisted on having her photograph taken in front of the last scene. So as not to tempt fate too much, I diligently rotated the "ring of luck" at our next stop, the *Schöner Brunnen* fountain.

After viewing the city from every angle by day, we decided to return for a floodlit perspective at night. To pass the time until nightfall, we took a train to the main railway station in order to visit the nearby Natural History Museum. At the end of kilometers of underground passageways we emerged from the station hopelessly lost. Approaching an intelligent-looking man standing nearby, I excused myself in my best German and, making a show of stabbing my finger about my street map, asked, "Vo sind vir bitter" (where are we?). Tight-lipped, he studied my map closely. Then, somewhat reluctantly, he pointed to a spot inside the castle! I must have looked up at him rather reproachfully, for he immediately came clean. "Sorry, bud, I'm American, and I'm as sure as hell lost myself!"

As he only wanted to find the railway station, we turned him around and sent him into the labyrinth. Heading north, we soon zeroed in on our goal. The local archaeological exhibits were marvelous and of special interest to us, for this area was the cradle of the Celts. From the material legacies of our own cultural roots, we went next to tread the aisles of the Germanic National Museum. After a superb historical display of European civilization, we were ushered out at dusk, back into the real thing.

Nuremberg seemed more relaxed by night. With most of the shoppers gone, there was space for an unhurried stroll through a beautiful, old world, artfully "rose tinted" by an array of floodlights.

Although the dark had been the primary consideration for the evening's entertainment, I had forgotten to take a torch for our return along the unlit canal towpath. On entering the eerie gloom, little Victoria, resourceful as always, piped up, "Here, Dad, I brought mine" (that's my pussycat). Thankfully, Father Christmas had shown more forethought on the dark night he had filled her stocking.

With the weekend approaching, we decided to spend it out in the countryside. Hoping to visit the section of canal still under construction, we set off in *Alea* to the Nuremberg lock. It was shut, and although the lock looked new, the chamber was full of algae and flotsam. The lockkeeper explained that this was the last operational lock, which gave access only to the industrial harbor. Our only escape was back in the direction we had come.

We were amazed to see that the acres of parked vehicles at the army base had all gone, presumably spirited away in preparation for the launching of Desert Storm, the liberation of Kuwait.

Farther on we came upon a slightly less violent launching as we nosed into a small recreational side harbor by a large forest. The only facility was a boat-launching ramp, on the edge of which stood a group of four boisterous men. Each held an arm or leg of a young man they swung between them. With a chorus of "Eins . . . zwei . . . drei," they sent him arcing through the air to land with a magnificent *splash!* Later, the happy young man presented us with two cans of beer so that we too could toast the launching of himself and his new speedboat.

We spent the night at anchor there and in the morning discovered that not all the natives were so amiable. When I went ashore I was attacked by a small, snapping lapdog. While it repeatedly lunged at my bare ankles, its unconcerned owner, a gold-bedecked matron, sunned herself nearby. Losing patience, I feigned a sudden charge at it while making a loud growling noise. This made the animal bolt off into the trees howling, leaving me to contend with its now stirred and howling owner. Within seconds a posse of her countrymen were gathered to the fray. Eyeing me suspiciously, as if I had done something unspeakable to her, they indicated that such behavior was *verboten* in this *Boot-hafen*. It seemed I was to be "let off" with a warning, until I appeared before my scandalized and snapping mate. In the time it takes to say, "I've never been so embarrassed," I was retried and condemned to do the honorable thing: "self-imposed" exile.

While the bustling matron went off into the forest, cooing for her stampeded weasel, I did hard labor on the anchors. Then, with the tiller between my legs, I moved *Alea* farther along the canal and found sanctuary for a while in an open bay. Soon after, a police launch came and stopped alongside. Fortunately, it had nothing to do with molesting elderly ladies. It just happened to be *verboten* to stop in this "turning bay" and *verboten* to use anchors in the canal. Let off again with another lecture in German, we were directed over to the other side of the bay to salvage the remainder of the day.

Salvage, in fact, put the kibosh on that "Carousel jolting" day. In the cool of the afternoon we climbed a nearby hill and were surprised to find a summit crater that was being used as a refuse dump. While Despina retraced her footsteps in protest, I led our children on a glorious scavenging expedition. Charles distinguished himself by utilizing a bottle opener to unbolt a stainless steel chair base, which made an excellent barbecue plate. Using the same technique I was able to collect a variety of stainless steel bolts for spares. Not to be outdone, Victoria rescued a bicycle bell that sported a picture of Mickey Mouse, which we later fitted to our ship's bike. Returning to *Alea* with our spoils, we wanted to boast about our "recycling exploits" but knew better to keep . . . "mum."

As if to make up for that day's trials, the next was perfect. We anchored back in the recreational haven and, with the rucksack packed, set off for a day in the woods. The forest turned out to be a national park with pleasant, well-trodden paths in all directions.

Right at lunchtime, we stepped out into a clearing in the middle of nowhere, to find a flag-draped *Bierkeller*. One result of the liter-sized proof that this was no mirage was our subsequent need for a siesta in the drowsy, resinous heat of the forest.

The weekend was over and so it was time to prepare for the haul-out. In order to make *Alea* as light as possible, we had managed to use up all our stock of petrol and water. In the same vein, I changed the oil in the outboard motor to clear my supply of engine oil. To avoid any spillage in the water, I had taken the motor ashore and drained the old oil into an empty milk carton. When I went to dump the carton into the club rubbish skip, I was ambushed by the local busybody.

He turned out to be a retired policeman who kept his "hand in" by keeping everyone under surveillance from the wheelhouse of his launch. Incredibly tall, he suddenly reared up from behind the skip and caught me red-handed. "Nein! nein! Das ist verboten!" he moaned, and with a great show of put-on concern, he started repeating, "Greenpeace! Greenpeace!" Excusing myself, I asked him where I could dispose of it. This he didn't know, for it was only the *verboten* side of problems he concerned himself with. So, with the honor of being the first boat owner to have "ever" changed his oil there, I was sent back with my carton of un-green waste.

Later on that day while maneuvering his launch for departure, Herr Verboten stopped just off our stern. Sticking his head out of the wheelhouse window, he thought he would show there were "no hard feelings" by reciting the dossier he had compiled on me. "Ah, zo you are Neu Zeelander, ja! Ah, zo you go to Regensburg tomorrow—gute, ja!" Then with a final wave he called, "Auf Wiedersehen." I felt my face burn as my reply inadvertently slipped out: "Gute Fahrt!"

Over the previous few days we had been having very hot, sultry weather again. The barometer had shown a sharp fall in the morning, but the storm still took us by surprise. We rushed to fix extra mooring lines, and just as the last hitch was tied, the full fury of the storm struck. Electrical storms and heavy rain persisted for the rest of the day and most of the next.

As it was the day of *Alea*'s scheduled road trip, I began to worry if Herr Push might call it off due to the weather. Fortunately, about 4:00 in the afternoon the rain stopped and a miraculous improvement took place. Herr Push was supposed to arrive at 4:30 P.M., but he didn't turn up until 5:45 P.M.

A friendly, athletic-looking man, he immediately swung into action like a video in fast-forward. Quickly, he backed the rather flimsy-looking tandem trailer down the ramp until the exhaust of his Range Rover was under water. At a run he led a strop round behind the stern cleats and winched *Alea* on as far as possible. Then, with a frantic spinning of tire rubber, the whole shebang surged up to the top of the ramp.

Alea was sitting too far back and listing to port. The back wheels of the trailer were so compressed I thought they might explode. As it happened, the only thing to explode was Herr Push's patience with the retired policeman. From the start Herr Verboten had been on the scene dictating how the job should be done. As rapidly as he did everything else, Herr Push sent the busybody packing with a guttural flea in his ear.

With the winch strop now placed behind the keel, he backed *Alea* down the ramp for a second go. This time he didn't stop until the water was lapping inside the trunk of the Range Rover. While I adjusted the trim, Herr Push winched *Alea* right on. The haul-out was a lot easier with *Alea* now sitting almost perfectly. Herr Push was pleased, although he judged by the compression of the trailer tires that *Alea* weighed 3 tons—close to the maximum safe load for the trailer, $3^1/_2$ tons—instead of my estimate of 2 tons.

Amid the airy good wishes of Herr Beigler and other helpful friends, we piled into the Range Rover and were immediately whisked away. We found that Herr Push was not a man of half measures. With the physical work done, he now went into relaxed mode. He forgot not only that he had 3 tons of boat in tow, but also where he was supposed to be going with it. An hour later, as we hurtled east toward the Czechoslovak border, he suddenly realized we should have been going south to Regensburg. He reset himself in "fast-forward" and we raced through winding secondary roads to reach Regensburg just as it was getting dark.

Now he started asking pedestrians for directions to the *Motorboot und Wassershportz Club*. After the fifth person, a U-turn in the main street, and the crossing of a soccer field, we found ourselves in a pitch-black forest at the back perimeter of the boat club. Rewind—we were off again on another tour of soccer field and suburbs before we finally arrived at the club's front gate. We were then told that, for safety reasons, the crane could only be operated during daylight hours. This was a bit of a blow for Herr Push, as he naturally wanted to return to Nuremberg with his trailer. The only boat-ramp near Regensburg was apparently out of service due to the low level of the Danube. Now Herr Push went into business mode, charging us an extra 50 deutsche marks for having to return the next day to collect his trailer. Although it was entirely his fault that we had arrived in the dark, we didn't have the heart to quibble. In spite of this hiccup, he had certainly worked hard, and we were thankful to have crossed the divide.

Un-hitched, the tall bulk of *Alea* looked out of place in the car-park berth, although the same cheery glow beamed out from the cabin ports. All things considered, we had come off lightly. It was eleven o'clock at night on Tuesday, August 14, and here we were, on the banks of the Danube. It was hard to believe that there, in the dark void that lay between us and the colored lights of the town, was the start of the next leg of our adventure—an incredible avenue that would take us all the way to the Black Sea.

Fourteen

Launched on the Danube

15 AUGUST

I AWOKE EARLY AND, from the companionway hatch, surveyed our new surroundings. The clubhouse looked like a colonial cricket pavilion, enclosed by thick stands of tall trees. Its spacious lawn swept down to the river embankment, where a large derrick crane stood incongruously on a concrete forecourt. The club's boats were moored out on an extensive pontoon, which was heavily stayed to the bank by steel hawsers. A 3-knot current scuffed and waxed the surface of the river as its dark mass slid relentlessly past. Its color gave the impression of depth, so I was surprised how shallow it was in the launching area between the pontoon and the bank.

The club caretaker who craned us in was a middle-aged bulldog type—short and gruff. Whenever he was about, we could nearly always hear his clipped, rasping voice haranguing someone or other. Nevertheless, he was an expert at operating the crane. *Alea* was placed precisely alongside a moored motorboat on the inside of the pontoon. After craning back the lifting strops,

"Grumpy" came down to direct me round to a berth on the other side of the pontoon.

The problem was a white boat fender being used as a buoy to mark a sandbank off the end of the pontoon. Grumpy, not the sort to make allowances for dumb foreigners, barked out what I took to be which side I was to pass the buoy on. But as events proved, he was in fact barking out which side the sandbank lay on. Thinking I understood, I sallied forth—and hit it fair and square. The strong river current immediately slew *Alea* round and pressed her over on her port side.

Immediately, Grumpy appeared on the end of the pontoon with three other Teutonic musclemen. Clapping his hands impatiently, he indicated for me to pass him a line from *Alea*'s bow—and to be *schnell* about it. Quickly I rummaged out and attached a long, 25-millimeter-diameter hemp rope. With his team lined up behind him for the "tug-of-war," Grumpy doubled as cheerleader: "Eins—zwei—drei—heave-hooo!" The instant *Alea*'s bow began to move, the rope snapped. With a frantic clattering of feet, the surprised troupe charged back along the pontoon and collapsed in a pile of arms and legs.

Thankfully no one was hurt, but suddenly my poor understanding of German became a blessing when Grumpy got to his feet. To the great amusement of the other victims, he waved the frayed end of the rope at me and began to rage.

Shaking my head in a show of exaggerated disappointment, I called back at Grumpy, "Englander rope—nicht gute!" Then, holding up a polypropylene rope, I added something to the effect that this rope would be better because it was made in Scotland—a despicable piece of diplomatic expediency, but it did the trick. It was the only time I saw a semblance of a smile on Grumpy's face. There were no problems on the second attempt, and once *Alea*'s head was hauled round I was able to motor off and moor at the correct berth. After my rescuers accepted my apologies, I paid Grumpy his due, 70 deutsche marks, for craning us in.

We spent the rest of the day reprovisioning. We got out the folding bicycle and, using it like a packhorse, made several trips to the local supermarket and petrol station. Returning from one of these expeditions, we noticed that Herr Push had retrieved his trailer. I was able to confirm this by speaking to a canoeist who was standing nearby. This fellow turned out to be an American, Bill Elgarton, who was minding his canoe while his companion went back by bus to pick up their car. In 50-kilometer stages like this, they were enjoying a camping vacation on the Upper Danube. Bill joined us for lunch and filled us in on the jazz scene in Germany, as he was working there as a musician.

While we chatted in the cockpit, the children were given permission to go paddling in the shallows behind the pontoon, as swimming was out of the question. Unfortunately, by hanging on to one of the pontoon mooring stays, Charles ventured out so far into the current that it carried away one of his sandals. This incident gave us quite a fright and jolted us back to our usually high state of vigilance, because we had now entered upon the most dangerous of rivers—a moody river, one that could change from a sleepy backwater one moment to a roused giant the next.

We got our first taste of the Danube's fickle nature the following morning. The water level had risen so much overnight that the white fender buoy of yesterday's folly was half a meter under water. We would discover later that the level could just as quickly drop almost 2 meters. Meantime, there was Regensburg, the twin city of my own Aberdeen, to discover.

Regensburg is one of the few German cities that was not too badly damaged in the Second World War. Most of the Romanesque and medieval buildings appeared to have undergone only an evolutionary blending to modern usage—so much so that one structure, the twelfth-century *Steinerne Brücke* (stone bridge), presented a frightening prospect for us, for we realized that *Alea* would have to pass underneath. With the level of the Danube at its lowest in living memory, the massive pier foundations were exposed, reducing the narrow openings even further. Foaming white water, cleaved by the bow of these boat-shaped bases, funneled into the dark archways in a torrent. We discovered we had been craned into the original course of the Danube, which was now only a by-water of the modern canal. Commercial shipping bypassed the city center, leaving the bridge rapids to whoever wished to shoot them. I waited some time before a speedboat proved that it was possible to squeeze through without touching the sides.

Our efforts to find a chart of the Danube here as well as in Nuremberg had been unsuccessful. In the end we gave up and bought a map of the cycleway that runs along the embankment from Regensburg to Vienna. Like our River Main pilot guide, this one contained a lot of tourist information, all in German. It seems this corner of Bavaria doesn't expect many foreign visitors.

We had an unexpected visitor when we returned to *Alea*. A friendly cat followed us onto the pontoon, and just as we were about to board, the cat jumped onto the boom-tent. In its panic at landing on the yielding fabric, it clawed a trail of holes up to the ridge. Needless to say, my displeasure was swiftly conveyed to the cat, who wisely made off. The damage was clearly evident that evening when it started to rain.

It rained heavily all that night, which increased the current and delayed our departure until after lunch. On the positive side, we found that the centerplate was now completely free. So, donning our life jackets, we cast off. The thrill of setting off on the Danube was somewhat tempered by the thought of negotiating the portal of the *Steinerne Brücke*. Although I held *Alea* at the minimum speed that would maintain steerage, the bridge still loomed up to us at a fearful pace. Passersby stopped and leaned over the parapet to watch the show. I concentrated on lining up *Alea* with the opening—we were committed. Suddenly *Alea* was snatched up on the accelerating current and propelled forward as if sucked down the bath plug-hole. We shot through the archway with barely a meter to spare on either side. In a split second the dark shadow of the bridge passed overhead and we were out in the sunlight again. There was no time for congratulations; everyone was on lookout as we swept round to the junction with the main branch of the river.

Fortunately, we found it all clear. We were lucky, for soon after a long convoy of black barges came upriver. Rafted together and pulled on long tows, they looked strangely antiquated after we had got used to seeing the modern method of pusher barges. With their racing, clunking engines, they sounded and looked old and dilapidated. We soon learned to recognize this as the stamp of the Eastern Bloc. At various sterns we spotted the flags of Bulgaria, Hungary, and Yugoslavia and got the distinct feeling we were a long way from home.

The landscape, too, seemed different on this side of the divide—bigger, more spacious. There was something exotic in the very air, giving us the impression that the East started here. And as if to emphasize how far we were venturing from the familiar, the 2370 km signboard hove into view. Yes, we were on the right course for the Black Sea, but we certainly got the message it wasn't just round the corner.

As we got farther from Regensburg, the river quickly broadened out into a majestic waterway. The turbulence disappeared as the current reduced in speed to as little as 1 to 2 knots. *Alea* seemed to glide on at an effortless 4 knots through wide, curving expanses of low, forested hills. Villages of red-roofed buildings nestled along either side, each one watched over by its own ornate parish church with a curious onion-shaped spire.

High above the river on a distant terrace was the massive white edifice of a Greek temple. Modeled on the Parthenon, this was the nineteenth-century Valhalla built by King Ludwig I, so that every two years a bust of a famous deceased German could be placed in its hall of fame. In spite of its grandiose proportions, it soon receded away astern as *Alea* ghosted on.

In the late afternoon we arrived at our first Danubian lock at Geisling and decided to call it a day. The children looked forward to these occasions when they could escape the confines of the boat and run free in the nearby fields. It so happened that these were cornfields and the crop was ripe. So while the sky put on a beautiful red sunset, we ate a few cobs of fresh sweet corn.

In the morning the lockkeeper let us through the huge lock by ourselves. The chamber was so high and intimidating that I made the silly mistake of thinking we were going to be raised. Charles, using his "Sherlock Holmes" powers of deduction, pointed out the impossibility of this because of the presence of spiderwebs above the water level. In fact, the river level was so low that we were lowered less than 2 meters.

Lofty castles overlooking the bends in the river made the route appear romantically Bohemian. We had several sightings of deer at the edge of the pine forests, and lots of white herons fishing their individual reaches. So far our cyclists' map had proved surprisingly accurate. Unfortunately, later on, when we started looking for a mooring for the night, nothing seemed to fit. The inlets shown on the map were either silted up or reformed due to the canal construction. To make matters worse, the current increased dramatically with the joining of the River Isar at Deggendorf. Wishing only to stop, we were carried on at a greater speed for another 20 kilometers before any semblance of an anchorage turned up.

What we finally settled for was an opening to a dead-water oxbow. With floating patches of green algae, it was far from idyllic. Nevertheless, we followed our usual habit of sitting in the cockpit after supper for a storytelling session. Unfortunately Victoria and I had to abandon the cockpit early due to swarms of mosquitoes. They seemed to ignore Despina and Charles and go straight for the tender steaks.

Despina had made a very effective set of mosquito nets that fitted over the open hatchways. Ever since our arrival in France, fixing up the mosquito nets had been a regular prelude to supper. Consequently, only on the odd occasion did an intruder get into the cabin, and very rarely did it survive long enough to dine. I slept with a torch and can of fly-spray at hand and would always awake if a mosquito approached within a meter of me. If I missed him on his first sortie, I could almost be sure of finding him a few moments later on the ceiling above Victoria's bunk. There were a couple of memorable misses. Once, groggy with sleep, I inadvertently picked up the spray can the wrong way round and shot myself in the eye. On another nocturnal raid, I was just about to snipe a "mossie" above Charles's bunk when he suddenly sat up and got his right ear fumigated.

One thing we had noticed about the German rivers was the absence of floating garbage, with the exception of discarded wine bottles. There is something very tantalizing about large glass bottles bobbing past on the water. They seem to invite destruction. After working on the project for the last few weeks, Charles and I now had a fine set of four catapults, straight off the production line.

With an arsenal of suitably sized pebbles, we set off. It wasn't until our second encounter that in a glorious free-for-all we scored our first kill. Unfortunately, the ammo ran out on the next target, which followed us unscathed into Passau.

We moored alongside a newly constructed quay on the deserted left bank. In contrast, the right bank was bursting with the arrival and departure of large tourist ferries, as Passau is the main northern terminus for Danubian cruises.

The old town itself occupies a very picturesque location, built as it is on the tip of a relatively slim finger of land between the converging Danube and Inn Rivers. Curiously, the limestone-colored Inn looks by far the bigger of the two rivers, which makes one wonder why the name "Danube" continues on after its apparent physical demise here. Even the Danube's color, a greenish brown, is quickly bleached to a milky gray by the flood from the Inn.

In our quest for a bookshop, we crossed the town bridge and entered a crush of tall, overbearing buildings. We encountered the same story: no one knew anything about charts for the river that passed not 200 meters from their door. Then one shop assistant brought out from a back room what was destined to be our navigational chart of the Danube: a miscellaneous second volume of a river guide, written in English, which we could have for 10 deutsche marks. Published more than ten years before by a shipping company for their passengers, it covered the 1,900 kilometers from Vienna to the Black Sea. The last forty pages consisted of a series of stylized sketch maps, marginally better than our present cyclist's one. Although we tried again in Vienna, this guide turned out to be the best we could do.

Passing the end of Passau's spit, we felt *Alea* being picked up on the 4- to 5-knot current of the Inn and carried forward. Ahead the broad, milky gray river swept on round a series of wide bends.

Although there was nothing to indicate it, the wooded hills on our right were now Austrian territory. Then, to our surprise, the Austrian Customs pontoon appeared 5 kilometers before the point where the Danube crosses the frontier. An elderly policeman in a very smart uniform helped Despina with the mooring lines. He spoke very good English, and when I said we hadn't seen the German checkpoint, he replied, "Don't vorry about zhem, conzider yourselves in Austria now."

Taking him at his word, we raised the Austrian colors to starboard. He obviously hadn't seen many British passports, for he got suspicious about Northern Ireland being printed on the front covers. Checking all our far-flung places of birth seemed to amuse him greatly, as well as satisfying him we were not IRA terrorists. With that little matter sorted out, he stood by our moorings and, with a friendly salute, cast us off.

Fifteen
Austria to Starboard

21 AUGUST

STEEP MOUNTAINS COVERED WITH BIRCH and pine forests rose away on every side. Isolated alpine-style farmhouses nestled in the corners of river flats or on high pasture terraces. Castles, preserved or in ruins, still dominated their stretch of the river.

We were not the only ones enjoying the visual feast. On the embankment, groups of brightly dressed cyclists tinkled their way along between the trees, at much the same pace as ourselves. By now there were special exuberant ringings and foghorn blasts with the ones recognized from previous days. We wondered whether we might see our Thames cruise companions Ivor and Ruth along this way. On comparing notes more than a year later, we found that they had cycled past here only nine days before.

Other river traffic was rare. Most of the time we were the only ones on that vast river vista, making it more akin to a lonely mountain lake than a major waterway.

At the Ottensheim lock we tied up against the entrance quay for the night. I had great difficulty getting the lockkeeper to understand we didn't want to lock through until the morning. Finally we appeared to agreed on *acht Oor,* eight o'clock, which I hoped didn't mean at night.

That *Oor* passed and we were left to have a peaceful night, but we got a rude awakening at seven *Oor.* Victoria's diary records the moment:

> It was still very cold. I was snoozing in my bed. I could hear a barge coming. I waited for the waves, suddenly a wave of water came splashing in our front hatch and got us soaking wet, me especially.

I was roused by indignant shrieks and scrambled to the forecabin to find two drenched pups. There was so much water about that at first we thought our main water tank had somehow burst. By *acht Oor* the flood victims had been evacuated to our bunk and the forecabin stripped and sponged out. Not that it was a day for drying out wet beddings, for it started to rain soon after we got going.

When we reached the industrial city of Linz, we moored alongside a central riverside park and ventured ashore to find a bank, for now we required the tinkle of the Austrian shilling.

While walking toward the city center we came upon a shop displaying the 3-kilo cylinders of "Camping-Gaz" that we used. As we needed a refill, we decided that I would return to *Alea* to fetch our empty cylinder while Despina and the children continued to the bank. When we met back at the shop, we would have the two ingredients necessary for the gas: the cylinder and the cash. This basically went as planned, but when we rendezvoused I found Despina waiting outside the shop alone. Cheerfully, she explained that she had left the children at the bank, happily playing with Legos in a playroom provided for customers' children. I needn't worry—they were "as safe as the money in the bank!"

This, to our dismay, was rather literally the case when we arrived outside the bank to find the doors locked and barred. Because of an outer metal grille, we couldn't even reach the door to knock. Standing on the gas cylinder, I managed to look in through an adjacent window. Across the dim foyer, I could see the shadows of Charles and Victoria behind the colored glass panels of the playroom wall. They were quietly playing on the floor, quite oblivious to their abandonment.

Luckily for us, through another window I met the puzzled stare of a woman in a back office. Teetering on top of my cylinder I yelled, "Ich murkter meine Kinder!" (I want my children—the phrase book's "I wish to withdraw some [cash/children] please" was too much of a mouthful). To this she gestured with two fingers that the bank was closed until *zwei Oor*, two o'clock. Ignoring this, I stood my ground, and after a lot of frantic pointing and shouting she finally went to check.

From behind the heavy door came the repeated rattle and clack of bolts being released; then appeared the rather bewildered prisoners. The embarrassed smiles and hurried apologies made it clear that none of us wanted to linger over this delicate transaction.

After our deliverance from the bank, we could appreciate the sentiment of the monument we found in the square: a richly gilded "plague pillar" erected by the townspeople in thanksgiving for their release from the plague. Although we could relate to that piece of Baroque art, we were stumped by the exhibition we viewed on the grounds of Linz Castle: sculptured concrete boxes that when approached gave out a noise such as a cough, a groan, or, most profound of all, the clinking of wine glasses. Things seemed even wackier when we entered a room where the furniture was set out on the ceiling.

From the rarefied air of modern art, we crashed back to earth when confronted by the prices exhibited in the local supermarkets. Austria's exceptionally high cost of living was a scourge we hadn't bargained on. Unfortunately, this was to have a significant bearing on the amount of long-term food supplies we would eventually carry with us into the Eastern Bloc.

Since France, where we had found the best-quality conserves, I had tried to encourage Despina to build up a stock of tinned foods. This, however, only served to raise the specter of *Alea*'s disputed suitability for the trip. "There is no room to stockpile tins!" I was lulled (very well then, cowed) by the cook's normally sound catchphrase: "We'll just eat what the locals eat!" In hindsight, we realize we didn't fully consider the situation that was waiting for us on the other side of the now defunct Iron Curtain.

With our "gilded" shopping stowed aboard and a strong following wind, we set off downriver again. After passing through a smelly industrial area that sprawled out of Linz, we came to the lock at Abwinden-Asten. Here, as if to make up for the traumas of the day, we met "The Five Bavarian Men," a raucous gang of Bavarian burghers who were apparently paying a social call to their Austrian neighbors.

Incredibly, they were all packed like tinned sausages into a sailing boat smaller than *Alea*. As the boat had no mast, a tubular framework was erected over the full length of the hull. Painted in the spiraling Bavarian national colors of blue and white, this frame supported a large Gothic printed banner: FIVE BAVARIAN MEN SAY GOOD DAY TO AUSTRIA (in German, of course).

It appeared that as much liquid was flowing into them as under them, so we prudently let their jolly-boat enter the lock first. To our surprise and delight, once settled, they all took out musical instruments and began to play German folk music. With an "oom-pa-pa" accompaniment from two accordions, a trumpet, a trombone, and a monstrous tuba, we were slowly lowered. The music waltzed around the cavernous lock chamber, and we applauded eagerly at the end of each tune. The climax came when the massive steel doors at the far end were opened to reveal the beautiful countryside beyond. In time with the slow movement of the doors, the brass played a Wagnerian fanfare that held us spellbound—it was terrific!

Five kilometers farther on, our cyclist's map showed the ill-defined feature *Lager*, enclosure—an inconspicuous word that is the German euphemism for a concentration camp. Here at the small town of Mauthausen, on the left bank, the beautiful scenery seems an unlikely location for such an infamous place as the word *Lager* seems as its handle. Well over two million people were murdered here among the wooded rolling hills, not to mention the basement of the local brewery.

Just opposite Mauthausen we turned into a small inlet. Because it looked shallow, Despina went up in the bow and sounded the depths with a long pole. Despite our cautious pace, a woman appeared on the only other boat in the inlet and abused us for causing a wash. This exchange having killed any likelihood of us rattling her crystal under friendlier circumstances, we anchored well away. Fortunately, we ended this mixed day on a happier note, with a recorder recital around a cheery campfire.

The following day wasn't good for Austro-*Alea* relations either. As we arrived at the hydroelectric dam at Persenbeug, the lockkeeper changed the control lights to green, then started shouting at us over the loudspeaker when we entered the lock. Completely at a loss as to why the lockkeeper was so infuriated, I looked back upstream and saw a convoy of barges coming. Realizing that the green light was not for us, we obediently returned to the outside of the lock to wait our turn.

As soon as the barges had maneuvered into the lock, four speedboats came screaming up and leapt straight in to grab all the remaining bollards. This had happened on a few occasions in Germany, but from here on to Vienna it became the standard boorish practice. We now had to pass the speedboats and secure to a recessed ladder uncomfortably close to the barges.

These were the first Russian barges we had seen. They appeared more modern and better maintained than other Eastern Bloc ones we had encountered. Four or five portly women in white uniforms, who appeared to be manning a centralized kitchen, watched us intently but refused to smile.

To top things off, as we left, the lockkeeper leaned right out of his control tower window and scrutinized us through a pair of binoculars. This was so we would be in no doubt that he was noting our number and reporting us to *zee authorities* for jumping the queue.

Sure enough, soon after we left the lock, *zee authorities* were on to us. Just as we were turning into the mouth of the River Ybbs to anchor for the night, a large police launch approached. We touched bottom twice in the shallow tributary before finding a suitable place, which may account for why the police launch did not follow. Instead, it held station at the junction while one of the policemen trained his binoculars on us. They watched us for a quarter of an hour, then, to our relief, quietly drifted off down the Danube.

Next day we locked through at the town of Melk, a quaint old town that is crowned by a huge Baroque abbey that overlooks the river. Unfortunately, there was just no space to leave *Alea* unattended in the tiny and crowded harbor. All we could manage by way of a mooring was to press the bow against a corner of a *verboten* pontoon. While the crew went shopping in town, I settled myself in the stern to operate on the outboard. It had begun misfiring at the last lock and had been coughing and spluttering all the way to Melk. The problem was that the breaker points needed replacing, though I was well pleased with the extended service the refurbished set had given since Paris.

With the returned shore-party stationed about the deck to push and shove, we disentangled ourselves from a boat jumble and set off. We had passed through some fairly gentle, rolling farmland in the morning, but just after Melk, the mountains came pressing in on the river again. This is the start of Austria's Wachau, a beautiful vine- and fruit-growing section of the Danube Valley. As well as draining the terraced vineyards, the steep encroaching terrain causes the river to narrow and increase in speed.

While we bowled along aided by the 3- to 4-knot current, we came upon the "Five Bavarian Men" drifting downstream side-on. Their placard-carrying boat, covered with sprawling, naked bodies, looked like the tragic aftermath of some maritime disaster. I slowed *Alea* alongside and asked if they had broken down. "Nein, nein," there was no problem, they were just sunbathing. "Vhy use zee Motor vhen zee Vasser moves?" This was indeed a novel view. We preferred to maintain steerage and so left them to their leisurely abandon, just as the riverside village of Willendorf hove into view.

This is where the early Stone Age statuette of a conspicuously obese fertility goddess was found, the voluptuous Venus of Willendorf. Looking back at the "Five Bavarian Men," I thought I could almost see her glee as she beheld her provocative offspring drifting past her patch.

We swept on through that spectacular landscape, inhabited since earliest times and fought over ever since. Ruined castles stand on nearly every high crag, the last of them having been wrecked by Turkish invasion and religious wars two hundred years ago. We anchored for the night in a sheltered inlet across from the lofty heights of Dürnstein Castle. Legend has it that it was under these tumbledown ramparts that the minstrel Blondel located the imprisoned Richard the Lionheart by singing songs from home that only Richard could respond to.

I thought it fitting that at the same place I should hear the tune I had been longing for: our radio picked up a very strong signal from the BBC. On these rare occasions it was a pleasure to listen to the news, given in that matter-of-fact way, as apparently only the BBC is able to do. Sadly, we had difficulty receiving this station throughout the trip, whereas "The Voice of America" was always loud and clear. While in Germany we tuned to the American Forces Radio, which gave out good local travel information. By luck, just as these stations started growing faint, we picked up an English-language broadcast from Vienna. This kept us company until we entered the East, where it eventually dried up, along with everything else except "The Voice of America."

Past Krems the surrounding countryside is marshaled into legions of vineyards, which probably accounts for pruning shears being invented here in 1849. On our right and well inland stood the massive bulk of the Monastery at Fürth. By the time its white towers had faded astern, the hills too had shrunk away from the river to form a low fringe on the horizon.

It was a hot Saturday afternoon, so we turned into an inlet at Altenworth, 36 kilometers from Vienna, for lunch and a swim. There we found an abundance of nude Viennese, many of Willendorf proportions, sunbathing on their anchored powerboats. For the more energetic Viennese there was a riverside cycleway, complete with a rustic "Gute Fahrt" sign, wishing them the best of luck on their break from the city.

Although we were heading in the opposite direction, I hoped that a little of the good wishes might apply to us, for, remembering our London experience in trying to get visas for the East, I knew we would need all the luck we could get to see us through Vienna.

Sixteen

Vienna: The Visa
Waltz

26 AUGUST

AFTER A LAST FREE-FOR-ALL with the Viennese boaties, we emerged on the downstream end of the Greifenstein Lock—and *down* was the operative word. Suddenly, the smooth surface of the river began to accelerate forward, and in moments we were riding on a seething millrace. We saw for the first time the rocket-shaped marker buoys that look as if they are skimming over the surface like racing powerboats. The current increased to 6 to 7 knots as we swept toward our turnoff for the boat club at Kahlenbergerdorf.

We were traveling so fast that I feared we would be shot past the opening if we didn't see it in time. I checked our cyclist's map: a cross marked the position of the entrance. In these conditions I had little faith in the map and even less in the cross, for it had been put there by an inmate of a boat club where we had sought a berth the night before. Curiously, the clubhouse was encircled by an outer as well as an inner barbed wire and chain-link fence.

When I found the door to this inner compound locked, I spoke through the cage to the nearest people seated in a courtyard café, not 2 meters away. It became clear no one was going to let me in, so I moved along the fence to opposite a thin, hawkish-looking man who was prepared to answer me. "Zhere are no vacant berths here!" But if I rolled up my map and poked it through the wire, he would mark other places I could try. I imposed further by asking him also to mark the position of the boat club nearest to the center of Vienna. As if filling out a ballot paper, he casually flicked three crosses on the map and posted it back through the fence. Touching my forelock, I left my haughty audience in peace to enjoy their *Lager*.

My guide may have watched the Danube from within a pound, but he certainly knew where to place his mark. Bang on target, the high embankment on the right suddenly ended. I heaved the tiller over, and *Alea* skidded round to face upriver. With the motor screaming we hung there for a moment, then started to slip back downstream.

I pushed the tiller over and felt *Alea* falling backward in a pendulum-like turn. As the bow pointed more downcurrent, she shot forward toward the bank, just inside the downriver end of the opening. Hauling round again to face upstream, she thankfully steadied less than a boat-length from the shore. Incredibly slowly, we ground forward against the gushing stampede. As we worked up the edge of the inlet, the current seemed to suddenly let go. With a wincing, earsplitting roar from the motor, *Alea* leapt forward and began to surge ahead up behind the embankment.

It was Sunday, August 26, and we had made it to the outskirts of Vienna. The rustic-style clubhouse stood on top of the 8-meter-high spitlike embankment overlooking a series of small pontoons. There seemed to be plenty of vacant spaces, but the water level was so low that some pontoons were beaching. We touched bottom at our first choice of berth and got ordered away from our second by the harbormaster, who half an hour later shifted us to a fourth.

Aptly named Rudy, the harbormaster was cast in much the same mold as "Grumpy Von Regensburg," short in both stature and manner. He had suffered a crippling car accident, so these traits were accentuated by his hobbling use of a single crutch. His agitated, rasping voice, accompanied by abrupt jolting movements, always made me feel I was taking a great liberty in talking to him at the most inconvenient moment.

I was therefore surprised when Rudy later invited me to join him for schnapps. He was sitting with some other people at a table in front of the clubhouse. This terrace commands a lovely view across the inlet to a range of small, wooded hills that hide Vienna from view. The picturesque village/suburb of Kahlenbergerdorf lay cradled in a narrow valley, directly opposite.

Rudy showed he could be quite affable, in spite of a disquieting tendency to boil with frustration when English words escaped him. Because of this, I was even more surprised that he should want to prolong his labors by suggesting we go across to the village for another drink. I excused myself by telling him that Despina had been preparing supper and it was time I headed back. He had obviously been drinking all afternoon, so in order to get away, I agreed to go with him afterward, thinking he was likely to forget all about it.

But no sooner had I finished my meal than Rudy appeared on the pontoon, ready for a night on the town. This turned out to be a veritable Camelot in more ways than one. As the club was marooned on the spit, we needed to take a punt over to the village side of the inlet. Waiting at the punt was Rudy's wife, Hilda, and another woman, Helga, who earlier had been seated at the table on the terrace. It transpired that Hilda was just there to ferry us across, and I was there as Rudy's chaperon while he set about dissolving their "eternal triangle."

A harvest festival was being held in the village, so its rustic facaded streets were crowded with vendors' stalls and revelers. We visited a tavern first, then a beer-tent where a folk band played. As conversation was limited by the hubbub of the festivities, I assumed Rudy and Helga were enjoying themselves as much as I was. Then, out of the blue, Helga burst into tears. My bewildered look prompted a sobbing explanation, the only English Helga ever uttered: "Rudy doesn't vont me anymore!"

Solace for all was sought in another stein of beer, which, on top of their afternoon's quota, anesthetized more than broken hearts. Stepping out into the night's fresh air was as effective as any "lover's leap." Still arm in arm, they ended their woes by collapsing like two sacks of potatoes at my feet. I had great difficulty getting both of them to stand up simultaneously long enough that I could support one at either side of me. Each time I stooped to pick up the second one, the first would keel over again. Finally, in a wild series of staggering tacks, I piloted "Long John Silver" and the heavily listing "Helganola" back to the inlet.

Finding the place in darkness, my allusions to the classics were further indulged while I pondered how we were to get back across. Faithful Hilda must have been keeping watch, for, dressed in a white flowing nightgown, "The Lady of the Lake" appeared—to claim her husband.

In the morning Rudy didn't look well at all when he ferried us over for our first visit to Vienna. We took the city's clean and ultramodern underground to the Karlsplaz and set out in search of the Bulgarian embassy. Eventually, we found ourselves outside a nondescript portal labeled "The Socialist Republic of Bulgaria." A closed-circuit television camera scrutinized us and a crackly voice from inside the bell button inquired as to the nature of our business. Then the heavy black door swung ajar, accompanied by a loud electronic buzzing. In the shabby waiting room, the sinister-looking embassy staff handed us over to a friendly chap who spoke English to help us fill out the application forms—seemingly a serious business, as one "instruction" helpfully pointed out in three languages, "No crossing out will be permitted." After taking down all of *Alea*'s vital statistics, he cheerfully announced that he would pass these on to the naval authorities in Sofia for approval. "Naval Authorities—for a small sailing boat—how long will that take?" Smiling, he shrugged, "Next Tuesday zee earliest—no problem!"

Seeking visas from these Eastern Bloc states was a gamble. What if one should refuse us passage? If it came to the worst, we were still within reasonable trucking range of the Adriatic. If only Romania should fail us, then there was the option of trucking through Bulgaria, either to the Black Sea or directly to the Aegean.

But for now we turned our attention to the sights of Vienna. Cast in an overdone, monumental classical style, Vienna falls somewhat short of London's solid dignity and Paris's grand spaciousness. Surrounding the central city, a ring of beautiful parks and gardens interlink with the grounds of many state and civic buildings. In one of these retreats, the Heldenplatz (Heroes' Square), we took a break from the busy and stuffy capital. Before us stood the statue of a dynamic horseman, frozen for posterity in his moment of valor. Above perched the empty balcony of the Imperial Palace, where in 1938 Hitler announced the annexation of Austria to the jubilant Viennese crowd.

Next day we hit the embassy trail again, which led to the Czechoslovak consulate in southwest Vienna. Luckily, we outdid the embassy gremlins by arriving twenty minutes before it was due to close at 11:00 A.M. We joined a feverish crowd darting about to fill in the forms and trim and glue on passport photographs "in the prescribed manner." To quote Victoria's diary,

> It was like being at school for adults, having to ask for glue and little scissors.

While waiting for the applications to be processed, I started speaking to an elderly woman who was sporting a bright new plaster cast on her arm. She was a Canadian music teacher, fulfilling a lifelong dream by making a pilgrimage to the haunts of her favorite composers. Unfortunately, things had gone badly wrong when she had tried to enter Czechoslovakia. Instead of being able to buy a visa at the border, as she thought, she was taken off the train and sent back to Vienna to get one. If this wasn't bad enough, when she arrived back in Vienna late at night, she was attacked by a thief. Although she managed to hold on to her bags, it cost her a broken arm. Despite this she was still full of pluck and preparing to try again, but this time dancing to the Czechoslovaks' tune.

When our number appeared above the cashier's booth, it was our turn to pay the piper. For the sum 420 shillings we were given our first key to the East. In view of the procedure the Bulgarians were following, I was pleasantly surprised how easy it was. They never even queried "sailing boat" as the answer to "mode of transport" on the application forms. And we were even exempt from registering with the police, because hopefully it would take a lot less than twenty-four hours to negotiate Czechoslovakia's 25-kilometer stretch of the waterway.

One spinoff of having to travel out to the embassy was that it brought to our attention the nearby Schönbrunn Palace. Walking through its spacious grounds and historical buildings, we found rooms that Mozart had performed in, and one in which Napoleon's son had died. We looked on beds that Napoleon himself had slept on, as well as the spartan-looking cot that Franz Joseph, Austria's last emperor, died in. Even as we made our way from Schönbrunn, our historical peep show continued when we came upon a plaque on a tenement building recalling that Stalin had stayed there in 1913.

Later in the week we tried the visa hall of the Hungarian embassy, where for the sum of 540 shillings we extended our range down the Danube to the Bulgarian border. Then it was on to the Romanians. No grand visa hall here, only a narrow, jam-packed hallway, where the smell of stale perspiration was overpowering. I tried asking about application forms but only got blank stares from the dark gypsy types that made up most of the queue. Taking my life in my hands, I began to squeeze through the press of people to make my way up to the front.

Just as I came to a standstill, about three-quarters of the way along, I looked back and saw a young chap making his way up through the queue. More determined than I, he burrowed past me but got stopped by a loudly protesting woman. I don't know what he said in reply, but the whole crowd, including the woman, started to laugh. He was fashionably dressed with a show of heavy gold jewelry. Obviously a natural comedian, he played to his captive audience, who laughed every time he spoke. And every time they turned to laugh, he cunningly moved up another place. While still some 2 meters from the tiny hatch in the end wall, he started a shouted conversation with the embassy official within. After some more hilarity the people in front of him passed his forms and passport up and through the hatch.

Now that his business was being attended to, he visibly relaxed and turned his attention to me. In excellent English, he asked if I needed any help. When I told him I wanted a visa, he looked at me as if I were mad and exclaimed: "Vhat do you vant to go to Romania for? All they vill do is empty your pockets!" He went on to tell me that nothing had changed in his country except one man at the top—Ceaușescu. Seeing that I wasn't to be put off, he shrugged and, with a look of disappointed resignation, asked me to hand him our passports. They were passed along to the hatch, accompanied by a set of obviously humorous instructions that had everyone laughing knowingly back at me. In no time at all, I was passing 800 shillings down the overhead chain in exchange for our stamped passports. No forms or photographs were required, it was just as my "silver-tongued" friend had said: "All zhey vant iz your foreign currency!"

By the time I made my triumphant reappearance before my amazed crew, I was dripping with sweat. No doubt realizing there must have been some divine intervention involved, a refined Romanian couple at the end of the queue reverently asked me, "Are you a priest?" I said I wasn't, but this didn't stop them following me out into the street to tell us their sad tale. They were Seventh Day Adventists caught in one of those "Catch-22" situations. Having escaped from Ceauşescu's Romania without passports, they now had to apply for them, from the "new" but still unsympathetic government, in order to return home.

They were trapped in a refugee camp; by contrast, we had just been given the freedom to pass through their country. When dealing with the awkward indifference of the embassies, one forgets that their own citizens have to put up with this attitude in every aspect of their lives. We were to become almost immune to such sentiments when faced with this everyday reality ourselves.

We headed off to the Schwarzenbergplatz, where we found a colossal Russian war memorial built "lest we forget" the 1945 "liberation" of Vienna. By the great number of dog turds around its base, it was obvious a lot of Viennese dog owners hadn't forgotten. In the short time we spent there, we observed three dogs being lifted up onto the monument's grassy dais to pay their respects.

Sunday was free admission day to the city's museums, so we wandered through the miles of our world's wonders. On Monday afternoon we climbed the hills above Kahlenbergerdorf. At the top of the 500-meter Kahlenberg we were rewarded with spectacular views of Vienna, which lay spread out to the far horizon beneath us.

On our way down we came upon a church that had a display on the 1683 Turkish siege of Vienna. One interesting anecdote of the conflict credits the invention of the croissant breakfast roll to a Viennese baker. Apparently, on starting work early in the morning he heard the sound of Turkish sappers tunneling under the city walls toward the basement of his bakery. His timely alarm allowed the defenders to save the city. Being a smart "cookie," he followed up his exploit by designing a roll in the shape of the Turkish crescent to commemorate his breakfast call.

Tuesday arrived, and we set off to hear what the Bulgarians had to say. The boat was apparently the problem. The authorities in Sofia wanted a list of all our intended ports of call and a schedule of visiting dates. Incredibly, they didn't have a map of Bulgaria in the embassy to help us compile the itinerary. The diplomat diplomatically suggested we could get a map at the Balkan tourist office in the city. Off we traipsed.

In the Karlsplatz park we made up a travel schedule, and I hurried back to hand it in. When I expressed concern about the delay, the good diplomat suggested that I ask the New Zealand embassy to contact Sofia on our behalf.

With this ray of hope I returned to the park and met the crew outside the Wagner Pavilion. This building had nothing to do with the composer but honored a city architect: Otto Wagner, best remembered for instigating one of the world's greatest *what-ifs*. As principal of Vienna's Architectural College in 1908, he refused the entry of young Adolf Hitler because the applicant didn't have a school leaving certificate. With the bureaucratic jungle we were having to struggle through here, I could see how some minds could get twisted.

We tracked down the New Zealand embassy, but unfortunately the Consul General couldn't do anything for us, because New Zealand didn't have an embassy in Sofia. I suggested they just contact them by phone, but this apparently wasn't protocol.

This was the end of the legitimate line for us. We figured out that all we needed was to get the visa stamped on our passport, and to have *Alea*'s transit application passed on to Belgrade (and hopefully dropped between the cracks) while we carried on. So we decided to have another go at the Bulgarian embassy.

The next day, Wednesday, September 5, we found Rudy in the process of locking everything up because he was having a day off. As we thought we might be able to get under way in the afternoon, we paid the mooring fee for the previous ten nights—1,000 shillings. When we arrived at the embassy, we were dismayed to find that it was not only Rudy who was having a day off. The crackly voice from the door intercom announced, "Geschlossen," closed. In desperation, I made a dramatic appeal to the cold eye of the closed-circuit television camera, and to our surprise the electronic buzzing sounded for the door to open. We charged up the stairs lest they should change their minds. It was the friendly diplomat from yesterday who had taken pity on us. I told him that we had been to the New Zealand embassy (true) and that the ambassador was doing everything he could on our behalf (diplomatic). He was pleased I had taken his advice and added that it was the Transport Ministry they should contact. Typically, when I asked for the telephone number, this couldn't be found, and a little shamefaced he gave me the Foreign Ministry's number instead. I believe it was this small embarrassment over the telephone numbers that actually carried the day, for when I asked if we could get our visas now and have the boat transit permission sent on to their embassy in Belgrade, he agreed.

Even in that joyous moment when we thought we had pulled the wool over the bureaucratic monster's eyes, it was turning quickly to even the score. Their visa regulations would only allow us one visit to Bulgaria within a twelve-month period. But we had planned to visit twice: once on its Danube frontier, then, after passing through Romania, once again on its Black Sea coast. When I explained this to the diplomat, he just shrugged and said, "Zhat iz zee rules!" We had no option but to choose the visit we wanted most, which had to be the Black Sea coast. In spite of this no-win situation, we still felt pretty good about getting the visas. At last we could leave Vienna, for now the political road, at least, was open—all the way to Turkey.

Seventeen
Czech-Mate

WE RAN LAUGHING from the Bulgarian embassy, happy in the knowledge that we would never kowtow at their door again—here or in Belgrade! They could roll up their boat transit permission and sit on it until their next revolution.

After spending the last of our Austrian shillings on supplies, we returned to *Alea* and prepared for departure. Due to the previous night's rainstorm, the Danube was running very fast. In a dipping, surging instant, we were drawn out and whisked away on the fastest ride yet. With an 8- to 9-knot current under us, we were flying down the deserted river.

We passed under a succession of concrete bridges that seemed to hang low over the rushing water. This included the replacement of the *Reichsbruecke*, which collapsed suddenly in 1976. The thought of that disaster caused us an uncomfortable split second each time one of its surviving neighbors swooped past overhead.

As the last of Vienna disappeared astern, we passed the low, scrub-covered nature reserve of Löbau. This is where Napoleon crossed in 1809 to receive his first military defeat at the battle of

Aspern, 5 kilometers distant. Things didn't bode too well for us here either, as black thunderclouds amassed in the southwest. It soon developed into a race as to which was going to arrive first: our next haven, or the heavens themselves.

Fortunately the thermal spa village of Bad-Deutsch-Altenburg hove into view. Situated just 5 kilometers from the border, its small, deserted works harbor made it an ideal starting point for tomorrow's run through Czechoslovakia. After a spectacular downpour the sun came out so strongly that steam rose from the deck in clouds.

With the air cleared, Charles and I went for a walk through what appeared to be a country park and came upon many Roman archaeological excavations. One was a graveyard, where Charles impressed me by translating the Latin on the headstones. It was amazing the interests that were surfacing in our children since the days when television ruled. Victoria had now taken up biology in order to study her pet ladybirds.

We were up with the lark the next morning and set off while the children still slept. Although misty and cool, the weather looked promising. The river current had moderated to about 5 to 6 knots, a speed that would have caused us concern before, but after the previous day it looked sedate. There was no other shipping until we reached the frontier town of Hainburg, when a noisy hydrofoil came charging up from behind. We were so taken aback by this dramatic encounter that we didn't notice the Austrian checkpoint until we heard the policeman shouting after us to "Halt!"

After another teeth-gritting effort to claw our way back, the elderly policeman only glanced at our passports. And when I asked about the Czech border post, all he knew was that it was somewhere in an inlet on the left bank. There was nothing else for it but to trust to luck and keep a better lookout.

I managed only a few tantalizing glances at the high, cobbled township of Hainburg as it glided past. Built as a demarcation between East and West, it has a history that is a study in the vagaries of fate. In 1683, when it was the turn of the Turks to burn and massacre the citizens, the grandfather of composer Joseph Haydn was one of only eight survivors from a population of nine thousand.

We followed the river round a high, rocky outcrop and entered a narrowing gorge. This was the Porta Hungarica, where the Danube breaks through the narrow spur of foothills that connect the Alps with the Carpathians. The latter, on our left, rose steeply out of the river to support the ruins of a castle on a high promontory. Dense forest scrub covered the surrounding hills and reached out from either bank, adding to the eerie foreboding that hung about the place. Although we had heard that border security had been relaxed, it still felt as if we were being watched from behind every bush. Then, on the rising hills above the trees to our left, the sinister silhouette of a POW-type watchtower came into view.

In quick succession others appeared, spaced out along the high ridge and down through the forest in a grotesque barbed-wire spectacle that defied belief. At the junction of the River Morava, which forms the border on the left bank, we stared back at the towers, transfixed by the array of binoculars that were trained on us as we swept on by, unchallenged.

Near where we thought the border post would be, we saw a dark-colored patrol boat moored under a steep rock face. Three young sailors stood smoking in the cockpit. Each had a machine-gun hanging from his shoulder. I crossed over, holding our passports in the air. One of the boys, as if in bored disgust, waved us on as he picked up the hand receiver of a radio and spoke into it.

We continued on for several kilometers with no sign of the checkpoint. Then, on the right bank, the continuation of the Austro–Czechoslovak frontier confronted us suddenly. A cleared tract of land was driven up through the forest as if the earth had split apart. Nearest the Austrian side two high, parallel barbed-wire fences, interspaced with watchtowers, roller-coastered over hill and dale as far as the eye could see. There was no ambiguity about this frontier: like a prison wall, its only function was to keep people in, and we had definitely crossed it.

Only a short distance on, we entered the outskirts of Bratislava, which looked rundown and seedy. On the left bank the mouth of a small harbor appeared, and I quickly steered across to it. It looked like a disused side canal, with no sign of a Customs post. Several derelict houseboats lay along one side, half afloat. I held station on the outgoing current and wondered what we should do. The only explanation we could think of was that the post was back upriver and that somehow we had missed it. There was no way I was going back now. If they wanted to check our passports, they could jolly well try catching us before we reached the Hungarian border.

As I headed back out across the Danube again, I noticed a person in civilian clothes running through the trees on the right bank, waving for us to turn back. It was too late—the die was cast. As casually as I could, I looked away downriver and eased the bow round to take advantage of the strong midstream current. My adrenaline started to pump—the race was on!

No sooner had we passed under the first central city bridge than we heard the approaching wail of a police siren. As it grew louder we felt as if the whole KGB were in hot pursuit. With lights flashing, the patrol car overtook us on the river promenade and turned onto the next bridge ahead. I really expected it to stop on the bridge and signal us to pull over, but to our relief it sped on across.

We sped on, too, and gained the open marshland south of Bratislava, where our next encounter was for real—"they" were on to us! A small, dirty yellow spotter plane swooped overhead at treetop level. Circling round, it returned to buzz us twice more. The glum, raw white face of the pilot peered down. I gaped back and resisted the urge to wave. Not too long ago that same predatory stare had probably hunted out his fleeing countrymen for the communists.

Not long after he had made off to the north, we heard the heavy roar of a powerful diesel engine coming up from behind at high speed. With only a kilometer to go before we reached the Hungarian border, we sat in dread and disappointment at the prospect of being caught. It wasn't until the terrible noise was right upon us that we dared look round at the vessel. For the second time that day that damned hydrofoil had played an unwitting joke on us. We breathed a grudging sigh of relief as the smoking aberration rocketed past.

In its noisy wake we made good use of our reprieve and raced to pass the mouth of the tributary that marks the border on the right bank. The instant we crossed, Despina snatched down the

Czechoslovak courtesy flag and raised the Hungarian colors—we had made it! Just in time, too, for soon after, a Czech naval minesweeper-type vessel came up fast from the south. It held station on the other side of the river while a bevy of officers scrutinized us through binoculars. This time we all waved happily over to them. To our great satisfaction, they immediately headed off upriver at high speed. Czech-mate! One down—three to go.

Eighteen
Hungary and the Buda Pests

6 SEPTEMBER

LIKE SIAMESE TWINS, the grubby harbor towns of Hungary's Komárom and Czechoslovakia's Komárno crouch opposite each other, hideously linked by two raw, rusting steel bridges. The river at this point gets noticeably wider, reducing the current to around 2 to 3 knots.

In contrast to the surrounding drabness, two bright new Hungarian flags marked the dilapidated Customs pontoon. To our surprise we were shown into a spacious reception area, neatly furnished in the style of a 1960s coffee lounge. A soft-spoken policeman helped us fill in a transit form and a sullen woman invited us to exchange our currency into Hungarian forint. Fortunately, we tendered only a token amount, for which they charged us a hefty commission that included one deutsche mark for an hour's mooring at the pontoon. This, we were to find, was all in the spirit of the new doctrine of "free market economy and private enterprise."

Being equally hard-nosed customers, we decided to use up our hour's mooring by taking a walk into town. Whereas in France and Germany the old buildings had evoked the past, here the people did as well. The way they dressed made us feel we had stepped back to the 1940s or 1950s. The women wore cardigans over floral print dresses, and those men not in Russian-style army uniforms wore baggy old suits. There didn't seem to be many cars. Heavy trucks and horse-drawn carts appeared to be the only users of the badly potholed streets.

Yet we could sense change in the air. A block of new shops stood half complete, while all the "entrepreneurs" were out on the streets with their wares. Teenagers, housewives, and old people had staked out their patch on the pavement with a meager display of merchandise: two pairs of shoes at one, a few acrylic cardigans at another. One hopeful stood over her stock of six plastic combs and a dozen miscellaneous buttons at yet another. It looked more like amateur participation than economic desperation, as if to trade was the new craze, and there were decidedly more sellers than buyers.

From this scarcity of consumer goods we reached the vegetable market, where oversupply reigned supreme. Here crowds of stall-holders watched over mountains of shiny peppers. Although we could buy any conceivable shape, size, or color of pepper, potatoes could only be got "under the counter." We decided to forgo the milk, which was sold in what appeared to be recycled plastic bags. They lay in a bulging heap on the ground, like a pile of amputated cow udders, while white rivulets of escaping milk snaked away in all directions. From that point on, it was fruit juice on our breakfast cereal.

One thing for which there was no easy substitute was petrol. We found the filling station and thus solved the mystery of where all the cars had gone. Moving to the front of the long car queue, we saw an attendant filling a cache of 20-liter jerricans. I chanced my luck and offered up my empty 5-liter can, which he willingly filled. Suspecting the apparent shortage might be an ongoing problem, I indicated that I wanted to buy a jerrican. The amused attendant shook his head, and when I asked where else I could try for one, he humorously held up his arms and rolled his eyes skyward.

This was my first and last attempt at speaking Hungarian, a distant relation of Finnish. It was impossible for us to read the string of phonetics from our phrase book. We soon discovered that miming and pointing was easier for all concerned.

The river grew wide and calm after Komárom with hardly a breath of wind to stir our flags. As if in a dream, we felt suspended on the great expanse of silvery gray, drifting through vast areas of farmland that looked neglected and bare.

In the late afternoon we arrived at Esztergom, the old capital of Hungary and the legendary seat of Attila the Hun. Although it occupied a magnificent elevated site, a moldering shabbiness seemed to hang everywhere as if we were inspecting a long-forgotten attic.

We were pleased to sail past the mouth of the River Ipoly, which forms the border between Czechoslovakia and Hungary; now both sides of the river were open to us for anchorages.

But soon another obstacle hove into sight: the Danube Bend, a sharp zigzag that sends the east-flowing Danube sweeping south for several hundred kilometers through the heart of Hungary. The left bank showed signs of huge earthworks having narrowed the river. This was the bottom end of the controversial joint dam and power generation scheme that Hungary has pulled out of—an environmental issue that hastened the end of communist rule in Hungary. Apparently, the Czechs are continuing with their dam and canal, which will reroute the Danube farther east from Bratislava. This will of course greatly change the flat river marshes we had just traveled through.

The traffic lights were at red, and although there was no other traffic we had to wait three hours before being waved on round—against all the red lights!

Where the bend turns south, two channels run down either side of the 40-kilometer-long Szentendrei (St. Andrew's) Island. The main shipping channel passes to the east, so we chose the smaller and more scenic western one.

On the island side of the channel we saw several powerboats anchored off a sandy beach and decided to call it a day and join them. A white-haired gentleman who was the spitting image of the author Solzhenitsyn invited us ashore, and to show his willingness, he paddled out in a canoe to act as ferryman.

I joined Lewis and his wife, Meloni, who were both locomotive design engineers and were learning English at evening classes. Lewis was very interested in our trip; in fact, it was he who first suggested I should try writing this book.

We sat with a clique of boat enthusiasts from Budapest around a huge campfire in a forest clearing. First we toasted each other with a delicious red wine, then rather dramatically their new democracy with schnapps, then we finished off by toasting bread and bacon on sticks. In the gathering dusk, Lewis and his friend Alexander paddled me back to Despina and the children. After a conducted tour of *Alea* and another dram, we launched our new friends back toward St. Andrew's Isle with as many good wishes as ever followed a Cunard Liner down a slipway.

Next day, Sunday, September 9, there was a definite autumn crispness in the air, the herald of a very cold snap that was to accompany us right through Hungary. On our way down to Budapest, we came across many leisure craft out enjoying a Sunday cruise, including, to our surprise, a smart 12-meter yacht. It was at anchor and had its mast stowed on deck. We were well past when a couple came up on deck and returned our distant salutes.

Boating was obviously very popular here. The riverbanks bristled with small boat jetties, each one leading to a semisecluded holiday cabin, and judging by the individuality of their designs, they were privately owned. From the river it all looked a charming, Bohemian holiday retreat.

We stopped at the local tourist town of Szentendre, once the long-time established home of an isolated community of Serbs. While strolling its quaint narrow streets we noticed several Serbian Orthodox churches, locked up and very dilapidated. One, festooned with rusting padlocks and chains, also had a graphical "beware of dog" warning. Mindful of past canine encounters, we ventured no farther and made our way back to *Alea*. Ironically, as we set off on the last stretch to Budapest, we headed straight into the jaws of our next dog drama.

Lewis had kindly given us directions to Bruno's, apparently the only marina in Budapest. We entered the city's sprawling suburbs and dutifully turned up "the first creek past the railway bridge"—a side channel that ran behind a large island called Obuda, Old Buda. We could see the marina at the end of the long, tree-lined fairway and hear the forbidding bark of large dogs.

We were directed to berth between two shabby launches by an equally shabby, middle-aged man. This was Bruno. After giving us a fleeting, melancholy smile, he indicated for us to wait while he made off up the long flight of embankment steps. He soon returned, followed by a short, bedraggled-looking woman dressed in a florid housekeeper's apron and sporting a shiner of a black eye.

To our great surprise, she introduced herself, in a strong south of England accent, as "Edith, Bruno's sister in-law." Her father was Hungarian, but she was born and brought up in Southampton. With Edith as interpreter I asked Bruno what the mooring fee was. He replied that the Germans gave him 20 deutsche marks per night but that I could decide on the fee myself. After getting him to agree that the Germans had too much money, I offered 15 marks for two nights, which he readily accepted.

Like any group of expats, we enjoyed the opportunity for a cup of tea and a chat with Edith. She told us that the government had just handed over the ownership of the marina to Bruno, who had been the caretaker all his life. It had been his parents' boatbuilding yard prior to the communist takeover. Now it had fallen into such a state of disrepair that all Bruno could do with it was hire out its mooring space.

A brief rain shower in the afternoon did not spoil our plans to visit the city center. Armed with our golfing umbrella–*cum*–shooting stick, we climbed up to the terrace, where two large mixed-breed German shepherds were going berserk at the end of their chains to get at us. Quickly we crossed the yard and gained the safety of the street, but unfortunately I decided to return—to see a man about a dog.

To my dismay, I found the dogs commanded the approach to the toilets as well as the back door to Bruno's house. Retreating, I knocked at his front door. As always seems to be the case, both Bruno and Edith declared the dogs "harmless" and indicated that their apparent ferocity was just excitement at the prospect of "meating" us. I asked if they could be moved elsewhere or their 5-meter chains shortened so we could use the toilet block. Bruno led the way into the yard, where he held both dogs by their collars while I nipped past along the side of the house.

In two shakes I was out again, expecting another free pass, but Bruno had gone, leaving his hysterical hounds baying for my blood. Trapped at the back of the house, I hammered at a bedroom window until Edith appeared. She came out and tried to hold my tormentors back. Seeing the first one break away from her, I took to my heels. Only 2 meters from safety, I saw, out of the corner of my eye, the racing blur of the dog leaping up at me. Half turning, I struck out with my umbrella and caught the brute a heavy blow on the snout. I got round the corner and slammed the yard gate firmly behind me.

Although I had escaped in one piece, I was badly shaken. We picked our way round muddy pools of rainwater on a footpath that had disintegrated and merged with the potholed street. To add insult to injury, several motorists swerved in to splash us. I was overcome with such a loathing of our seedy surroundings that the thought of staying here for two days and putting up with those dogs was just too much. Turning about, the silent crew followed their unhappy skipper back to the ship.

We had just started taking down the boom-tent when Edith came down onto the pontoon. The poor woman was terribly embarrassed at having to inform us that Bruno was so upset at me for hitting his dog that he wanted us to leave. We had no wish to make it any harder on her and just agreed to "go quietly."

Despina was mortified at the thought of being "thrown out of Budapest" before she had set foot in the place, and the consideration of "going quietly" was only to be extended to Edith. As for me—I would have got more sympathy from the dogs! Charles and Victoria disappeared down below to let their parents get on with their scrap. Not wanting to tempt fate out on the Danube, we anchored for the night alongside Obuda Island.

With rage and fury spent, we had just settled down when the yacht we had seen earlier in the day drew alongside. The owners of the *Faun* introduced themselves as Tibor and Katherine, both university lecturers, who, after taking ten years to build the *Faun*, used it as their permanent home. On hearing about our incident with Bruno, they were determined to improve *Alea*-Hungarian relations and invited us aboard the *Faun* for a tour of Budapest by night.

Budapest is the only capital city on the Danube to have the river pass right through its center. Curiously, it was once two separate towns, Buda and Pest, both names in fact meaning the same, "kiln or oven," in different languages. While the sun set behind the low hills of Buda, we passed the shadow-etched, neo-Gothic facade of Hungary's parliament. Katherine got quite animated when telling us about being in the jubilant crowd that watched the communist star being plucked from the building's domed pinnacle by a helicopter. After forty years of the "Red scourge," their prayers were at last answered. Next to be remodeled, they hoped, was the dominating "Statue of Liberation" that commemorates the arrival of the Red Army. The monument has been guarded day and night ever since the 1956 uprising, when the freedom fighters had "worked" on it.

It was quickly growing dark, and by the time we reached the Elizabeth Bridge, on our way back upstream, its flamboyant display of draped, colored lights was in full blossom. To the left the floodlit, high, terraced walls of Buda Castle shone out more like a ghostly apparition of a Tibetan temple than a medieval stronghold. Then on our right came another view of the Parliament building, this time in fairy-tale splendor.

The *Faun* plugged purposefully into the dark, winding channel behind Margaret Island and Obuda. Tibor steered with supreme confidence through the enveloping blackness, hunting out the channel with the warning bleeps of the echo sounder. Watching this impressive display made me regret that I still hadn't been able to fix *Alea*'s depth-sounder.

Soon the ghostly sheen of *Alea*'s hull appeared through the inky murk to starboard. In no time the boats were rafted together, and over a cup of coffee we sat enthralled as Katherine and Tibor told us about their steady progress toward fulfilling their long-cherished dream of sailing to Tierra del Fuego. Tibor even showed us his treasured charts of the area, bought when there seemed little chance they would ever be allowed to leave Hungary. Now, after years of being confined to the limits of the Hungarian Danube and the occasional trip to Lake Balaton, they were at last politically free to cruise farther afield. Of course there were still great economic hurdles for them to overcome, but there was certainly no lack of willpower.

When we bid them farewell in the early hours, Katherine promised to speak to Bruno in the morning. Sure enough, they returned after breakfast with a full pardon and an invitation to return. We thanked them for their kindness but felt it was best to continue on our way. So after another hearty farewell, we raised anchor and slipped out onto the Danube.

Flowing gently, the broad river wound its way south through a dense industrial area before stretching out over the flat Hungarian plain. On either low bank, a thin, continuous verge of leafy willows blinkered our view, leaving an immense expanse of sky to surround us. From here on a wonderful sense of idle rhythm set in; time and space seemed to merge with the eternal flow of the river. I fell under its spell, resenting the intrusion the stops for provisions made on this blissful harmony.

It was this intoxicating laziness and the sudden sharp drop in the temperature that put me off raising *Alea*'s mast. Three days later, in the quiet calm of the access canal that meanders around the town of Baja, I finally managed to raise myself. As if in homage to the return of the warm sun, we gathered on deck and hauled the mast erect as though it were a shiny totem.

Following the flat, wooded landscape, we reached the border town of Mohács, 30 kilometers downstream. Here, in 1526 at the catastrophic Battle of Mohács, the Ottoman Turk won the prize of Hungary, which he held for two hundred years—thus giving rise to the Hungarian saying that belittles any disaster they face: "Worse things happened at Mohács."

To our surprise we found the Yugoslav passport control office next to the Hungarian one. The Yugoslavian policeman was very friendly in spite of having to fill in lots of forms, each requiring four carbon copies. This took some time, between making jokes about the task, showing us photographs of his children, and deciphering each other's German. When the paperwork was complete, we were given a copy with instructions that we must get it stamped by the police in Belgrade.

With handshakes all round he told us to go back and wait for the Customs officer, who would make an inspection of *Alea* shortly. After waiting three-quarters of an hour on the quay, I returned to the policeman to ask what had happened to the Customs officer. Laughing, he indicated quite graphically that the young man was otherwise engaged with a Hungarian girlfriend. "No problem," he would make the inspection himself on behalf of the missing Casanova. When he arrived at the quay, it was obvious he didn't want to make the awkward climb down onto *Alea*'s deck, so with a magnanimous wave of his arm, we got clearance. To show our appreciation, Charles ran up the Yugoslavian colors on the starboard spreader and Despina handed up a nip of whiskey to our friendly "Bill." Although still 14 kilometers inside Hungarian territory, we were now officially in Yugoslavia.

Nineteen
Yugoslavia: The Beginning of the End

WE CROSSED INTO YUGOSLAVIA and after only a few kilometers anchored for the night behind an isolated breakwater of heaped-up boulders. Although we were to find these L-shaped havens all through Yugoslavia, we never saw any other boat using them. A vast plantation of silver birch stretched away from the shore as far as the eye could see, giving the place a very Slavonic air.

For the first time in about a week it was warm enough to sit out under the stars after supper. From the surrounding forests came the most incredible animal roaring noises. A distant, deep-throated groan was echoed by others that stabbed from the darkness all around, making their direction and nearness as startling as their fiendish tone. "Perhaps stags," I said, but Charles, a growing expert in such matters, whispered gravely, "We're in Transylvania."

With such spine-chilling sound effects laid on, it was indeed an ideal time for a rendering of *Dracula, Prince of Darkness*.

Surviving the night, we set off early in bright sunshine and not a breath of wind. Right away we had to perform our first limbo dance with the mast to pass under the road bridge at Batina. The mast-lowering apparatus was designed to be left in place, allowing us to tilt the mast down at a moment's notice. After negotiating another two bridges in the day's 90-kilometer run, we had perfected an efficient operating procedure. Victoria took the tiller and steered, while Despina stood by at the bow to work the forestay release pin. I positioned myself on the cabintop to haul on the block and tackle, and Charles controlled all the sagging stays to prevent them from fouling the motor. In every instance, the operation went like clockwork.

By contrast, the operation that never seemed to go smoothly was obtaining the first issue of a country's currency. Although we carried a reserve of deutsche marks, we had been warned that it was still illegal to exchange these outside the official banking system. We stopped at several sizable villages only to find that none had a bank. Next day, September 15, we found out that the exchange rate was an incredible 67,000 dinars to the dollar, and that there were in fact two types of dinar in circulation, "old" and "new." Apparently due to galloping inflation, 10,000 "old" dinars were equivalent to one "new" dinar.

Confident of finding a bank at the Croatian town of Vukovar, we moored for the night alongside an anchored barge. Little did any of us know that within a year, this quiet riverside town would be the first to be devastated in bitter civil war.

A talkative Croatian woman explained the mystery of the dual currency to Despina and with great pride volunteered to show off her hometown, especially its well-stocked supermarket—"just like the West," she had apparently said. We got the impression that here was a people much happier with their lot than their Eastern Bloc neighbors, a recurring observation that makes their subsequent hateful civil war all the more baffling to us.

I went in search of petrol and water along a dusty, tree-lined suburban street and asked directions from a giggling group of high school students. One girl was summarily pushed to the front to act as their "English" spokesperson. Bravely she explained that the petrol station was far out of town, but that she could get me water. In embarrassed haste she returned with the heavy container, after the school bell had rung, then rushed off to her class with a highly original excuse for being late. Every time I see the tragic images of Yugoslavia's civil war, I remember that young girl and wonder how she fared.

We left Vukovar in our wake and headed out on the ever widening Danube. The day before, we had passed through a very contorted stretch of the river, caused by the influx of the powerful River Drava. Horseshoe bends and large sandbanks had followed each other in snaking succession. Although the buoyage system was not as comprehensive as in Germany and Austria, we had picked our way through without mishap. Today the Danube was more open, stretching out ahead in a gentle curve to the southeast. Now only the odd distant buoyed gate marked any change in the line of the channel.

We had just passed through one of these gates near the right bank when *Alea*'s centerplate hit bottom. I pressed the tiller over and turned to port but came to a grinding halt on a submerged sandbar. Despina raised the centerplate while I tried reversing, but the river current on our port quarter just pushed us farther over on the shoal.

Standing on the sandbar stripped off and with the river gushing around my middle, I put my shoulder to the starboard bow. Slowly *Alea* pivoted round to face upstream. While I held the bow in position, Despina put the motor into forward gear. As she had not operated the outboard before, I had to call back the instructions. *Alea* didn't move, so I called on her to twist the accelerator—"a bit!" Instantly, the motor gave a noisy shriek and *Alea* shot forward. This caught me off balance, my upper half being propelled upstream with *Alea* while my bottom half was carried back by the current. As I floundered alongside the hull, I got hooked up in a tire-fender and used it to pull myself up the side. No sooner had I managed to crawl over the gunwale, half drowned, than I was crossly seized upon by Despina, who demanded to know what she was to do next!

I got her to helm *Alea* round, well clear of the sandbank, while I lay on the cockpit floor and scrubbed the black tire marks from my chest and legs. The encounter was soon forgotten in the orgy of wicked glee with which Victoria rinsed me down with buckets of water scooped up from the river. After I recovered from that chilly trauma, it was all hands to their positions for sneaking the mast under the bridge at Bachka Palanka.

Completing a day's run of only 60 kilometers, we anchored behind another deserted breakwater. In the morning we awoke to our first river mist since leaving the Swale in England. By the time we were ready to go, it had lifted to treetop height. This foggy gloom made the modern city of Novi Sad look even more drab and depressing with its concrete high-rise boxes. The only redeeming feature was the impressive terraced bulk of an eighteenth-century fortress overlooking the right bank. Our guidebook mentioned that Marshal Tito was once held prisoner in it, so we decided to have a closer look. Nothing stirred along the embankment; houses as well as boats lay abandoned in moldering neglect. We moored alongside what appeared to be a defunct floating hotel and climbed up the dusty approach road to the fortress.

Although it too lay open and seemingly deserted, it had a far more appealing atmosphere than the dilapidated streets we had just passed through. At least one expected an old castle to look timeworn. In fact, there were more signs of life inside the fortifications than out. Large areas were cultivated into vegetable gardens, as though the place were holding out against some long siege.

On the way back to *Alea*, Charles and Victoria thought they had stumbled on a fortune when they scrambled to pick up the scattered fragments of several discarded banknotes. They spent the rest of the day taping the jigsaw together, eventually reconstituting two and a half 1,000 "old" dinar notes, worth less than the amount of tape they used.

We ducked under reputedly the lowest bridge on the Danube; it was possibly 7 or 8 meters high, although it was very difficult judging the heights of these potential dangers to the mast. They always looked threateningly low, especially the new overhead hazards we came upon that afternoon: electric power lines. We dutifully lowered the mast for the first couple of sets, but as their frequency increased, so did our nerve. Seeing how they sagged in mid span and rose up to their pylons on the riverbank, I started sneaking past close inshore. Although we risked grounding in the shallower water, it saved disturbing the crew from their school-work.

The time for disturbing the crew came later that day. With the sky threatening rain, we began looking for an anchorage. After a fruitless hour, we opted for a slight cove on the left bank, where a small creek entered. We tried to nose into the mouth of the creek but ran aground just as it started to rain. Backing off, we dropped the anchor about 5 meters from the riverbank. There was the expected splash, and then the prolonged rattle of the anchor-chain as it continued to run out, until the anchor was hanging straight down at the end of its 25-meter chain—without having touched bottom! All our previous anchorages on the Danube had been no deeper than 4 meters.

We tried dropping it 10 meters farther upstream but with the same result. Up anchor again. Tried back closer to the shore. Ran aground. Reversed off and went round again while the mate's short fuse hissed loudly. It was clear that if this one didn't work, I'd be doing the next on my own! Close in by the downstream riverbank, I helmed *Alea* round sharply to port and tossed the pick over the stern. Then, cutting back across the cove to almost the upstream point, the bow anchor found bottom at a depth of 5 meters. The rain was now bucketing down.

Alea was pointing diagonally out toward the river. When I checked my transit before turning in at 8:30 P.M., it showed we hadn't moved. Before falling asleep I remember being rocked by the wash from several passing ships. Then, just after 11:00 P.M., I was awakened by Despina shaking me and shouting, "We're moving!" A loud noise of rattling chains filled the cabin as *Alea* drifted rapidly sideways. Just as I reached the top of the companionway steps, we ran aground with several crunching jolts, then tilted over to starboard.

We had come to rest athwart the small stony spit that formed the downstream point of the cove. *Alea* now pointed toward the shore with her stern sticking out into the current of the Danube. The rain had stopped and the night was starry clear. "How could this be happening on such a beautiful night?" I thought illogically as I quickly got the motor started. Despina clambered forward to the bow and started pulling on the anchor, which just came sliding in over the shingle. Although the stern anchor broke out when

I pulled on it, it had thankfully held enough to keep us from going off down the Danube.

With the anchors in, Despina decided it was time to abandon ship and rushed below to dress the children in their life jackets. Abruptly awakened from their slumber, they quietly complied with trusting bewilderment. I tried to reverse off with several churning blasts of the motor, but *Alea* wouldn't budge. Frustrated, I disengaged gear and was just considering my next move when, miraculously, I felt *Alea* tipping back and down by the stern. Looking about me in puzzlement, I noticed Despina in the cabin, shepherding the children aft, out of the forepeak. As they all reached the companionway, *Alea* started to slide backward as if on a launching ramp. I crashed the motor into reverse, and with one tweak of the accelerator, we were free—and taking off down the black Danube, sideways.

It had all happened so quickly that our release was as great a shock as the stranding. Of course, as with every pickle we ever got into on the waterways, a barge came bearing down on us at the worst possible moment. From downstream, two shafts of dazzling light swept across us, then in an instant darted back to search along either side of the river. Like some fiendish creation from a science fiction epic, the two beaming eyes advanced on us. I quickly helmed *Alea* round to head back upstream and found to my horror that I couldn't see where we were going. The glare of the searchlights had completely destroyed my night vision.

The small cove was the only place we had to run back to. So Charles was sent up onto the cabin roof, where he bravely held and directed the searchlight, while Despina went up to the bow, ready to take a line ashore. As there was deeper water at the up-stream end of the cove, I planned to moor bow to the shore. I ran *Alea* straight in. All was going well until *Alea* gave a sudden lurch and stopped dead—3 meters from shore. Shining the light down into the water, I saw the black tentacles of the monster that held *Alea* fast: we had run onto a sunken tree.

As if on cue, the barge convoy pulled abreast of the cove and caught our folly in a blaze as bright as day. I was just able to sink two tire-fenders alongside before the wash came in to jibe us. With a branch jammed at either end of the keel it was clear *Alea* wouldn't be going anywhere else tonight. Just to make sure, I rashly lowered the bow anchor down through the tangle of branches and regretted it the moment it was done. The problem of how I was to get it back up again troubled my fitful slumber for the rest of the night.

Luckily, *Alea* didn't move at all during the night, allowing the bow anchor to be raised up through the branches without snagging. With the intention of cutting the branches, I climbed down onto them and found that the one stuck behind the keel flexed when I jumped on it. While I jumped, Despina worked the motor. On the third bounce *Alea*'s keel rode back over the branch. We were free again, and I got only my bottom half wet.

Unfortunately, there was a greater price to pay. The whole episode had taken its toll on Despina. Shaken and weepy, she suggested we stop the trip at Belgrade and transport the boat from there to Greece. I was able to pooh-pooh this on the grounds of the high costs involved, but her alternative plan of taking the children and waiting for me and *Alea* to arrive in Greece was harder to squash. It was shelved only after I gave an undertaking to review the situation at the Bulgarian town of Ruse, where the transporting of *Alea* was certainly more feasible.

By late afternoon the dreary suburban spread of Belgrade was passing to starboard. The metropolitan scene did brighten up a bit when we turned in behind the island of Vojno Ostrovo, which sits just before the mouth of the River Sava. Here ornate pavilions and boat clubhouses of a bygone era stand within spacious grounds. At first glance, it had an almost Greenwich of London look. But the nautical display reminded us that we were definitely east of Greenwich. Starkly functional naval gunboats lay next to neglected, tall-masted yachts that had obviously not left their moorings for a very long time.

We turned up the placid River Sava and slowly cruised the kilometer or so to the first bridge. Here we had to keep clear of the grime-smeared hydrofoils maneuvering about their terminal. It looked as though they had seen busier times, for several of these aerodynamic monsters were laid up high and dry, as if in some futuristic scrap-yard for spaceships.

The only attractive feature we could see was the remains of the buttressed foundation walls of the Kalemegdan citadel, which overlooks the junction of the Sava and Danube. However, by reasoning that we were probably seeing the best aspect of Belgrade from where we were, we decided to give it—and their police along with the Bulgarian embassy—a miss.

We spent a quiet night anchored back behind Vojno Ostrovo Island and set off early next morning. It was a dull, overcast day, memorable only for the number of sagging power lines we had to duck under. This was quite galling, for ever since we had erected the mast, it had proven to be nothing more than an awkward flagpole. There hadn't been a breath of wind for us to use the sails.

We called a halt at the town of Smederevo, where we moored to a deserted rowing club pier. It started to rain in the evening and developed into quite a storm during the night. *Alea* was being bounced about so much by the chop kicked up on the river that I had to get up to attach a set of spring lines. This settled her down a bit and allowed us to get some sleep.

Next day dawned bright and sunny, but best of all, there was wind. With the Danube running east at 1½ to 2 knots, we now had a willing 12- to 15-knot northwesterly to help as well. Charles hurried forward to help Despina with the jib, while I ran up the main and shouted instructions to Victoria on the tiller. She was trying every which way to turn *Alea* into the wind, but I had left the motor turning too slowly. We unashamedly completed the hoist while *Alea* crabbed backward down the Danube at 45°.

Sheets in and we were off! I cut the motor and the silence was deafening. After we had got used to the driving vibration of our little motor, the sudden sense of stillness was rather disquieting. It wasn't until we had checked that the inshore sandbanks were indeed slipping past at an easy 4 to 5 knots that we began to enjoy the sensation. When dealing with the day's quota of power lines, we dropped the sails at the first set, but from then on we sailed round the others.

We sailed all day, across the last of the great central plain we had entered in northern Hungary. In the distance, the foothills of the East Serbian Mountains and the Transylvanian Alps crept slowly into view. Several rivers join the Danube on this stretch, first the Morava and the two wide arms of the sluggish Rama, then the little Nera on the left bank, which, along with the line of khaki-colored watchtowers, marked the beginning of Romania.

Twenty
Through the Iron Gates to Romania

A STRING OF MANNED WATCHTOWERS led along the left bank to what our guidebook described as the border station of Bazias. Of the village, only a few dark roofs could be seen through the trees, but on the waterfront a low building stretched along a deserted concrete quay. It looked like a derelict railway station, but it was festooned with barbed wire—some of it shiny new. A one-meter-thick wall of the stuff blocked off either end of the platform-type quay and continued up and over the roof. The whole entangled edifice, along with its attendant watchtower, looked diabolically unreal, like some macabre diorama from a Jewish Holocaust museum. And just as if it were an exhibit behind glass, we slipped past, strangely remote from the brutish reality it represented. It was too disconcerting to contemplate that we were about to visit a land where the need for such a monstrosity had recently been thought necessary.

Our guidebook mentioned only one other Yugoslav town, some 130 kilometers farther on, so we decided that in order to keep our options open for supplies, we would check into Romania at the next town.

Taking up all the available space at the high timber wharf at Moldova Veche was an old steamer ferry and a police launch. We made to go alongside the police launch but got shooed away by two panicky, armed soldiers standing guard above. A ragtag group of gypsy civilians, who appeared to be waiting to board the ferry, crowded along the wharf's edge to stare down at us. One of them, a thin man whose oversize black trench coat was tightly tied at his waist with a heavy leather, brown belt, directed us round to the downstream end of the wharf.

As we had been unable to get a Romanian phrase book, the only words we had at our command were a few basic phrases printed in our guidebook. To our surprise, the language was very much like Italian. Its origin in the days of the Roman Empire accounts for the country's name, which means "land of the Romans."

My rendering of "Buna sera," good evening, to the "Scarecrow" in charge got as a response a very officious "Pazzporto!" Both soldiers pulled *Alea* in so that I could hand up our New Zealand passports. After scrutinizing every page, he handed them back down, then, pointing downstream, uttered his second word to me—"Orsova!" This was a town some 90 kilometers farther on. I tried giving an impression of an Italian asking if there was a bank in town—"Banka—Moldova Veche?" Showing impatience with our "conversation," he broke in, "Noo banka!" and, pointing more insistently, "Orsova!" I glanced at the nearest soldier, who joined in woodenly—"Orr-so-va." I expected the whole crowd to solemnly repeat it, but they just silently stared down with their fixed black eyes.

There was nothing for it but to give Moldova Veche a miss. We set off and soon came upon a vast flood lake some 4 kilometers wide, created by a bottleneck called the Iron Gates. Here the east-going Danube enters a defile 700 meters high by only 150 meters wide that leads to the Iron Gates Dam 80 kilometers farther on.

After a peaceful night anchored off Moldova Island, we were up at six o'clock. This was early indeed for us, because before going to bed we had turned the clock one hour forward to Romanian time.

It was Thursday, September 20, and although it promised to be another sunny day, when we set off across the flood lake we could see thick clouds of mist billowing out of the canyon mouth. On arriving at the opening we couldn't see more than 30 meters past the threshold. A great, ragged white tower of fog swelled up from within the chasm, to be dissolved in a wild tearing vortex high above our heads. There was certainly no question of venturing in there until it had completely cleared.

With a quick change of courtesy flag, we headed over to the Yugoslav side of the lake to wait it out. We moored under a high rocky outcrop that had the ruins of a fine castle upon it. This was Gulubac, a name meaning "dovecote," owing to its spectacular position. Apparently it had been occupied down through the ages by Romans, Hungarians, and then Turks. Charles and I were the only ones willing to make the steep climb up to add our names to the list.

The girls had other ways to while away the time, as Victoria's diary records:

> Charles and Dad went away to look at the castle. Mum and I did lots of washing and I'm a real professional at getting water with the bucket. I tie a rope to the handle of the bucket and then tie the other end to the life-line. Then I throw the bucket in so that the top of the bucket is face to face with the water. While it tips over it scoops up the water and you have a full bucket. But I can do this quickly, that's why I'm a professional.

By the time we returned from our raid on Gulubac, the fog had all been blown out of the chasm. So with *Alea* decked out in all our smalls and the Romanian flag once again at the crosstree, we turned into the narrow canyon. Instantly we could feel *Alea* being picked up and accelerating away. Sheer cliffs that dwarfed us began to zip past on either side. Huge protruding rocks near the river's edge seemed to steam past with fierce bow waves as if fighting their way upstream. The headwind had weakened, but it was still kicking up whitecaps on the now surging river. We were on an undulating, fast slide that was taking us where it willed. At 9 to 10 knots and with 60 meters of water beneath us, there was definitely no turning back or stopping. *Alea* sped on like an autumn leaf being carried down a swollen drain, having little option but supremely buoyant.

Mile after mile, these conditions prevailed. Despina and the children sat out in the cockpit, their heads craning to take in the wild scenery. We passed several barge convoys plowing their way up the gorge. To us, on the roller-coaster ride down, they looked as stationary as the rocks. After 25 kilometers of heading due east, the river passes through an even narrower defile, then immediately starts a huge sweeping loop that takes it north. At this bend the current slows dramatically as it enters another flood lake about 2 kilometers wide.

With the building of the Iron Gates Dam, many long-established settlements had to be relocated before their sites were submerged under the generating reservoir. Fortunately, extensive archaeological excavations were carried out on these sites before their abandonment. The most important discovery was at Lepenski Vir; this settlement had fifty-nine houses eight thousand years ago and was one of the first civilizations in the world to develop farming.

The mountains became less steep, with farmland and large tracts of forest stretching up their slopes. I regretted not having the time to spend a few days here, as it looked very inviting.

But we had to press on to make up for lost time. Heading north, we entered the next straight passage, the Kazan, which leads to the most constricted gorge of all, the Klissura. On this stretch the wind was on our starboard quarter, which gave us a run of over 12 miles under full sail.

Ahead, the scrub-covered mountains appeared to completely encircle the end of the fairway like an impregnable fortress wall. In the middle stands the high, white cliff face that highlights the entrance of the Klissura, where the Danube suddenly disappears. We approached cautiously, not knowing what to expect. The current was down to less than 3 knots and there wasn't a breath of wind. With the motor just ticking over, we more or less drifted through the narrow opening formed between two razor-edged buttresses of sheer rock. The river turned to the left in a sharp Z bend, through what looked like the narrow chamber of a huge open cave. Cliffs rose vertically out of the black depths that were just beginning to swirl ominously in slow, laborious eddies. I gave the throttle a tweak; although spectacular, it was certainly not a place to linger.

We were very lucky not to meet any traffic in these narrows. The river current hardly increased, and we were able to circle round for Charles to take a photograph of Trajan's marble slab. This commemorates the Roman emperor who had a road built through here, which was suspended out from the rock on a wooden gangway. The memorial plaque and a Roman sundial were raised from their original positions, which now lie 40 meters below the Danube.

Once past the Klissura, the valley opens out again into another flood lake, the Orsova Basin. Nearing the Romanian shore, we couldn't help but notice a seemingly abandoned construction project. On a partially built pier stood the rusting hulk of a pile driver, which had obviously driven its last pile here years ago. After our long and exhilarating day, the pier presented an ideal mooring for the night. Victoria and Charles were still full of energy and had great sport catching frogs until bedtime.

At midnight we were awakened by the noise of a motorboat mooring in front of us and a bright spotlight being directed at our cabin. I was about to look out the window when I heard the boom-tent being pulled back. I called out, "What's the problem?" and rushed up into the cockpit. When I poked my head round the stern end of the boom-tent, I was shocked to see a short, scruffy man, dressed like a farm laborer and holding an automatic rifle at the ready.

Surprisingly, he hadn't seen me, and holding the gun in the air with one hand, he started banging on the cabin wall. Stupefied by either fear or sleep, I couldn't think what to say. Forgetting the Romanian we had learned, I tried to dredge up some Italian, which came out sounding more Mexican—"Bunas diass!" His head shot round and he seemed to stagger back as he leveled the weapon at me. I froze.

"Pazzporto!" he snapped, then, "pazz-paperz," which sounded a little more controlled.

Just then, Despina called out from below, in her most challenging voice, "Who is it? What do they want?" and, not waiting for an answer, added indignantly, "What the hell's going on?"

As calmly as possible I said, "There's a man here who wants to see our passports—give me them out."

When I stretched down the companionway to receive them, she held them back and demanded to know, "Does he have a uniform?"

"No," I replied, "but he's got a gun!"

He slung the rifle over his shoulder and took the passports back to show the person operating the spotlight. From all the shrugging of shoulders and waving of arms, it was clear they were unsure of what to make of us. Then trudging back he returned our passports with the single-word proviso "Orsova" and an incongruous childlike mime of the sun rising. Yes, I agreed, we would get them stamped in the morning at Orsova.

The spotlight was turned off, but the motorboat remained at the pier. We felt uneasy about their presence. Just as we got settled down again, the gunman returned and knocked on the cabin. This time the charade was for "cigaretta?" I had to apologetically mime the discomfort of the nonsmoker before being left to crawl back to bed. They hung about for several hours before suddenly roaring off for maximum wash-making effect.

After our nocturnal encounter Despina and I were not in the best of humor, first thing. No sooner had we pushed off than we were in the thick of a bow versus stern slanging match. Our guidebook described Orsova as a large and busy port, which somehow didn't ring true for the settlement we were heading toward. Unfortunately, the skipper needed more convincing that this wasn't Orsova than the "super-perceptive" mate thought necessary. To settle the matter, I decided to leave the open channel and head over to ask a person fishing from a deserted industrial wharf.

This required Despina to keep lookout in the bow in order to guide us round thick patches of weed that rose up from the depths like kelp. I complained that I couldn't hear her instructions. Although there was a noticeable increase in pitch at the bow, there was still no more comprehension at the stern. Foolishly, I complained again and, as she stamped off below, got it loud and clear that the problem lay in my ears.

To my chagrin my other informant on the wharf indicated that Orsova was over the headland in the next bay. After a penance of having to clear weed from the propeller, twice, I made it back into the channel—solo.

The correct port of Orsova is indeed part of a large town. Like a tidemark along the foot of the steep, wooded hills, a dense fringe of concrete high-rise buildings crowds around the edge of the bay. We zeroed in on a police launch moored by a narrow concrete quay. Finding the launch unattended, we moored in behind and I went off in search of someone to check us in. The waterfront seemed to be strewn with drunk gypsy men, dark in complexion, dark in dress, and apparently dark in mood.

I entered an official-looking building and mimed our passports being stamped to a man at a desk. Smiling to show his understanding, he ushered me back outside and passed me over to one of the gypsies. There was a brief exchange in Romanian, then, after a fleeting tipsy smile, the gypsy took me by the hand and led me, childlike, to a crowded pub!

Just as I was beginning to question what signals I had been giving out, my guide presented me to a couple of gray-uniformed policemen seated at the bar.

The older and obviously senior of the two looked and acted like a tough weather-beaten gunfighter out of a crass western movie. He set down his small glass of spirits and, with something akin to amused arrogance, sized me up and down, as if I were to be the next notch on his gun. I caught myself staring in astonishment and tried to disguise it by offering him the passports. Maintaining his "top dog" status, he took them in his own good time and began casually to flick through them. Then, to my surprise he spoke in English, "Vhere ship?" After I explained, he gave me the thumbed "beat it" gesture and said, "Vait ship—I come," and added in German: "Zen Minuten!"

While we waited, Victoria took my photograph alongside the Romanian flag on the police launch. We had only seen "the flag with the hole" at a distance before, flying defiantly at the stern of the Danube's most decrepit fleet. Our own Romanian flag, which Despina made, must have been one of the most up-to-date in the country. Only ten months before, we had all watched the dramatic television coverage of the Christmas Revolution. When a scene was shown of an ecstatic crowd cutting the communist party symbol from their flag, Despina had piped up,

"Thank goodness, I was wondering how on earth I was to make that!"

"Top Dog" arrived on the quay and, in his "endearing bull-dozer" manner, started to interrogate us. "How long you stay Orsova?" and "Vhat you vant (in) Orsova?"

I was quite intimidated by him and answered promptly: "One night"—"Petrol and food."

His eyes narrowed: "Vhat money—you (got)?" At this, I added that we needed a bank as well, to which he decreed: "I take you Orsova banka—get ready—zen Minuten!" There was no question of contradicting this gangster; it was clear he was totally used to people doing as he ordered. And as if to dispel any doubts on the matter, a sharp yell from him brought an armed soldier running down the quay to stand guard over us.

We hurried to get ourselves organized with the necessary documents for the bank and the 20-liter jerrican. But when we climbed up onto the quay, the guard came charging over to shoo us back on the boat. It all happened so quickly; red-faced, with no-nonsense agitation, he waved his extended arm as though herding cattle. Despina called out in alarm and tried to explain. I held up the jerrican and said an Italian-sounding "Petrola" but got it shoved back in my face. Just then Top Dog seemed to appear out of nowhere and curtly called off the bovine moron.

Although we were quite shocked by the incident, Top Dog appeared to think nothing of it and made no attempt to apologize. In his now familiar tone, he told me to put back the jerrican, as he had a container in his car. I complied, feeling we were somehow being hijacked by this man and unable to get out of it. He ushered us into what I assumed was his own car, an unmarked, drab, Russian-made saloon. His driving was an expression of his boorish self; slapping the horn and stamping from the brake to accelerator, he bullied his way through the narrow streets. The more we winced and gasped at the near misses, the more aggressive his driving became.

At last we drew up outside a rundown prewar suburban house. Heavy prison-type bars were on all the windows, making it look more like the local "Securitate" headquarters than a bank. We followed him up a short flight of crumbling concrete steps to the front door. The bank was obviously closed, but that didn't bother

Top Dog. He just kept hammering on the door as loud as he could until somebody came.

Hardly waiting for the door to open properly, he barged his way in and strode off down the dark corridor. Pressed up against the wall with the door in his face was the still formidable bulk of an elderly all-in-wrestler type. Unshaven, he wore a grossly tight-fitting pullover that sported several food stains that had slalomed down either side of his fat gut. This sleazy cutthroat was obviously the security guard, for a chipped and battered automatic pistol was stuck in his trouser belt.

Taken aback, I hesitantly made to follow Top Dog. I had just taken the first step inside when the guard, who had scarcely glanced our way, pushed me back out with a powerful sweep of his forearm and slammed the door shut.

For the second time within half an hour we found ourselves piled up on each other. In our stunned silence we suddenly heard Top Dog, at the far end of the house, start to yell with rage. Instantly, footsteps came padding quickly back to the door, and in a nervous panic the chastened guard waved us in.

We were shown into a large, dimly lit room that looked like the bank office. Only two women were there (one I suspected to be Top Dog's wife). They ignored us and continued to gush over several pairs of shoes they were trying on—no doubt spoils from the black market. When they had finished, Top Dog did all the talking. He informed us, "Banka change cassa (cash) only!" This peculiar policy of the bank's got somewhat passed over when we saw the high rate of exchange they were offering—over twice the "official rate." Thinking it a very good deal, we agreed and Despina handed him over $100. Little did we know that in the rare event of finding something to buy in Romania, we would have the greatest difficulty getting them to accept their own worthless currency.

Holding a large wad of crisp new Romanian lei, Top Dog approached me. Then, instead of placing the money in my hand, he pinned it against my chest with a practiced expression of menacing arrogance that said, Ask no questions—let alone a receipt!

At the filling station, a queue of cars stretched out of the forecourt and down the street, disappearing up a side street. Top Dog drove right up to the front and, taking a large plastic container from the trunk, ordered the attendant to fill it. As soon as I paid we were hurtled back to the harbor. When Despina asked where she was to do the shopping, Top Dog replied, "Noo problem—everything (at) Orsova!" He clearly meant it wasn't going to be a problem to him, for he had got what he wanted from us.

I siphoned the petrol into our jerrican, taking care not to disturb the half liter or so of water lying in the bottom of his filthy container. No sooner had I finished than Top Dog appeared with our passports. Accompanying him was a thin, vacant-looking Customs officer dressed in what looked like a 1920s Red Guard's uniform.

In disbelief, we watched this ridiculous man search *Alea* without opening one drawer or cupboard. He obviously thought contraband could be heard if he listened hard enough. Stooped and with his ear cocked to one side, then the other, he slowly crept forward through the main cabin toward the children's. Charles and Victoria, who had been playing an ongoing game of Monopoly, shrank back in horror as he approached. Then, suddenly, he darted his hand under the Monopoly board and flipped it over, which sent all the playing pieces flying.

After this inane piece of lunacy he seemed satisfied and declared us "cleared" as well. Almost reluctantly, Top Dog handed down our stamped passports. Unbeknownst to us, he had invalidated our visa by stamping it twice—in the same instant we officially entered Romania, we had officially left. Unfortunately, we had already started to feel that if such a thing were physically possible, we would have jumped at it.

Twenty-One
A Last Look at Yugoslavia

21 SEPTEMBER

WE CUT ACROSS ORSOVA BAY, to where we judged the shopping center would be. A pontoon that formed one side of a defunct recreational area provided us with a convenient berth. After Despina and the children had left on their shopping trip, I had a host of visitors. Most were young students who just wanted to practice their English. Apparently speaking to foreigners had been illegal the year before.

Over two hours later, the bedraggled shore-party returned with five loaves of bread and an open tray of twenty eggs. Despina collapsed, exhausted, in the cockpit and wearily exclaimed, "Well, that's the grimmest yet—we queued ages for the bread and had to fight for the eggs!" She said they would have been queuing at the baker still had not the people in front let them go first. The eggs had been an elbowing free-for-all when a supply truck (evidently a rare sight in these parts) had suddenly arrived in the street. As for the supermarkets, they were empty.

Yet in view of later experiences, Despina was to remember Orsova as a successful shopping spree. And it wasn't quite over yet, for I had arranged a second sortie at five o'clock, when the shops opened again after the midday siesta. One of my young friends, who spoke English very well and called himself Ernest, had offered to take us to "zee best supermarket in town." When we arrived outside the building, there were two large queues stretching back from either side of the entrance doors. Ernest explained we could go right in, because these queues were specifically for bread and meat. We pushed through the glass doors to be confronted with racks of vacant shelves glaring at us from every side, like the rib cages of famine victims. We stood looking about us in stunned amazement, until Ernest beckoned us to follow him. At the back of the hall were the only shop items on display. Along the front edge of several shelves were sparsely stacked pyramids of small, unlabeled preserving jars, the discolored contents of which could only be guessed at. With Ernest's help Despina managed to identify a jar of jam and one of fruit juice.

We were just turning away from the cashier when a great crashing roar came from the front of the shop. Staff had opened up the doors to let the meat queue in, and the crowd was now surging in. Once through the entrance they ran, desperately racing each other to a row of empty meat display counters to our left. A heavy tubular steel barrier, designed to funnel the shoppers to a single file, was brutally effective. With more people pushing in from behind, the throng of wild, jostling people suddenly seemed to freeze, as if the "pause" button on a video had been pressed. People hung doubled over the barrier rail, squeezed motionless by the crush of bodies spilled over on top of them.

Although faces winced as if in pain and mouths gasped for air, none were willing to give up their place by escaping under the rail. We could do nothing but stare, and shamefaced resolve not to give an inch stared back at us from desperate eyes. The idea of taking a photograph came to me, because for once I had remembered to take my camera ashore. Although I regretted it later, I didn't have the cheek to capture their humiliation at having to behave like this in order to feed their families.

Thankful that we were not in such dire straits yet, we made our escape. We wanted potatoes, so Ernest led us round to another building where the potato queue stood. The potatoes on sale were smaller than walnuts. Taken aback, I asked Ernest, "What kind of potatoes are these?" After a mildly quizzical smile he shrugged and replied: "Vee call them pig potatoes!"

We decided to leave these and followed Ernest to an open marketplace. Here stallholders sat in attendance over the most meager quantities of vegetables we had ever seen—and no potatoes of any kind. On one desolate table lay only nine undersized radishes and two cigarettes. Ernest made all the little haggling purchases for us that would just about keep scurvy at bay.

In the evening, we took down the mast in preparation for locking through the Iron Gate Dam first thing the next morning. This huge dam is built over the set of impassable rapids historically known as the Iron Gates. The kilometer-long dam is jointly owned by Romania and Yugoslavia, who each operate a power station at their respective ends.

Next day dawned calm and bright, but unfortunately the same couldn't be said for Despina. She was brooding over the implications of yesterday's events. For her, the family holiday was now completely at an end. Romania at the moment was clearly not a place to visit but one to escape from. I assured her that we would be passing through the place as quickly as possible, and to this end decided to set off right away, before breakfast.

We motored down the 10 kilometers or so to the dam, which lay at the end of a steep, pine-forested valley. Unfortunately the Yugoslav lock was out of action, forcing us to use the Romanian one. The main road from Timişoara follows the shore, and a great long queue of cars was stretching some 3 kilometers back from the dam. A border-crossing road runs along the top of the dam, and clearly Despina was not the only one with escape on her mind.

Like a refugee column fleeing a war zone, every car was packed to overflowing with people and belongings. None seemed to be moving. Several groups of people were gathered around campfires lit at the side of the road, as if they had been there all night. Nearer the frontier post, the cause of the delay could be seen: a squad of police were overseeing the unpacking of every suitcase and bag; even the spare tires and car seats were being hauled out for inspection.

We turned into the lock fairway and found the quaysides littered with the rusting paraphernalia of another abandoned construction project. There was no telephone, so after an hour's red light wait, I decided to go round to see the lockkeeper.

I might have guessed I was heading for trouble when I saw a group of armed soldiers patrolling the other side of the lock. To get to the control tower I had to climb up through some construction scaffolding, which brought me out on top of the dam's parapet wall and directly above two very startled peasant soldiers, who pointed automatic rifles at me. With agitated shouts they motioned for me to come down.

They took me to a nearby sentry box, where the corporal made a long and involved telephone call that appeared to entail a description of me. The result of this was we all had to wait; "somebody" was coming. After ascertaining that I didn't have any *cigaretta*, my two captors lost interest in me. They were there, it seemed, to bully on the unfortunate refugees who had just escaped from the clutches of the border police. Inevitably, the motorists would try to stop on the bridge to repack their cars, which now resembled laundry baskets. If a shout didn't move them on immediately, the soldiers threatened to strike the car with the butts of their rifles.

Luckily, it was the lockkeeper who came to see me. Looking rather embarrassed by the situation, he explained in German that the next commercial ship wasn't due until two o'clock in the afternoon—we would have to wait.

We were really quite puzzled when, after a four-hour wait, we were lowered some 12 meters in the huge chamber by ourselves. But when the end gate opened it revealed a barge in another chamber. It was a gigantic step-lock. The barge swapped chambers with us and we continued down another 12 meters.

We were just clearing the fairway exit when I had my second encounter of the day with armed Romanians. Just abeam of us, a group of four small boys came running down onto the beach. They all had catapults. The first lad to reach the water's edge aimed high and lofted a shot at us. We were a good 60 meters off, but astonishingly the stone zipped into the water only a few meters away. Fortunately, this crack shot prevented the others from firing until he was ready to join them for a mass volley. In the time it took him to reload, I was able to snatch up my own cata-pult and let fly. Although my shot fell embarrassingly short, it quite surprised the "firing squad." In unison, they lowered their weapons and, after a quick glance at each other, just stood staring after us.

Out on the turbulent river again, we were picked up and swiftly carried down to the Yugoslav town of Kladovo, 7 kilometers below the dam. After seeing what shopping was like in Romania, we wanted to stock up with whatever we could find on the relatively bountiful shores of Yugoslavia.

Despina hurried off in search of a supermarket and a bank, while the children and I watched over *Alea*. It wasn't long before we noticed that the Danube here was the clearest we had seen it. Immediately my young tars wanted to go swimming, for it was still sunny and warm. After seeing the fun they were having in the lee of the pontoon, I decided to have a dip myself and inspect *Alea*'s bottom.

One of the rubber strips I had fixed over the centerplate slot to keep out England's east coast mud was hanging half off. Sometimes while steering, I thought I could feel its drag slowing *Alea* down. With Charles as lookout I set about cutting it off.

By the time the diving operations were completed, Despina returned from the fairly well stocked supermarket that looked like Harrods compared to the "People's Co-op" in Orsova. Despite this, there was still a distinct lack of conserved foods. It was evident we were competing with other fugitives from Romania, who were arriving by the carload. They easily stuck out from the Yugoslavs with their shabbier clothes and the way they invariably caressed a carton of cigarettes to their bosom.

Later, I went off to explore a harbor I had noticed farther along the waterfront. In fact there were two, one completely silted up and the other so crowded with workboats that I decide to stay where we were. To see a bit more of the town, I cut up a side lane and made my way back along a street running parallel to the river.

While walking down this quiet suburban street, I came upon some sort of army barracks. The building looked like a nineteenth-century library, set back some 10 meters from a set of metal fence railings. In the small courtyard, thirty to forty off-duty soldiers were lounging about in small groups.

As soon as I came into view, several of them began to jeer and shout abuse at me. It was getting dark, which is my excuse for being taken for a Romanian refugee by the battalion thugs bent on a bit of ethnic cleansing. I walked on, but one of the armed and helmeted sentries at the gate stepped out onto the pavement to bar my way. With an expression of great distaste, he appeared to be asking me if I was Romanian. Trying to keep on moving past him, I answered with a forced smile and a Russian-sounding "Neyet—Scotska!" This seemed to disappoint him, and as he followed me round I could see him making a laborious mental search, checking to see if he had anything against Scotsmen. While he was still juggling with his other brain cell, I hurried on, feeling I'd had quite enough of apes with guns.

Next morning, as we swept past the Romanian town of Turnu Severin, we kept our eyes peeled for any sign of the old Roman bridge that had once stood here, but we saw nothing. Our guidebook mentioned that submerged pillars can still be a danger to shipping when the water level is low. The emperor Hadrian had the bridge demolished as part of the same defense strategy that produced his famous wall in Britain.

In brilliant sunshine, we headed round the first of a great series of snaking loops that leads the Danube south. By afternoon, the combination of these bends and the backed-up waters from the next dam at Prahova had reduced the current to nothing. The wind dropped away, and as the temperature soared we found ourselves on an immense, glassy lake bound by a far-off, hazy shore. The children were still in swimming mode and badgered us until we agreed to stop. We found an idyllic shallow bay on the Romanian side and moored *Alea* between two half-submerged trees.

While we frolicked in the crystal-clear pond, a shy young fisherman in a rowing boat watched us from afar. We waved him over and asked if he had any fish to sell. This took a combined family effort, for he appeared a bit simple. When the "penny" finally dropped, it was our turn to scratch our heads. When Romanians mime, they play to the strict rule that not a word must be spoken. After a silent enactment of all the intricacies of him putting out his nets at night, we gathered the answer was *neyet*, but maybe tomorrow.

Before climbing aboard for the night, I had pushed *Alea* out into deeper water and anchored in just under a depth of 3 meters. The night was so calm and peaceful that we never felt her settle on the sandy bottom when the water level dropped some 2 meters by morning. Luckily all it took to get free was for my weight to come off and a gentle shove.

When the fisherman returned the next morning, he was accompanied by a small boy who was watching over their still-flapping catch of a few dozen fish. Despina chose five and had the price of 30 lei silently traced out in the air before her. With that settled, the fisherman noticed my pair of "theft-preventive" sneakers. Although the sole was hanging right off of one, he did a rather good Charlie Chaplin mime of instantly falling in love with them. I handed them over and was thanked by soundless cheers and humble bows.

As they were about to leave, Despina presented them with a lolly each. It appeared that this was the first time they had ever seen a conventional, cellophane-wrapped lolly. Mystified, as if inspecting some strange insect, they prodded them around in their open palms and exchanged puzzled glances. With some prompting from us the small boy worked it out first and pulled the wrapping off as one does a large parcel. The fisherman, with focused concentration, copied every step of the smart youngster's technique, even to the unceremonious way he dropped the paper overboard.

When they rowed away, the two brightly colored wrappings were left floating buoyantly in the vacant, still water. I was reminded of the modern art exhibition we saw in Linz. What profound statement lay before us now—the vagaries of the human experience, perhaps, or was it just rubbish?

We raised the anchors and motored down to the Prahova Dam. When we entered the fairway, we could see that a huge Russian tour liner was coming out of the lock, but its path was blocked by a Yugoslavian barge. The barge was sitting at right angles to the quay, with its stern right out across the channel. Between dramatic appeals for help the bargee would either disappear into his wheelhouse for a few seconds or run down the deck to the bow for a look over the rail. *Alea* charged to the rescue.

Apparently his propellers had suddenly stopped revolving, and he had drifted round on the current caused by the lock being filled. In a trice we lashed *Alea* alongside his starboard quarter. Then, with our little eggbeater of a motor skewed round at 90°, we slowly pushed some 300 to 400 tons of barge around and into the quay. Typically, the liner immediately barged past, its slopping wash the only acknowledgment that *Alea* had cleared the channel. The bargee was more forthcoming, and had it been up to him, the Order of Lenin would have been ours. Instead, we got the order of the "green light" and were lowered another 12 meters.

Soon after leaving the lock, I looked over to the Yugoslav side, and there, on top of the embankment, was a policeman watching us through binoculars. He waved for us to come over and pointed to a pontoon farther downstream. This was the proper Customs post, and although it didn't fly a flag of any kind, Duty Free Shop was painted across the building.

The bumptious little policeman came bustling down the jetty toward us. Angrily he pointed at our Romanian courtesy flag and gestured it being snatched down with the greatest contempt. Abashed, I apologized profusely while Despina and Charles reverently set up the Yugoslavian colors on the boathook. Not prepared to let us off the "hook" so easily, he demanded "Pazz-papers" and thumbed me to his office.

He picked up that we hadn't got the transit papers stamped in Belgrade and, throwing them down on his desk, cried, "Zashto! Zashto!"—Why? I "huffed and puffed" and mimed a great storm sweeping us helplessly past the great capital. I even added in some tragic disappointment at having missed photographing such a famous city. He bought it! Grudgingly he forgave us and, after doing some "huffing and puffing" himself, stamped our passports.

After my sin of shameless lies, we were free to visit the duty-free shop, which exclusively catered to three other human vices: alcohol, nicotine, and fraud. Because we don't smoke, we succumbed to the former but rather proudly sidestepped the latter. It transpired that although customers could pay with any "hard currency" of their choice, any change was paid back in the Yugoslav "toilet paper." When our purchase of a bottle of whiskey and a dozen cans of German beer was tallied up in deutsche marks, the cashier refused to let us pay with a Euro-cheque. This of course would have avoided the need for any change to be given back. Using simple arithmetic we achieved the same result by returning two of the cans. Judging by the cashier's indignation, this fiddle was clearly a source of extra income for him.

There is a universal law that states, "We must pay for our sins and, like as not, our pleasures." So, with our "duty-free spirits" high, we set off for the Bulgarian border, quite unaware that we were about to settle a heavy bill. Nor did we suspect that this would be our last look at a united Yugoslavia. Even then, its final account was being tallied up by forces that would exact payment in a very hard currency. . . .

Twenty-Two
Between the Devils and the Neap Blue Danube

24 SEPTEMBER

WE RESET THE ROMANIAN FLAG and headed out across the breadth of the hurrying Danube. Owing to the pre-*perestroika* visa rules still in vogue, we couldn't land on Bulgarian territory until we reached the Black Sea. We reasoned that if we kept well over to the Romanian side, we could avoid any dealings with prying Bulgarian bureaucrats until then—but it wasn't to be! No sooner had we passed the mouth of the River Timok, which forms the frontier, than a squat, gray patrol launch came bounding over toward us.

In a roaring fury of noise and flying spray, it swerved into a beam-on halt just off our starboard bow. A uniformed sailor appeared on deck and picked up a vicious-looking boathook. Through the wheelhouse window, I could see the helmsman signaling me to slow down. I waved him away and pointed to the

Romanian courtesy flag. He was having none of that and angrily insisted we stop. I throttled down.

Once alongside, it was "Pazz-papers!" With an air of furtive haste the officer-*cum*-helmsman thumbed through our British passports. Then, as he thrust them back, he pointed upstream and asked in German, "Are they with you?" About a kilometer away was a small red sailing boat with its mast lashed on deck.

This was *Garnet*, a 5-meter trailer-sailer manned by a pair of Bulgarian bachelors, Pieter and Ventchi. They had rail-freighted *Garnet* to Germany, primarily in pursuit of Ventchi's very special *Fraulein*. Then, with one love quenched, they slaked another by traveling home on their beloved Danube. And how do I know all this? Anon . . .

While the launch sped off to intercept the then still mysterious yacht, we continued drifting downstream, waiting for them to catch up. The little yacht, offering the happy prospect of introducing us to "fellow voyagers," had somewhat captured my attention.

There were no channel marker buoys, and we had, by design, been following a course to the left side of the river. Suddenly, some 60 meters up ahead, I noticed a dark, broken patch of shoal water extending out into the center of the river. I changed course to starboard by 90 degrees and headed toward midstream. *Crunch!* The centerplate hit bottom but instantly freed. I immediately helmed *Alea* round another 90 degrees to head directly back upstream. After only a few meters we grounded hard and heeled over to port as the current spun us back round to face downstream again.

It was just then that *Garnet* arrived. Here was Ventchi, stocky and vivacious, who positively glowed with the prospect of executing a rescue, and Pieter, lean and pensive, foreseeing wasted time and effort. Ventchi, speaking a mile a minute in apparently well-practiced German, took command of the situation straightaway. Confronted with a whirlwind of emphatic confidence and resolute commands, I acquiesced to them giving us a tow. This was more out of a feeling akin to good neighborliness rather than need, for by now we had developed quite a laid-back attitude to running aground, because we had always got off so easily before. We were about to discover just how difficult it could be—especially with help!

A line was passed from our bow to *Garnet*'s stern. Then, to my surprise, Ventchi signaled the direction of the tow as downstream, cutting across the current at 45 degrees. I called, "Nein!" and pointed back upstream, to which both Pieter and Ventchi indicated adamantly that downstream was best. I surrendered.

The strain was taken up and so was our centerplate. *Alea* moved off easily and followed in behind *Garnet*. We got about 9 meters across the current when both of us simultaneously ran aground on a bank of shingle, small river-rounded stones. We were now really in trouble! With the centerplate fully retracted, *Alea* was sitting down firmly on her stub keel. I cursed myself for having thrown away our trump card of the rising centerplate, but recriminations had to be tempered, for we really needed help now.

Ventchi stripped down to his underpants and got into the water with me. With this loss of ballast and the raising of their centerplate and rudder, *Garnet* came off easily, but again I couldn't get them to push or tow *Alea* in an upcurrent direction. It was clear they thought it ridiculous to even suggest it, especially in view of the obvious difficulty Pieter was having controlling *Garnet* in the 3- to 4-knot current. This was partly due to their weak Russian outboard motor but mainly to the fact that he wouldn't lower his centerplate again. (Do you think I could get them to understand this?—it was impossible.)

Eventually *Garnet* went aground again, in the same place as before, and of course with no protruding centerplate it took a great effort to free her. When brute force prevailed, Ventchi and I started to make our way back to *Alea* against the rushing current. The water was cascading around our waists and I felt it dragging heavily at my Bermuda shorts. With all the hauling and pushing on the two boats, I was beginning to weaken. Leaning into the stream, it got harder and harder to press one leg past the other. The shingle on the riverbed was continually on the move, escaping from underfoot and rattling past our ankles. Suddenly, to my horror, although I was still bent forward and wading, the ground and I began moving backward. I called out for Victoria to throw the towrope, which she had meantime gathered in. My alarm brought Ventchi back to catch me by the arm. This saved me until the current brought down the rope and I started to pull myself up hand over hand, but even this got to be too much. Thankfully,

Despina, seeing the trouble I was having, scrambled up to the bow and hauled me in—like a sodden old boot.

Curiously, because I survived, it's difficult to imagine I could have ever drowned, but no doubt that is the way some people have. Back safely in the lee of *Alea*'s hull, I breathlessly thanked everyone for saving me. Ventchi smiled and nodded his understanding at my gratitude but showed distinct alarm when I began to scorn the part my Bermuda shorts had played in my near demise. Stripping them off I threw them contemptuously into the cockpit, at which Ventchi edged away round behind the stern, preferring to take his chances with the current.

Being naked made it far easier to move through the water, giving me a new lease on life. It also seemed to cow Ventchi's opposition to everything I suggested. I got him to help me pivot *Alea*'s bow round to face upstream. Then, with Victoria feeding out the towrope from the bow, I carried its end out to Pieter. This was the nearest I came to getting a tow into deeper water. As soon as it was attached, off he went, *downstream*, to pull *Alea* harder onto the shingle bank and to ground himself again—yes, in the same place.

It seemed as if the water level was going down. In desperation I suggested they anchor *Garnet* there and the three of us push *Alea* back into deeper water. It was never tried, for in spite of Ventchi being willing, Pieter had clearly had enough. He said he would go back and ask the Bulgarian patrol launch for help.

Ventchi came aboard *Alea* to wait. As well as telling us about his trip to Germany, he mentioned what Pieter and he did for a living—they were both Danube River pilots! It was small compensation to know we were in the hands of professionals.

It took over an hour for the patrol launch to arrive, accompanied by black storm clouds from the west. I could see the wind whipping the sand and spray into a swirling mist that was blotting out the distant landscape. The launch's opening gambit was to come charging down on the current and wind to take aboard our towrope, ramming into our port bow with such force that *Alea* was knocked round some 60 degrees. We now lay facing Romania, athwart the current and beam-on to the developing storm.

Ventchi shook his head in disgust as the launch extricated itself from our side and passed downstream of us. Then, its skipper decided on another tactic, so they threw off our rope and came round to stand about 50 meters off our port bow. It was beginning to get dark and the wind was stirring up waves. Nevertheless Ventchi got back into the water to carry our line over again. At this, a sailor came off the launch with a very thin line. He moved across the current in a peculiar leaping fashion, using a kind of Japanese wrestler's stance, no doubt as he had been trained to do. Both Ventchi and the sailor came back to *Alea*, and to my amazement the thin line was gathered in by the launch. It appeared no one knew what the next plan of action was.

Although Ventchi came back aboard, the sailor refused, preferring to stand in the waist-deep water with waves breaking over his shoulders. He looked very cold but incredibly cheerful, as this was his last day of military service. Using this as an excuse and our bottle of whiskey as a lure, we finally coaxed him aboard. In the middle of that dreadful situation, we toasted his good fortune, and he in return presented us with the collar of his tunic as a memento.

The party was broken up when the launch approached, flashing its navigation lights. It was completely dark and the storm was at its height. Without hesitation Ventchi and the sailor disappeared over the side. After a lot of shouting back and forth, the launch roared off and Ventchi appeared alongside by himself. The launch would return to the rescue—tomorrow.

We had seen Pieter return earlier and anchor over near the Bulgarian shore. Conditions were now so bad that it went without saying that Ventchi would have to spend the night with us—in his underpants! We offered him a dry pair, but he was happy just to wrap himself up in a tartan plaid. Despina was in no mood to cook, so we had a shipwreck's sandwich and a "cuppa" instead.

When we settled down to get some sleep, *Alea* had only a slight list of 8 degrees to starboard. This allowed us to sleep in our normal places, with Ventchi bedded down in the central aisle on the cockpit squabs. It was quite warm but very noisy. The wind howled across the decks, and the waves slapping against the hull caused the keel to grate on the shingle. If that wasn't enough, Ventchi started to snore like an old steam boiler. At about 4:00 A.M. *Alea* began to pound badly, which woke even Ventchi. The list to starboard increased to 15 degrees, forcing Despina to move in with the children, where they all had to sleep athwart the bunks. Ventchi moved to crank up steam on the port-side seat, while I took up his place in the aisle. After this redistribution of weight *Alea* listed no further.

At 6:30 A.M. it was still dark, but I got up and roused everyone with coffee. Ventchi was anxious to contact Pieter and tried flashing Morse code with the torch but got no response. He then tried our VHF radio, although I showed him that the aerial was disconnected with the mast down. Then he struck on the idea of rowing over in our dinghy. The wind was still some 20 knots, which I thought too strong when added to the fast river current, but he was adamant. I pumped it up and off he went, rowing like the clappers, clad only in his underpants and my heavy jacket. He did very well and reached the shore about a kilometer downstream from *Garnet*.

It hadn't rained at all, and sadly the water level was almost 300 millimeters lower than when we struck. We had to wait until 10:00 A.M. for the launch to appear. It went over to *Garnet* first and picked up Ventchi and the dinghy. Then, taking up station some 40 meters upstream from us, Ventchi came off in the dinghy.

As he came swishing down on the current, he appeared to get into a pickle with the oars, which spun him round and out of the dead run. To keep from being swept past us, he tried to jump out. This looked like someone rolling out of bed. Stretched out horizontally, he disappeared underwater as the dinghy tipped over him like a lid closing. I vaulted over the stern rail and in two strides simultaneously grabbed a loose oar and the dinghy. Ventchi was still underneath it, desperately struggling to get on his feet. Then, discovering my leg, he successfully clawed his way up it.

With the loss of only one rowlock and a few acres of skin from my thigh, Ventchi was safely back with us again. Although speechless for once, he bravely indicated, with a locomotion gesture of his arm, that he was eager to get started. When we set off to carry the end of the towrope up to the launch, the current exerted such an incredible drag on the rope that it needed all our strength to haul it through the water. Seeing the difficulty we were having, the crew on the launch floated down a thick line on a lifebuoy. Curiously, Ventchi tried joining the two lines with a granny knot! Although I have seen this done several times since by foreign yachties, I stopped him and retied it using a sheet bend.

Without any signal and while I was still in the water, the tow began. Ventchi took the tiller, while I had only enough time to scramble up onto the starboard coaming and hang out to heel *Alea* over. Despina and the children did the same from inside, which must have raised the keel quite a bit. *Alea*'s bow was dragged round as we moved off, smoothly and swiftly—upstream! The speed built up faster and faster until we were going as fast as any water-skier. We hit several shingle banks but just plowed through them. On reaching the main channel, Ventchi and I whooped with exultation. Despite my often sorry despair at his audacity, he had certainly worked valiantly to get *Alea* free.

Following the launch's example, we went alongside *Garnet*, and by way of appreciation, I handed round the cans of beer we had providentially bought yesterday (seemingly eons ago). However, the skipper of the launch was anxious for us to remove our Bulgarian courtesy flag and set off, because we didn't have a visa. So, with handshakes all round, we cast off and headed out into the channel.

When Despina went to lower the centerplate, she discovered that it was jammed inside the case. This was a serious handicap, especially in these treacherous and poorly marked shoal waters. So why (oh, woe) didn't we anchor, there and then, and fix it? Anon . . .

Just as I was having a fiddle with the centerplate winch, *Garnet* caught up with us. Of course, to the indomitable Ventchi, this was "Nein problem!" Weren't they river pilots? They would guide us (oh, woe)! . . . Before you could say "repel boarders," *Garnet* was alongside to starboard and lashed fore and aft. They switched off their motor and climbed into our cockpit, Ventchi clutching a bottle of wine and Pieter his Russian-made binoculars.

While Ventchi called for a corkscrew, Pieter took over the tiller from Despina. Thus disarmed by this continental demonstration of camaraderie, we surrendered ourselves into their hands once again. Pieter diligently scanned the empty river vista ahead at regular intervals with his binoculars. To show how good they were, he passed them to me to have a look at the next buoy, which was practically invisible to the naked eye. I was impressed—we were truly in professional hands. Ventchi got out some photographs of his holiday to show us, and we exchanged addresses. Everything was going well.

Suddenly, there was an agitated conversation between Pieter and Ventchi. I jumped to my feet in a panic and looked ahead. A 3-kilometer-wide expanse of dark, ruffled water stretched out to a thin strip of sand dune that formed an all-encircling horizon. We were to the right of midstream and approaching the dancing ripples of an extensive shoal, some 30 meters ahead. Pieter was pointing to the right and Ventchi to the left. I made a grab for the tiller to go about, but in the same instant *Alea* touched bottom. I put the motor into reverse, but to no avail, for the current pressed us forward onto the sandbar. After only 15 kilometers we were aground again.

While Pieter and Ventchi were still arguing about which way the channel was, I snatched the binoculars from them and climbed onto the cabintop. Scanning the horizon, I saw a green buoy far off on our left, but whitecaps covered the area between us and the buoy.

When I turned round, Ventchi and Pieter had already boarded *Garnet* and were casting off their lines in complete panic. I wasn't feeling too much savoir faire myself and foolishly called on them to "Stop!" This got the same consideration as all my other utterances, as they scurried to get their motor going. As they moved off, I threw my towrope to Pieter. He held it over their stern cleat, then, thinking better of it, cast it off and overboard. They set off over the rough water toward the left bank, and sometime later I spotted them passing the green buoy to disappear downriver.

I had no option but to strip off again and get pushing. This time the riverbed was of a deep, coarse sand, the top layer of which was in constant stampeding flight. I could feel it being stripped away from under the stern and heaped up around the bow. This made it imperative to turn *Alea* round to face upstream as quickly as possible. We tried with the motor and me pushing at the bow, but *Alea* wouldn't budge. Despina was unwilling to risk herself in the cold current, so I set out the anchors so she could haul on their warps from the bow. By progressively resetting the anchors farther round off our port quarter and judicious digging and levering with the plank, we slowly managed to pivot the bow round.

With only short breaks to rest and warm up, we hauled and shoved all afternoon. We made tries with the motor, with anchor warps back onto the sheet winches. My last effort had all these, plus Victoria and Charles sitting astride the end of the plank, rigged up to cantilever out abeam. Although it heeled *Alea* over considerably, it wasn't enough to lift the keel free. Exhausted and very cold, I set out both anchors in line, 45 degrees off the starboard bow, and gave up for the day.

Several barges had passed, revealing that the channel lay far over on the Romanian side. Due to our hasty abandonment this morning, we found ourselves in possession of a very good pair of binoculars. With these I exchanged curious binoculared stares with the passing helmsmen, from whom understandably we could expect no help.

When I awoke the next morning, the cabin was bathed in bright sunshine, and I felt my senses alert. Then I heard the slight scuff of the keel on the sand—we were afloat! Oh, joy! Although my whole body felt as if it had been beaten with a stick, I creaked out of bed and climbed on deck. *Alea* had moved over in line with the first anchor. I started to haul up on the chain and built up such good momentum that the plow broke out easily. I hauled away on the warp of the second anchor, and after about 15 meters *Alea* slid to a halt. Curses! We were stuck fast again.

What puzzled me was that I had waded all round here yesterday, and it had been the deepest part. Then it dawned on me that the sandbanks were constantly shifting too. Nevertheless, I was heartened that we had moved some 20 meters nearer the channel. So, with renewed determination, we set to and raised the mast for our next stratagem—to sail her out. A chilly reconnaissance revealed deeper water 30 meters upriver. But despite the genoa and main being set, the motor screaming, and everyone praying out on the side coaming, *Alea* remained fast.

I got into the water again to push and was baffled to find the water level high up my middle—*Alea* should be floating! Hanging on to the rubbing strake, I stretched my legs under the hull and began to dig and kick away the sand from around the keel. To my amazement I discovered the centerplate was sticking down almost half a meter below the keel. Full of hope, Despina tried winding it up, but it was jammed solid.

Just then I saw a tugboat steaming upriver toward us. There on its deck was Ventchi, waving madly. He hadn't let us down after all. We hurried and dropped the sails, ready to put ourselves in his hands again. Two crewmen rowed him over and happily exchanged him for the end of our towrope. To this they joined several other ropes and set off back toward the tug. The drag on the paid-out towrope became so great that the rowing boat couldn't haul it across to the tug. Instantly, Ventchi went over the side in his underpants, and I followed in the buff.

The only way we could relieve the pressure on the rowing boat was to stand like power pylons and hold the line out of the water. Slowly they inched across, but the line was about 10 meters short. It took three half-hearted throws to get another line from the tug. As well as this bit of light entertainment while we stood with aching arms, the Danube turned on a little something of its own: a great armada of aerated mud islands, which looked like giant cowpats, came floating downstream. They slapped into our bellies and scurried round our waists like an army of tickling spiders.

Eventually, they got the line aboard the tug and we were relieved of our assorted tortures. They started the tow—downcurrent again! *Alea* pivoted round 90 degrees as the last rope to be joined at the tug snapped. After a dreadful haul against the current just to retrieve the loose line, Ventchi and I were once again back to being human pylons. When the tow began again the line never even lifted from the water before it parted. Ventchi shook his head and said they wouldn't try again. And sure enough, the rowing boat came over to take him off.

As consolation Ventchi explained that the "cowpats" were a sign that the river level was rising and in two or three days we would float free. Poor Ventchi also had the skipper of the tug to console. Rather shamefaced, he asked if I had a bottle of schnapps or something to give to the skipper for coming to our aid. Although it went against the grain to reward such a ridiculous effort, for Ventchi's sake we handed over our last bottle of wine. We also gave him back Pieter's binoculars. This prompted Ventchi to mention that the tugboat was going farther upriver to check the channel. He indicated that with the shifting sand, the navigation buoys kept on breaking out and being swept away.

Be that as it may, when Ventchi rowed off, we knew no one else was going to help us. We would have to get out of it by ourselves and as soon as possible, for to wait for the water level to rise was to risk being completely boxed in by the shifting sandbars.

The first task was to undo the "aid" our would-be rescuers had wrought and get *Alea* facing back upstream again. When I was out resetting the plow anchor, its 25-meter length of chain gave me an idea. By shackling the block and tackle from the mast-raising mechanism onto the chain and running the tackle back to the sheet winch, we could greatly increase our kedging power—hauling us toward the anchor. This seemed promising but incurred two major difficulties. The first was that the plow anchor was taking an incredible hold in the sand and needed digging out each time I shifted it to a new kedging position. The second was caused by the block and tackle having to lie along the chain, where it twisted and jammed against the chain links.

Despina, frightened of the current, had previously refused to get in the water, but seeing that we were truly on our own and that this was our best chance, she overcame her fear. White-faced, she clung to the anchor chain and twisted the troublesome pulley back into line, while I worked the winch from outside. In this way we gradually dragged *Alea* around. She was now not only facing upstream again but also about half a boat-length nearer the channel.

By this stage we needed to rest but decided to raise the sails again to catch any likely breeze. No sooner had I sheeted them home than a gust hit us. *Alea* heeled over—and took off! I sprang to the motor and got it started. We sailed and motored right round the whole radius of the bow anchor rod, not daring to approach it directly for fear of grounding again.

Just as we got abreast of it there was a loud *crack* and the mast wobbled back as if to fall. The backward pull of the anchor chain had snapped the bronze rigging screw eye on the forestay. Fortunately, the genoa luff wire saved the mast from falling. With half a dozen things needing to be done at once, a bit of a panic ensued—the climax of which came when I jumped from the bow with the fisherman's anchor cradled in my arms and discovered the only spot where the depth was greater than neck-level. After some underwater cursing and coughing, I was finally able to re-anchor and retrieve the plow.

The damage to the forestay was incidental; the main thing was—we were afloat! Strangely, our mood was hardly euphoric; it had all been such a struggle we could only muster a dizzy glow of weary satisfaction. Despina put the kettle on and I replaced the broken rigging screw with a piece of chain. As I finished, I noticed the tug returning from upstream and traveling quite slowly. Fearing that they might stop to attempt another rescue, we decided to forestall them by setting off.

We motored over to the channel and passed the solitary green buoy, where the tug caught up with us. Ventchi waved from the wheelhouse and indicated that we mustn't forget to write to him. We didn't forget, for in spite of all the problems, we felt he had tried his best to help us.

Twenty-Three
The Battles of Calafat and Corabia

BY CAREFULLY FOLLOWING THE COURSE of Ventchi's tug, we made it safely to the ferry port of Calafat. As we passed along the shabby waterfront looking for a place to tie up, an armed soldier on a pontoon beckoned us over to him. At the same time, a friendly civilian greeted us in English and came to help us moor there but got rudely ordered away by the soldier. In that awkward moment, it seemed the whole tenor of our stay in Calafat was set.

We were not allowed ashore until the soldier made a series of telephone calls. Then, under guard, I was taken with our passports to the port police station, situated some distance away at the ferry terminal, where long queues of "refugee" cars were waiting. After fielding half a dozen requests for cigarettes from soldiers and civilians, I was finally passed on to a high-ranking police officer who looked a fatter version of "Top Dog" from Orsova. I was beginning to notice that there appeared to be three distinct racial groups in Romania. Everyone with any authority looked northern European, while most people who stood in the queues were dark-haired Mediterranean types. The third component were the gypsies who just hung about in ragged groups everywhere. Fortunately, this "Top Dog" had his mind on other fry and only glanced at the passports absentmindedly.

In our desperate efforts to get afloat, the motor had swallowed a lot of petrol; we had less than 20 liters left. So, with our suitcase trolley stacked high with empty cans, we set off into town. The queue of cars waiting for the ferry to Bulgaria stretched out of the dockyard gates and up the main road. In Romania's ruthless quest for "hard currency," priority was given to trucks exporting the country's resources. One motorist, cooking his supper on a camp stove by the side of his car, offered us directions to the filling station in German. I asked how long he had been waiting: "Zwei Tager," two days!

Needless to say, the filling station was miles away on the outskirts of town. On our way we wandered from empty shop to empty shop. Apart from our concern at the lack of provisions, it was a very mild and pleasant evening for a stroll. While following a long, tree-lined street through a relatively tidy suburb of modern blocks of flats, we came upon a woman fetching water from a community well. It looked like a bus shelter and was fairly new. The woman, seeing how intrigued we were, happily demonstrated how it worked and offered us all a taste from the metal communal cup.

At the filling station, we found seven cars waiting in line. As this didn't seem too bad, we moved into the forecourt to wait under the petrol company's logo of a fiery Lucifer. I sensed trouble the moment we entered the place. The two young women who were running the station coldly ignored us, although I noticed them discussing us when they got a periodic moment together.

When our turn came and I offered up my cans, the darker of the two women brazenly demanded "deutsche mark!" Rather taken aback, I showed her our Romanian lei. Abruptly she waved this away in disgust and said something that made the other woman laugh. Trying to go along with the spirit of the joke, I mimed my car running out of petrol, by way of showing how serious our situation was. To match my effort, this hard-bitten imp mockingly answered, "Noo deutsche mark—noo benzina!" and waltzed off to serve the next customer. From then on she smirkingly ignored us, which clearly gave her great satisfaction. Even when Despina tried asking her, she just shrugged her shoulders and hurried by.

We wanted to hang on to our foreign currency in case of extreme emergency, and besides, by now I would have seen her in hell before I gave in to her. So, after a "council of war," we decided to stand our ground in the hope of a change of heart or the appearance of the police. We waited there half an hour, with no sign of either. It was 8:45 P.M., and I felt ripe for edging down that fire-and-brimstone road. We cornered the imp in the service office. Her smirk broadened into an impudent laugh, as I tried to offer extra lei for the petrol. "Noo!" she scoffed, then—"Noo deutsche mark—noo benzina!"

Just then, the imp's husband arrived to drive her home because the filling station closed at 9:00. Being more communicative than his wife, in an international mixture of languages, he gave us to understand that foreigners in Romania could purchase petrol only with coupons, and these could only be bought with hard currency at hotels. He went on to demonstrate how the police would handcuff him if he didn't obey the rules. I laughed at this, saying that all that had surely changed with their recent revolution— Ceaușescu was dead.

They obviously had their own views on the country's new "democracy," for they became quite animated in their efforts to convey to us how little the "old" regime had changed. It seemed that airing their misfortunes made them more sympathetic to ours—they would sell us petrol, although we had "noo coupon" and "noo deutsche mark."

When the forecourt was finally emptied and blacked out, we were surprised how furtive and genuinely nervous they were. The imp's husband first parked his car in the darkest corner, in order to place our empty cans on the floor of the backseat. He left the car to check if "the coast was all clear," then returned to move it over to one of the pumps. After another "safe period" the imp filled them—inside the car. My schoolteacher instinct warned me that this would be too much of a temptation for her, so I went out to check the pump. She had just finished with the 20-liter jerrican when I approached to remind her we wanted the containers *full*.

She angrily muttered something but went back to the jerrican and topped it up with the missing 5 liters.

We got our fuel and paid 600 lei, well over the market price but the best of a bad deal. As a consolation they gave us a lift back to the ferry terminal. In a carefully chosen, unlit side street, and amidst lots of *shhhh*s, they quickly unloaded us and our cans before speeding off. We made our way back to *Alea* past the queue of refugee cars. The friendly chap who had given us directions earlier had met with some limited success himself—he had moved along about three car-lengths.

The next morning, I was out early repairing the bronze rigging screw. Luckily, I was able to salvage enough thread on the end of the screw eye to reassemble it, making up for the loss of length by using an extra shackle. While I was engaged with this, an armed soldier on guard (a particularly nasty-looking piece of work) watched over me. He first asked for cigarettes and then schnapps but found himself out of luck both times. I thought that was that, but when Despina and the children tried to leave on another foraging trip ashore, he ordered them back aboard. When asked why, he reluctantly pointed to his shoulder, the miming euphemism for an officer. We assumed one was coming, but after half an hour we were still waiting.

Fortunately, a friendly sailor who spoke very good English came to our aid and went off to get a policeman. To our surprise our unsavory guard was instantly stood to attention and given a very vicious dressing-down. Then, with a dismissive salute, the policeman gave the shore-party the password—"Nooo problem!"

Despina had anything but, as Charles's diary records:

Thursday September 27, Mum and I went shopping, saw the rubbish we put in the bin yesterday lying around a park bench in town! There is a long queue of cars wanting to go by ferry to Bulgaria, saw some people we met in the queue last night and they have only moved 5 spaces!! Went to many supermarkets, nothing to buy except "gungy" preserved fruit and veggies left from the war!!!

After trying all the shops, she began asking at restaurants, but most had no food to serve to their customers! Finally she got lucky and found one that was able to sell her some bread and a piece of cold ham.

Meanwhile I tried to lever down the centerplate, but it wouldn't budge. I suspected a small stone was lodged between the plate and the slot in the keel. This, unfortunately, could only be got at from the outside. In view of our "shopping" experience here, we did not fancy putting ourselves even further at the mercy of the facilities at Calafat, so we decided to head over to some small islands by the Bulgarian shore, where there might be sheltered water in which we could try fixing the centerplate.

One advantage of the river current was that we needed only to lie close-hauled on one port tack heading upstream to arrive straight opposite and directly upwind. With Despina sounding the depth with the long pole, we cautiously motored our way in and found a shallow shelf of sand that would allow me to stand by the side of the hull. Unfortunately, this meant trespassing in Bulgaria, although the isolation of the area made the chances of detection remote.

We anchored fore and aft while Charles and Victoria swam ashore with the bow and stern lines. These they attached to short pieces of timber that they then buried deep in the sand as "dog anchors" on which we warped *Alea* close in to the side. The keel was now about 400 millimeters from the sandy bottom.

I dived down and, by lying on my back under the keel and passing the blade of my handsaw up the sides of the slot, I found the culprit: a 20-millimeter-diameter stone was stuck high up inside the slot on the port side. On my next dive I tried striking it out using the back of the saw blade (in deference to a strict apprenticeship in carpentry). Unfortunately, the tapered edge of the blade wedged itself between the stone and centerplate on the very first resolute blow.

Several dives later, the stone and my saw were still pinned there. I was having great difficulty diving down and holding my breath for any length of time. I tried breathing through a 2-meter section of plastic tubing with a clothes-peg on my nose and found out how a vacuum cleaner feels when a sock gets stuck in its pipe! However, by slinging a rope right underneath the hull, I was able to pull myself down a lot faster, allowing me more "puff" to do something constructive once I got there. After hammering a wedge up the slot to ease the pressure of the centerplate, I was able to tap the saw free. Then, to my eternal shame, I turned the blade round and smashed the stone to pieces. Incredibly, my own clenched teeth seemed to suffer more than the teeth of the saw—not one broke off.

One more ducking and the job was done—the centerplate was free. But oh, what a price! I've never been so cold. They speak of the body's "core temperature." Well, that day I physically felt my body's core; it sat inside my chest like a length of cold, cast-iron drainpipe—decidedly unpleasant. To thaw out I had to lie in the forecabin with Charles and Victoria, swaddled in everyone's sleeping bags, while Despina administered a hot toddy—a marvelous treatment for a drainpipe up your middle!

When I felt a bit more myself, we moved back out on the anchors and tidied up, happy in the knowledge that *Alea* was whole again. To celebrate, Despina prepared a delicious meal with the Calafat ham, cooked again to ensure that it was completely dead.

The next morning was cool and gray. We put up the boom-tent and carried on in the rain until we ran into fog, which forced us to anchor at the side. When the visibility improved, we were able to continue by following a succession of barges, although we could never keep up with any particular one for long.

We had a bizarre affair with the first barge we tucked in behind—a huge Russian brute. The skipper, of like description, realized what we were up to and, coming out onto the afterdeck, signaled us to follow. I waved my thanks. Then he began to point his finger back at us and mime an action, like bundling up a newspaper—ripping it to pieces and throwing it away? Hoping that this symbolism didn't refer to me personally, I shrugged my shoulders, mystified. To this he disappeared inside the wheelhouse for a moment, to return holding the Romanian flag. Now, with even more exaggerated expressions of malice, he bunched it up, threw it on the deck, and proceeded to jump up and down on it. We got the message and removed our courtesy flag from the rail, to the beaming satisfaction of "Ivan the Terrible."

This brought us opposite the Bulgarian port of Lom, where we spent the night moored alongside an anchored, unattended dumb-barge. In the morning we awoke to find ourselves fogbound again. I tried fishing, without any luck. When I was called in for morning coffee, we discovered a major quartermaster's disaster. Victoria's diary relates:

> The sugar was finishing, so Mum took out the packet we bought in Hungary. I told her to taste it before she put it in with the other sugar, but she didn't listen. Instead she started to pour it in, then she stopped and tasted it, "Yuk!" Mum said "It's salt!" "I told you" I said. Dad told us all to get a plate each and see if we could separate the salt from the sugar. We gave up, it was impossible!

We were spared a little from this bitter fate when a harbor tug came alongside to check the unattended barge. The skipper was very happy to swap some of his yellow, unrefined sugar for some Viennese coffee.

At noon we got away, to clock up another short run of 50 kilometers. All along this stretch, the Bulgarian shore consists of high, eroding cliffs, while the Romanian side is low-lying tree plantations. We saw several work gangs of men and women being ferried out to the many large islands to collect timber. Apart from their tractors, they reminded me of typical peasant scenes from the Volga in czarist times. It was behind one of these plantation islands that we found an idyllic sandy anchorage, where the children played until dark. Fortunately, we had just got them and the plank aboard when a motley gang of cutthroats appeared on the riverbank, wanting the usual cigarettes. One spoke Italian and wanted us to move *Alea* closer to the shore, but I wished them "Buona notte" and, to our relief, they left.

The next day, we came upon a large tree that appeared to be growing right in the middle of the channel. We thought it prudent to anchor and wait until a guiding barge appeared. When a Bulgarian barge finally came, its wash caused the huge piece of flotsam to topple over and continue on its way. As the barge was going downstream, we quickly followed, and lo and behold, we got our second signal to take down our Romanian courtesy flag—not so flamboyant as Ivan's, but with the same spiteful sentiment.

This didn't seem to say a lot for good neighborly relations in the region, but we certainly couldn't complain when we arrived at the port of Corabia. The skipper of the tugboat *Rasinari* waved us over to moor alongside, and the whole crew turned out to help. They invited us aboard for a glass of "wine" that was just at its first fermentation and tasted more like fruit juice. The engineer spoke fluent French, so we were all able to converse through him and Despina, although Charles and Victoria seemed to be doing all right on their own. They and the youngest crewman were having great fun watching cartoons on the ship's black-and-white television and swapping mimed tales.

During this impromptu party a soldier appeared, ostensibly looking for us. Our hosts immediately invited him in for a seat and a glass of "juice" as if he were an old friend. When he was finished he said he would now have to fetch an officer to clear us. Unfortunately, the welcome the officer received couldn't have been more of a contrast. Made to feel as though he was a bad smell entering the cabin, he didn't linger but said he would get an immigration officer to deal with us. The only explanation we could get for the crew's hostility was that they didn't like "them!"

In the morning the *Rasinari* left and we remoored in the vacated berth. When I tried to go ashore, the soldier on guard wouldn't let me pass. As I was trying to explain I was only going to get water, the immigration officer arrived.

He was overweight and wore an army officer's uniform with no hat. Black, greasy hair capped a sweaty, unwashed, podgy face. His opening statement was a French-sounding "Passport!" Although appearing satisfied and returning them to me, he stopped Despina and the children as they left to walk into town. At first Despina thought he was offering them a lift, but it transpired he wanted her passport to hold as some sort of security until they returned. It was hard to imagine anyone would want to be an overstayer in Romania—least of all Despina!

He looked very shifty, which made me concerned that he might take the passport away, but he indicated he was going to wait there until they returned. We had to agree.

Just then, out of the blue a group of peasants came up and presented us with a crate of apples! Quite blatantly, the immigration "greaseball" tried to make out that they were a gift from him, which was totally denied by the embarrassed, silent scorn shown toward him by the benevolent group.

Thinking that everything had been sorted out, I picked up my water container and made to leave in search of a faucet. Incredibly, Greaseball would only allow me to do this if I handed over my passport.

When I got back, he was trying to put on a serious, bumptious air as he paced up and down, rechecking the passports again and again. Seeing that he was working himself up for something, I thought the sooner it was out the better, so in passing I asked for my passport back. At this he waved it in the air and gravely announced, "Problem!" He had noticed our visas were for two adults and wanted me to pay for the children. I explained that we had got the visas stamped in our New Zealand "family" passports to avoid this, for the Romanian visa rules stated that children on their parents' passports didn't require separate visas.

He was obviously unsure of his ground and finally gave me back my passport, but after another period of pacing thought, he wanted to see it again. This time he asked if I had changed any money and wanted to see the receipt, which of course I didn't have. This encouraged him to get agitated, and he jabbered on in broken French, that I had been "compromised" and that there would be "grand problems" when I got to Constanta. There was nothing I could say, and he seemed to run out of steam. I got the distinct impression he wanted to manufacture a situation in which he could extort a bribe but didn't quite know how to go about it. This time he refused to give me back the passport, indicating he would have to stamp it.

The crew were gone over two hours and had precious little to show for it—the shops in Corabia were as bare as in Calafat. But with everyone aboard, I now had to face the problem of getting back our passports. Taking a leaf from Aesop's fables, I closely approached the Greaseball and smilingly slapped a clenched fist down on the open palm of my other hand and ordered: "Stampa passports—merci!" He pouted his bottom lip at my impertinence, and just to show me how "grand" a Greaseball he was around here, he handed the passports back with a truculent "Noo stampa!"

Twenty-Four
Comrades in Olteniţa

THE BULGARIAN TOWN OF SVISHTOV is situated on a sharp left-hand bend. At this strategic yet bridgeless spot the German and Russian armies chose to cross in both world wars. Right on the bend and in midstream lay the thin, golden crescent of an exposed sandbank. There were no navigational buoys, but this was no problem to us, for we now had a snaking Biro pen line to follow on our little guidebook chart, thanks to the skipper of the *Rasinari*.

With confidence we took the channel on the right—or so we thought until we grounded some 100 meters farther on. Just as I went over the side to push *Alea* off the sand, a barge appeared upstream, and we watched it pass down on the left side of the sandbank. How he knew to do this was a mystery.

With Victoria stationed with her ear pressed to the floor of the cabin, we slowly plugged back upstream. "I think we're scraping—there's a funny noise!" Like a submarine crew waiting anxiously for enemy depth charges, we all listened intently for the centerplate to strike. When we made the channel unscathed there was a loud sigh of relief.

The weather was very pleasant, so Despina, with the help of her "professional water scooper," took the opportunity to wash our beddings. With these set like additional sails, we covered the 50 kilometers to Ruse.

On the eastern outskirts of the town we approached the "Friendship" bridge. At 2,224 meters, it's the longest on the Danube—and no doubt the longest seeming in Europe for the crowds of Romanian refugees held up by their customs police at the northern end. Standing by to lower the sails and mast if need be, we glided through with just barely a meter's clearance.

Our map showed a large island about 5 kilometers past the bridge, but it turned out to be just a long, barely exposed sand-bank. Nevertheless, we anchored off the downstream point, and the crew went over the side for a swim.

While I relaxed in the cockpit, I watched thousands upon thousands of crows in continuous ragged lines come flying up on the other side of the river. It wasn't until I perceived their raucous squawking getting louder that I realized they were coming round and landing on the sandbank. The once vast stretch of golden sand had turned black with the swarming mass.

Sometime later, I noticed the first vanguard of birds fly past on their way back downstream. Glancing back at the sandbank, I was confronted with a most spectacular sight. With wings out-stretched, the great throng were hopping along the ground in a mass circular movement. In an increasing frenzy they loped around in a counterclockwise spiral toward their center, from where they then took off. This formed a black, swirling vortex that rose into the air in a central tornado-like column 3 or 4 meters in diameter. It appeared as if the birds were being sucked high into the air and spun out into wisps of black smoke that drifted off downriver. It took ten to fifteen minutes for the advancing rim of golden sand to reach the base of the revolving spout. Then sud-denly the column seemed to dissolve upward into a dazzling noth-ingness that left us all gaping.

Nature provided us with a more mundane phenomenon the following morning when we awoke to find *Alea* riding to the stern anchor in a 20-knot easterly. With this being a headwind, it wasn't until after lunch that we motored out into the channel, in a steady cool breeze.

We had gone only about 5 kilometers when suddenly I became aware of a strong smell of rotting fish. Following my nose, I turned round and, to my horror, saw steam coming from the back of the motor. A quick glance at the water outlet confirmed the problem: no cooling water was circulating around the motor. I cut the motor and checked the water intake at the bottom of the propeller shaft—it was clear. This put the cause of the problem inside the motor, making an immediate pit stop imperative.

The only convenient place was a small bay I had noticed about 2 kilometers back. As we raised the sails, right on cue the inevitable troublemaking barges appeared like vultures. The headwind that a moment ago was a curse was now a blessing. With the sails full, I looked carefully at the near left bank and saw that we were moving upstream—just.

A barge traveling slowly upstream approached on a course 10 meters off our port side. Typically, just at the point where I could begin my reach across to the anchorage, the barge was close enough to deter me from crossing its path. We were effectively jammed in a narrow channel between him and the river's edge. Forced to continue on upstream, we were shepherded a kilometer past the bay before he finally overtook us.

We now set off to beat back downstream. It took three tacks to enter the bay, and when the sails began to flag under the lee of the point, I briefly risked the motor to position *Alea* into the current. It took only a few seconds for it to start steaming again—but the job was done.

When *Alea* fell back on the anchor chain, all was peace and quiet—but not for long! Despina had had enough. She wanted to sail on back to Ruse and take *Alea* overland from there. I temporized with "Let's see what's wrong first." She gave up and stormed below.

Taking refuge in the world of simple problems, I turned to the motor. My first thought was that it was a blockage caused by the excess of gasket cement I had applied at Compiègne. The first task was to test the many galleries that surround the cylinders. As it was an outboard motor, it was a relatively easy matter to tip it up in any direction and pour water through all the entry and exit points. With water flowing freely from all of them, the idea of a blockage had to be set aside. Next I had to look at the water pump, situated at the bottom of the propeller shaft. Fortunately, I had greased all the bolts last winter, so it didn't take long to dismantle—and find the trouble.

A metal T-shaped key that holds the water impeller to the driveshaft had disintegrated. As I didn't have a spare, my only option was to try making one—a job that would have to wait till morning, for I knew better than to ignore the mate's first summons to supper.

I started work at first light and cut out a replacement key from a piece of scrap stainless steel that by good luck was the correct thickness. Everything went so well that in less than two hours the motor was ticking over on the transom with water issuing from where it should.

Despina was still unhappy about continuing and suggested I go on by myself while she and the children took the "Ruse option." The impasse was suddenly resolved when I pointed out that I would need at least Charles to help get *Alea* through the Constantsa Canal locks. This was "out of the question!" She might be prepared to leave her husband in the empty larder of Romania, "But never my son!" So, thankfully, we forgot about Ruse and agreed that united we would proceed to the sea—then see.

We raised the anchor and set out round the point to spend the day threading our way through the flattish, wooded terrain. Now that the course of the channel marked on our chart was suspect, I kept a sharp lookout for barges coming upstream so that I could see on which side of the river they steered and at what point they crossed over. A rare boon would be when a barge passed in our direction, providing me with an infallible guide through the increasing labyrinth of sandbanks.

Without too many mishaps we reached the Romanian shipbuilding port of Olteniţa. Row upon row of empty slipways lined the shore. A civilian launch, the *Petunia*, was moored at the port captain's pontoon, and we were invited to tie up alongside.

Stripped to the waist, with longish hair and a thick beard, the engineer of the launch looked like Robinson Crusoe. To our surprise he announced, "My name John Adams"—apparently an inheritance from an English grandfather or great-grandfather, we couldn't quite understand which, for our curiosity soon out-stripped his endowment of English.

John beckoned me over to see the huge diesel engines, which I was amazed to see filled most of the hull space. With a fair bit of mime, he explained that he was servicing them for the return trip to his home port of Sulina, which is at the mouth of the Danube.

We were also introduced to the skipper of the launch, Valentino, who in spite of the name had the appearance of a boxer who had dropped his guard too often. He spoke a little French, so over a beer we got on handsomely.

It wasn't long before the inevitable armed soldiers arrived, but close on their heels came the port captain. This time there was no question of army officers being summoned, for it was evident that this port captain was in command here.

He was in his mid-thirties and had the bearing and features of an Italian welterweight boxer who had kept his guard up. In very good English, he politely introduced himself as Dinu Tudorel and welcomed us to Olteniţa. As there are situations that start badly and seem to head downhill, there are ones that from their pleasant beginnings just get better. Olteniţa was to prove one of these. As soon as the formalities were completed, Dinu offered to accompany us into town and help us with provisions.

Because Dinu's car, a Romanian Dacia, was laid up at the moment awaiting a spare part, we set off to walk the 4 kilometers inland to the town. Outside the port gate we passed a large, derelict-looking factory, which, Dinu told us, was the town's domestic hot water and central heating system. Thinking that this was a clever byproduct of some other manufacturing process, we asked what the factory made. "Nothing else, hot water only." Water from the Danube was heated in oil-fired boilers, then pumped the 4 kilometers to every house in Olteniţa. It had been closed down, along with the sugar refinery across the road, due to lack of money after the revolution. Dinu seemed to have hopes that the Japanese might come and operate them.

As we were trying to comprehend the prospect of this unlikely event, we turned a corner onto the main road. There, running parallel to the road, was an extraordinarily ugly vista of looping and snaking water pipes stretching out toward the town. With most of the heavy pipe insulation hanging off and blown about the countryside, it looked hideous. Talk about a blot on the land-scape!

In contrast, the township looked much more cared for than the other places we had seen. Dinu was obviously very proud of his town and showed Despina the better shops, where she was able to buy some—albeit very few—groceries. Then Dinu invited us to his home for coffee.

Dinu lived on the third floor of a high-rise apartment block. Although the housing estate looked a bit seedy, his flat was as well furnished as any we had seen in Britain. The only blemish was where the recently installed electric cables had been sunk into the walls and ceiling. After eight years of using candles, they had finally got electric lighting. Dinu gratefully announced, "Things getting better since zee revolution."

As it had been six months since we had sat in a proper home, Despina and I really enjoyed the hospitality. We met Dinu's wife, Maria, who was kept busy with their twenty-one-day-old daughter and rather precocious four-year-old son. Charles and Victoria had to diplomatically field most of his boisterous attentions and reserve their judgments for their diaries:

> Michael was a pain in the neck. When I was looking at the Captain's English learning book, Michael showed me the scribbles he had done on it and laughed! He kept trying to kiss Victoria—there must've been something really wrong with him!

Happily, there were no such misunderstandings between the parents. Indeed, of all the kindnesses that we received from the many helpful and friendly people we met on the tip, none moved us more than the simple openhandedness of Dinu and Maria. When it came time for us to take our leave, they most generously presented us with about 4 kilos of potatoes from their own scarce supply. This was an incredibly thoughtful gesture, for these were now unobtainable. No matter how bad the food situation got for us, we knew at worst we could always abandon *Alea* and leave the country. But Dinu and his family were stuck here with the specter of a very difficult winter approaching.

We got back to the harbor in the dark to be met by a large dog charging down on us. A massed volley of stones quickly put it to yelping flight, but our victory was short-lived. Its outraged owner, an armed soldier, came purposefully across to belligerently point out the error of our ways. With the odds now decidedly in favor of the snarling dog, I ardently mimed how sorry we were and fortunately managed, at least, to appease the growling brute with the gun.

Safely aboard *Alea*, we stowed away the day's shopping and considered the situation. Our stocks of pasta and rice were dwindling and we had again been essentially unable to restock. We had already used our last tin of meat, and we were obviously all losing weight. Since our arrival in Romania, all thoughts of being on holiday had been dispelled, leaving only the serious resolve of an expedition to get through. After Oltenița, this resolve deteriorated to a desperate need to escape and with it a willingness to accept almost any risk.

Twenty-Five
"Fool" Speed Ahead through the Constantsa Canal

IN THE PORT OFFICE the next morning, Dinu voiced his concern that I didn't have a proper chart of the Danube, especially the next stretch, which he said was "very difficult!" I was put further to shame when he began to rummage out a series of old, folding charts that showed the river from Oltenița to Cernavoda, where the Constantsa Canal begins.

As these charts were 20 years out of date, Dinu resolutely set about revising the position of the channel and all the navigational buoys. Before long, other people in the office got involved and added their bits of information, including Valentino, who was still filling in departure forms. When the revisions were complete, they all agreed that it was now the most up-to-date chart on the Danube. It was incredible to see that in 20 years the channel had shifted more than a kilometer in places.

Then, just as I was leaving the office, there was a telephone call. Suddenly, at the end of an intermittent staccato of Romanian, a worried Dinu announced, "You von't make it!" I was thunderstruck. "Why?" He had just been told that the water level 45 kilometers upstream of Cernavoda was only 600 millimeters. I said I couldn't believe this, because I had seen barges pass in both directions this very morning. "Ah," Dinu replied, "zhey go through zee Bala to Giurgeni."

The "Bala," it turned out, is a narrow creek that connects into a side loop of the Danube. This detour is called the "Borcea" and runs parallel to the Danube for some 140 kilometers. Unfortunately, it doesn't merge with the Danube again until 60 kilometers downriver of the entrance to the Constantsa Canal. This, of course, would have to be made up against the river current, a situation we had always tried to avoid. And as a further twist to our sudden change in fortune, Dinu had to explain all this on my guidebook chart. The port office didn't have a chart of the Borcea.

I walked back to *Alea* and broke the news to Despina, who received it like yet another hammer blow. However, putting on a brave face, she stood by the moorings and smiled at our well-wishing friends as we cast off and turned downstream. At least we would have the benefit of the newly revised chart for the next 85 kilometers until the turnoff into the "Bala."

We had traveled about 20 kilometers from Oltenița when Valentino and John in *Petunia* caught up. With a heavy, coughing roar of the engines being throttled down, they came gliding up beside us. John indicated they wanted to give us a tow. I was a little apprehensive about this, but surprisingly Despina was keen, saying, "We'll get out of here quicker!" Before accepting, I made sure that Valentino understood *Alea*'s draft was far greater than *Petunia*'s 400 millimeters.

With assurances given, I led their 40-millimeter towrope under the bow-roller and made fast to the Sampson post. In an effort to strengthen this anchor point, I braced it back to the mast foot and sheet winches. When I stepped back and viewed my handiwork, I felt someone "walk over my grave" so decided to belt on my sheath-knife—in case knots should need undoing in a hurry. So with catastrophe briefly considered and spurned, I gave Valentino the nod, foolishly casting our fate to the wind.

The throaty throb of *Petunia*'s engines quickened and we were firmly borne away. As if waterskiing, *Alea*'s bow rose and the stern seemed to sink into a trough of white, foaming water. The crew were all holding on nervously in the cockpit. Suddenly Victoria gave out a fearful scream. We all shot a glance at her terror-stricken face, then immediately to where she was pointing aft. The stern coaming was below the level of a gushing wall of white water that reared up over the tilted motor. Looking down, I saw the after cockpit was being flooded by water coming up the drain. Fortunately, it stopped when it was 300 millimeters deep.

At the beginning I hung on to the tiller, but later I found I could let it go and it would stay firmly amidships as we whizzed along behind *Petunia* at 8 to 9 knots. My greatest fear was hitting something on the riverbed. I imagined at such a speed either the keel would be ripped off or the Sampson post and half the fore-deck pulled out. With this very much in mind, I diligently followed our course on the updated chart.

After a while we got accustomed to the speed and began to admire the spacious riverscapes. Low, forested shores would recede rapidly away into the distance, then come gliding up close as we swept round another bend. At Danube kilometer 375 we passed the waterfront suburbs of the Bulgarian town of Silistra, which sits on the border with Romania. Incredibly, the last houses of the town look out across the street to the concentration-camp-style fence of the frontier.

At about 4:00 P.M. I breathed a great sigh of relief when I heard *Petunia*'s engines throttle down. Thankfully, we had reached Danube kilometer 345 and the parting of the ways. Over on the left bank was the gaping entrance to the Bala, and just ahead lay the now impassable channel, twisting between several exposed sandbanks. Typically, there was no buoy or sign warning that the river was closed to anything other than extremely shallow drafted vessels like *Petunia*.

When *Petunia* came to a halt, we skimmed up alongside. As so often happens in foreign parts, the plans had changed: now they were going down the "Bala" too, and it went without saying that we would tag along, but first they had to go somewhere to refuel. While they roared off, we headed over to wait by a huge dredger platform that was aground near the right bank. To our surprise a striking young couple appeared on the deck of the dredger and helped us moor. She looked a sort of peasant version of Princess Di and he a more carefully sculptured Rudolf Nureyev. They apparently lived in a large garden shed erected in the middle of the open deck. This unlikely setting was also the playground for their two-year-old son, who ran about the open deck quite unrestrained.

Before long we were drinking to each other's health while being serenaded by Romanian folk music from a speaker that "Rudolf" set up for our benefit. The woman was obviously very fashion conscious and asked Despina if she could give her any dress clothes and lipstick. All Despina could spare in clothes was a T-shirt, and as for lipstick, she had none herself.

John and Valentino came back, and without further ado, the towrope was made fast and off we rushed again. In a flash, it seemed, we passed from the spacious sandy Danube to the winding, muddy creek of the "Bala." Thick beech forest crowded to the edge of the high banks that flanked the 20- to 25-meter-wide waterway. It was like water-skiing through the French Canals.

Valentino really showed his skill here as he guided us round the sharp weaving bends. It started to get dark soon after we turned into the wider Borcea. A cool headwind sprang up, causing a bit of a chop, which our speed dashed into flying spray. Despina passed out my wet weather gear and I prepared for a long night. I hung out my trusty kerosene lamp and rigged up the plank athwart the cockpit as a seat so I could see over the cabin roof. Not that there was much to see ahead. *Petunia* was now just a dark shadow, dimly outlined in the ghostly glow of navigation lights and the flash of bursting white spume. Now I was more worried about hitting any solid flotsam, so I steered to keep *Alea* directly in behind *Petunia* just thundering on, seemingly oblivious to the dangers. How Valentino managed to follow the snaking channel I do not know, but our pace never slackened.

It was a clear, starry night with no moon. Distant lights of all colors and clusters approached and receded on the far shores. Despina put the children to bed and handed me a sandwich for supper. We had no idea how long or how far *Petunia* was going to tow us. I began to feel tired as the hours dragged by. Each time I saw the loom of shore lights, I prayed that this would be where

Petunia would stop for the night. I listened intently to the dull throb of the engines, willing it to change pitch, the first indication that we were slowing down—but always we careered on past. Then at last my prayers were answered, but again I was in for a surprise.

I had made a rough calculation as to our estimated time of arrival at Giurgeni, which was the appalling hour of two o'clock in the morning. It was now just after nine o'clock, but I was nonplussed to see towering above us the distinctive-looking Cernavoda railway bridge. I recognized it from a picture in our guidebook—it's the same sort of lattice design as the Forth Bridge in Scotland. Could it be that Valentino had towed us right to our destination via some secret backwater? I called to Despina to read out the passage on Cernavoda, and the mystery was soon solved. The bridge, it proudly stated, was nearly 15 kilometers long so as to pass over the delta swamps. We were obviously at the opposite end from Cernavoda, and it was most galling to think we had to travel another 130 kilometers of meandering river to get there.

Petunia found a berth next to a large barge, and we tied up alongside. Our feeling of relief was euphoric, and all of a sudden the evening felt warm and nine o'clock didn't seem so late. With the children tucked in bed, Despina and I got ourselves suitably armed and climbed aboard *Petunia* to toast the river gods for our deliverance. We spent a relaxing hour with Valentino and John, who gave us their thoughts on the collapse of communism. They were very concerned about their uncertain futures, being, as they emphatically put it, "Not young men!" And of the old regime, "Not all bad!" was their verdict, "for at least then a worker could look forward to a state pension."

We awoke the next morning fogbound, which forced us to wait a couple of hours before charging off again. This section of the river ran almost due north and was much more twisting than the first. At 7 to 8 knots we swished round bend after bend. The rising and plunging bow wave didn't look so fearsome today, although it was still more comfortable not to look at the foaming geyser erupting from under our stern. All morning I sat up on my perch and watched the green forestland pass by.

At noon we came out of our last flying bend, and there before us was the great expanse of the Danube again, with the Giurgeni road bridge forming the distant horizon. For the first time we saw several barges lying aground, and we moored up to one of these to remove the towrope. Our considerate friends wanted to see us enter the main channel safely before they left, so on Valentino's advice, Despina sounded the depth with the pole as I slowly headed *Alea* around the junction's low sandy spit. Following the course instructions to the letter, we soon turned up against the 2- to 3-knot current without Despina finding bottom once. Our concentration was suddenly broken by the yodel of *Petunia*'s siren as John and Valentino gave us the all clear and a last farewell.

A light southerly was blowing, and as the channel turned more to the east, we were able to raise full sail to aid our valiant little motor. We managed to hold that one tack for about 15 kilometers. Then, as the river began to snake again, we got into a pattern of raising and lowering the sails so we could alternately get the maximum benefit of favorable winds or remove the extra windage caused by the flogging sails.

By late afternoon the wind had strengthened to a good 15 knots and we were able to tack up across the channel. Navigation buoys were few and far between, with land-based markers very hard to see because of the dense vegetation. Although numerous barges lay aground, some abandoned well out from the shore, we rarely touched bottom. On the odd occasion that the fully extended centerplate did ground, I would immediately spin *Alea* round on the next tack, which saved us every time.

The following day's effort was much the same: a fog-delayed start, followed by a motor-sailing slog against the current. As it was a Sunday, we heard church bells for the first time in ages. This somehow mellowed our "desperate escape" back to the bounds of a recreational sail. Victoria's diary describes her day:

October 7th, We are getting short of food. The shops here are just bare rooms with shelves. In Olteniţa, we bought a jar of cherry jam and this morning we tasted it. I felt sick just looking at it on my bread. It had heaps of hairs in it, from some animal's fur. We set off. The weather was very nice. On one side of the river there were woods and on the other villages. We saw lots of little boats, coming from the woods to the village, full of firewood, probably getting ready for winter. We put the sails up and the boat tipped to one side and all the things from our game fell to the floor. Charles got the good idea of us all sitting out in the cockpit. So with handfuls of walnuts and the nut cracker we sat out in the sun. I filled my pant pockets up with nuts but when I stood up my pants nearly fell down with the weight. I cracked some nuts and gave them to Dad, while he was steering. When the boat leaned over Charles and I dangled our feet in the water from the low side.

This family sail was to be the lull before the storm, a quiet respite bestowed as a parting token from the mighty Danube. At two o'clock we arrived before the latticed bulk of the Cernavoda bridge. It seemed to lie across the river like some forbidding barrier, and somehow we were free on the outside of it. There was no doubt that many aspects of the trip had soured on this difficult leg, but in spite of this, to this day we consider the Danube to be the most spectacular and majestic of all the rivers we have traveled on.

The waterfront of Cernavoda lay to our left, deserted in a siesta-like calm. As *Alea* glided over the dead water of a large sheltered bay, we could see straight down the fairway of the Constantsa Canal. The white concrete sides looked stark compared to the green, curving riverbanks we had just left. After a *pazz-paper* check, the port captain called the canal controller on his VHF radio. To my surprise, he handed me the microphone to make my halting request for passage. To my relief the controller's excellent English crackled back from a loudspeaker on the wall, but I didn't care much for what he had to say:

"You must 'ave a pilot—over."

"How much does it cost?—over."

"Four 'undred American dollars to pazz alone, $20 if you pazz with a commercial ship—over."

"I will wait for a commercial ship—over."

"Vee expect a ship at six o'clock tonight, a pilot vill come to your boat at five—over."

"But I want to go through tomorrow—over."

"There vill bee no ships tomorrow—over."

"I will go through tonight then, how long does it take?—over."

"Six to seven hours—over."

It was going to be another long night! As well as the fatigue of traveling in the dark, I was disappointed that we would miss what there was to see along the canal. Despina's response was "The quicker the better!"

We had three hours in which to prepare for the passage, so while I readied the mast for lowering, Despina prepared a potato stew. We had to choose between our last two tins: peas or carrots? Peas it was; the "donkey carrots" would be our reward for reaching the sea tomorrow.

Once the mast was stowed on deck, I turned my attention to safeguarding our motor. The port captain had asked me several times how fast we could travel and was obviously unimpressed at our 4 to 6 knots. I didn't fancy the prospect of a Romanian pilot forcing the motor at full throttle for six hours. The motor had done well going at half throttle for an average of seven hours nearly every day since April. However, I could sense it was getting tired and needed gentle nursing if it was to see us through to Greece. After having a good look at the throttle cable and its fittings, I tied a piece of wire round the throttle lever and the body of the carburetor to prevent the throttle from being moved more than halfway, thereby regulating our maximum speed to our usual 4 knots.

The pilot arrived by launch at 6:15 P.M. He was a carefully groomed young man dressed in civilian clothes and speaking good but sparing English. Immediately he indicated for us to cast off and be ready to follow the barge we could see entering the bay. It was a huge Romanian pusher pushing two empty dumb-barges lashed abreast of each other. We had seen these monsters out on the Danube pushing as many as sixteen fully loaded barges, four abreast and against the current. Heading out into the fairway, the pilot turned to me and, nodding at the motor, asked: "Is zthis your top speed?" I shrugged my shoulders and made a big display of throttling down and then twisting the handle back hard. He shrugged and, taking out his two-way radio, said: "I vill ask zee Kapeetan if he vill give uz a tow."

The first lock was some distance down the entrance canal, so we chugged on, flanked on either side by the high, grubby embankments that sloped back from the water's edge. Because of the low water level, these slopes looked massive—concrete landscaping on a grand scale. But even these huge expanses of concrete shrank to insignificance when compared to the monstrosity in a high valley behind Cernavoda. It was a gigantic nuclear power station that seemed to blot out everything else. With relief, we heard from the pilot that it wasn't in operation and that work had stopped on it soon after the revolution—another dream, or in this case nightmare, left to rust.

The pusher had just berthed inside the lock when we arrived. Lined up along the port rail were ten very eager crewmen, each, in typical "Ventchi" fashion, whistling and shouting at me to pass up the ends of our mooring ropes. With this barracking competition, the language problem, and the terrific noise of the engines throbbing in the cavernous lock, chaos reigned. The lines would be secured at one end, and by the time I went down to the other, someone would be undoing them to tie on in some other way. The pilot had disappeared and I was just beginning to despair when suddenly a short, stocky fellow appeared holding a two-way radio. This was obviously his baton of office, for when he started to bellow, crewmen jumped in all directions.

All the ropes were untied and *Alea* was pulled forward to sit in the corner formed behind the left barge that stuck out past the width of the pusher. Other crewmen came with thicker ropes, which they passed to me to make fast to the bow and stern. The "little marshal" impressed me further by indicating for me to double these lines; he obviously knew what he was doing.

Because of the large fluctuations of the Danube, this lock is designed to raise or lower ships from the river side to the relatively constant level of the canal. In our case it raised us about 4 meters. The gates opened and the "Kapeetan" appeared at the rail of the bridge, three decks up, and asked the pilot if we were ready to go. A moment later those mighty diesels began to race. The noise was deafening. Unfortunately, we were positioned directly in front of the open engine-room door, and I found myself knitting my brows in an effort just to think. At first we traveled quite slowly, but when clear of the lock fairway, the pusher very quickly began to accelerate.

Alea steadily heeled over toward the side of the pusher as the speed increased, then just seemed to hang there. A torrent of foaming water came cascading back from the dumb-barges' wake to be forced up between *Alea*'s starboard side and the pusher in big, curving sheets. In nervous fascination, I watched these flow smoothly, like clear plastic, up the pusher's metal plating to arch over, well above the height of our cabin roof, before breaking in a welter of foam and spray.

We all hung on and Despina and I exchanged anxious looks. We both knew that what we had got ourselves into was totally irresponsible, but there seemed no way out. We were going through the water faster than when *Petunia* had towed us. I asked the pilot what the speed limit on the canal was; he replied that it was 6 knots. I then asked, "How fast do you think we are going now?" "About 9 knots, zee Kapeetan is in a hurry." He was right about the hurry, but I would have put it nearer 12 knots. The stern lines were under a lot of pressure, constantly tightening and slackening. I began to worry: we were relying on two 8-millimeter brass bolts that held the cleats on.

The pilot had concerns of his own. "I 'ave coffee now please," he said. Despina and I were so nervous that it took a muddled joint effort just to light the stove, let alone produce a coffee. When he finished his refreshment, he asked me to accompany him to see "zee Kapeetan." Like a zombie, I followed him up onto the cabin roof and over the pusher's rail.

We went along a series of deserted metal corridors and up several flights of stairs, then out onto a large, open top deck. We had to lean into the cool wind and stagger forward to reach the door of a glass-sided control room, as if we were walking on the roof of a speeding train. The room was full of electronic control panels, and the air was heavy with cigarette smoke that glowed with the eerie green light from the hundreds of switch diodes.

To complete the impression I was in the backseat of a "Star Wars" strafing mission, I peered out through the glass windscreen. We appeared to be hurtling down a tunnel of misty white light produced by the beams of two powerful searchlights mounted on either side of the bridge. This shocked me back to my senses: "I've left my family down there! . . . What on earth am I doing up here!" Quickly, I thanked the Kapeetan for the tow, then bolted back down through the labyrinth to ride out the nightmare on my own ship.

Studying for a moment how the boats were working together, I decided to try to prevent the alarming heeling to starboard that

Alea did every time we went round a left-hand bend. Doubling up my hemp rope, I put a slip knot round the starboard winch drum and hanked it onto a stanchion directly above on the pusher. No sooner had I climbed back down than she heeled again, snapping the hemp ropes as if they were thread. This gave me quite a shock, and I hurried to replace them with my last short length of nylon rope, doubled, which did help to hold us upright to some extent.

It was a clear, starlit evening and getting colder as the night wore on. The wake behind us seemed gigantic. Its rolling, 1½ to 2-meter waves hit the side of the canal and exploded over the banks. At one lamp-lit place, I saw large tree branches and other debris being flung high into the air by the crashing flood.

I sat in a daze, my mind frozen with the noise and the spectacle that thundered on every side. As the night dragged on I began to long for the last lock to appear. I scanned ahead for the lights of Constantsa, imagining they would be the first sign that this torment was about to end. I even welcomed the idea of finding a berth in a dark and unfamiliar harbor—anything was preferable to this madness.

Finally, while still surrounded by darkness, we started to slow down as we passed under a sinister-looking suspension bridge. The pilot appeared and told me to get ready to cast off when the pusher came to a stop. It was just after midnight and, with the help of willing hands above, *Alea* was soon released.

As the pusher churned away toward the lights of the lock, all my senses seemed to bask in the relief from noise, vibration, diesel fumes, and fear. But the pilot put an end to any emotional overindulgence with his next disquieting order.

Pointing over to the right bank he said: "Moor zthere for zee night."

"But I must pass through the lock with the pusher!"

"Do zthis tomorrow."

"But there are no ships passing tomorrow."

"Noo problem—zhey vill let you through by yourself!"

I was too tired to argue further. We had just survived the most foolhardy escapade of the entire trip, and at that moment all we wanted to do was stop moving.

Twenty-Six

Marea Neagra: The Black Sea at Last

WHEN I AWOKE, the bright water reflections shimmering on the cabin ceiling told me it was late. But I sensed something else, more significant. Was I still in shock from last night's lunacy? The memory of it caused me to draw a deep breath, and suddenly, I realized what it was—I could smell the briny tang of the sea!

Dressing quickly, I climbed up onto the quay and breathed in my fill. Only a thin, distant horizon of insipid blue-gray could be seen of the Black Sea. Below this weak backdrop ran a filigree of merchant ship superstructures. The foreground and most of the surrounding area was a bulldozed-flat wilderness of reclaimed land.

Ahead lay the rusting steel and concrete of the double lock, seven years old but already taking on a decrepit guise. Behind me, dominating the flat landscape, stood the single-tower suspension bridge we had passed under the night before. It apparently carried a motorway to Constantsa, 8 kilometers to the north. Somehow its stark outline personified our isolation, for we were obviously miles from anywhere.

The pilot had told us that there was a canteen at the port office, near the lock, but when Despina took the children there for breakfast it was closed. He had also pointed out, in the dark, the direction of Agigea, the town we were supposed to be in, but in daylight it was still invisible. Undaunted, they set off in search of the place. After a long walk they finally arrived in the township only to find their quest had just begun.

Like the canteen, the shops and restaurants were either closed or empty. Having obtained only two bunches of radishes from a man selling them outside his house, they noticed some people eating small dumplings in the street and eventually tracked down their breakfast. Victoria's diary takes up the story:

> The dumplings were very nice, so we went back and queued for three more. Even although we were dying for a drink, we didn't buy the lemon juice, because we saw little black bits floating in it. We walked back down the road and saw the radish man again. Mum asked him why no one had any bread, he said that it was coming. Mum said "So is Christmas" (it was a bit cheeky). We went back to the baker and joined a big queue. I got sick of standing up and there was no place to sit down, after a while I had a tummy upset, it was horrible. After two hours Mum came out with some bread. We went and waited by a closed shop where some other ladies were waiting. My tummy was . . . I don't know . . . but it was worse than horrible. After half an hour Mum decided to ask the ladies, what time would the shop open? The answer was two o'clock, that was in three hours time! We started heading back to the boat. As usual soldiers were all over the place.

Back at the boat, we had a visit from a policeman and two immigration officials who arrived in a chauffeur-driven car. The formalities were completed with surprising ease, but before leaving, the shifty-looking driver handed me a printed form and a pen and indicated where I should sign. When I returned the form, he wrote "$30" on it and holding out his hand demanded, "little dollar?" Rather puzzled, I asked him what this was for, to which he indicated, "the hire of the car for the officials." He accepted my emphatic "Nooo!" stoically, and to my relief the car drove off.

Next came a small, thin, port officer, who looked very dapper in his smart naval uniform. This turned out to be an extraordinary character, who came across as a complete enigma to us. He spoke excellent English and introduced himself as—Pop! He was as vivacious as any fizzy drink, and we couldn't help but be charmed by his exceptional friendliness. He had come, he said, to help us through the lock and take us to a new berth. So with Pop aboard we were dropped 7 meters to the greenish harbor water of the Black Sea. This was our very last lock, and after having negotiated hundreds of the things, we were more than pleased to see the back of them.

Before leaving, Pop offered to accompany us into Constantsa— he said it was unsafe for foreigners to walk there alone, for fear of theft. We readily agreed to this but thought his offer to ask a soldier to keep guard over us a bit superfluous, for our obligatory sentry had already followed us round. Until this disquieting conversation with Pop we had always looked on these armed guards as an imposition, but perhaps they had always been intended for our protection.

At the appointed hour a car came speeding along the rough dirt road and skidded to a halt in front of us, and out stepped Pop. Pointing to the shadowy figure behind the wheel, he said his "colleague" had offered to drive us all into the city.

From the crush of the backseat, Constantsa appeared to be an airy and well-laid-out city. Even the suburban multistory buildings showed some attempt at architectural design, compared with the concrete crates we had become accustomed to seeing. The port facilities were huge, with dock and shipyards stretching all along the coast from Agigea to the heart of Constantsa.

Our first priority was food, so the "colleague," to whom Pop seemed unusually beholden, dropped us off at a large open market. Pop insisted on being our buying agent, saying that because we looked like tourists, we were sure to be "reepped off!" The market was better stocked than we had seen anywhere else. There was even margarine, although we didn't buy any, because the wrapping paper was so discolored with age.

Pop bought a bottle of vodka and invited us back to his home, a high-rise apartment only a short distance from the market. It surprised us to hear that his mother actually owned the flat, having bought it from the late Ceauşescu regime. This was also home for Pop's sister and her husband and two young children. Pop laughingly told us that his mother was fearful of their being seen with foreigners, as they all still worked for the government. Although he wouldn't hear of us leaving, we couldn't help but feel the women's tense remoteness as they busied themselves in an adjacent anteroom.

It came as a complete surprise when they suddenly presented to us a most exquisite meal of stuffed cabbage, with various side dishes of vegetables and cheeses. Though embarrassed by the way our children wolfed it down, we felt very grateful.

The family chose to eat their meal in another room, thus leaving Pop to get on with his bit of entrepreneurial business or whatever it was. After a few vodkas I had difficulty keeping up with all the different propositions he seemed to hatch at the slightest provocation. I had only to admire the parquet floor in the room we were in and I was instantly projected as his overseas agent for the export of Romanian timber. He was looking for any opportunity that involved foreign exchange.

When he saw that all his most fanciful hopes were foundering on the poor capitalist shore he had spied, he turned to a more modest export prospect—himself. Even this, he conceded, was "very difficult," as he could be sacked if it was found out he was applying for jobs outside the country. As he thought it a foregone conclusion that his mail would be opened, he asked Despina for an address in Greece where he could pick up his application replies.

Pop also offered to help us buy petrol. For this we had to wait until it was dark, and then Pop's brother-in-law drove us to the local filling station. As we joined the small queue, Pop warned us that we mustn't talk at all while in the filling station—such was deemed necessary to obtain 15 liters of petrol for a foreigner!

As a fitting finale to this daring mission, we had to withstand the torchlight scrutiny of an army checkpoint at the dock entrance. Even Pop, who was still in uniform, had to show his *pazz-papers.*

Next morning, while the port captain made out our clearance certificate, I inspected an office model of the canal and harbor development. Seeing my interest, Pop rummaged out two information brochures on the canal, but before handing them over, he felt obliged, in front of the other staff, to attempt to remove the photographs of the Ceauşescus at the official opening. I said I would prefer them left in, as it was all just history now. They seemed a little nervous, but I was allowed to keep them without further censuring. As Pop had to go somewhere else, we said our farewells there. Although we later sent him a Christmas card, we have never heard from him since.

We had restepped the mast the previous day, so in no time we were motoring out of the canal fairway. Unfortunately, it took almost an hour to work our way north through the labyrinth of rusting merchant ships to clear the only exit to the harbor, which is in front of Constantsa itself. I was overjoyed to feel *Alea* dip once again to a strong sea swell, but my poor mate couldn't help feeling she was going from the frying pan into the fire.

Many people had warned us about the sudden changes of weather here. Apparently the "black" in Black Sea derives from its character—a fact that was made abundantly clear by every insurance company refusing to cover us for this leg. The sky seemed more sullen than yesterday. A watery grayness hung all around, printing its steely gloom on the sea. Nevertheless, I felt we could chance the four-hour run south to Mangalia, the last Romanian port before Bulgaria.

With the sails raised to catch the accommodating 15-knot nor'wester, I set our course on the compass and headed down the coast. *Alea* also seemed to be reveling at being back on the briny. Every now and again we would go slicing through a squadron of large, pulsating jellyfish, which gave the children great sport as they tried to count them. The carefree mood was infectious; soon we were all counting.

After an hour I took our first compass fix using a tall television mast abeam and the distant silhouette of Cape Tuzla on the starboard bow. This put us 4 miles southeast of Agigea and just over 2 miles offshore. The land looked low and hazy, raised on a continuous gray line of short mudstone cliffs. It was exhilarating to think we were now looking on a coastline scanned by the ancient Greeks and Phoenicians. By the time of our second fix the cape was astern, but an east cardinal buoy that was marked on our new chart was nowhere to be seen. Then a prominent chimney stack marked as being right on the shore couldn't be found. This was very disappointing; after all the trouble we had gone to in ordering the chart in London, we had hardly improved on our tourist guide map.

Just as we turned into the harbor entrance of Mangalia, the wind increased to 20 to 25 knots. No sooner had we maneuvered alongside the deserted quay than the inevitable soldier appeared to escort me to the port office with our *pazz-papers.*

The elderly port captain called in an interpreter, a tall, distinguished-looking man with almost the aristocratic air of an English public schoolboy. He introduced himself as Romano. While the port captain checked through our papers, Romano asked me about our trip. He was very interested in *Alea*, having been a keen dinghy sailor himself.

Just then a heavyset man came into the office, dressed in what can only be described as theatrical garb portraying a dockyard laborer of the 1920s: two-tone golf shoes, oxford-bag pants held up by braces worn on the outside of a sleeveless jumper, scarf tied at the neck, and oversize cloth cap. I could have easily burst out laughing had it not been for the sudden chilling of the atmosphere the moment the port captain and Romano saw him. Romano turned to me and in obvious disgust said, "This person is from the port police and he wants to look at your passports."

His fat fingers flicked over every page as he examined them minutely, looking for trouble. I had unwittingly stumbled upon a microcosm of the new Romanian reality. Here was the dispossessed aristocrat emerging from the woodwork and the jumped-up peasant boy desperately hanging on to the reigns of power. Unfortunately, I was going to be the butt that showed everyone who was still in charge.

Finally, after holding the passports up to the light, the flamboyant "Docker" announced to Romano that both the entry and exit permits of our visa had been stamped in Orsova. Glowing as if holding all the trump cards, he played his hand. We would not be allowed ashore unless we paid for another visa!

Romano seemed more exasperated about it than I was and began to argue our case forcibly. In the end Romano had to admit defeat; the Docker was unmoved. For my part I didn't particularly need to go ashore in Mangalia, and the relief that this hadn't been discovered earlier far outweighed any irritation. The Docker capped the situation by deciding to keep our passports until we left. Then another policeman came in to ask me if I was carrying any guns or explosives aboard. Romano scornfully laughed at this and, to my chagrin, joked that I was a drug smuggler! Although the policeman seemed to ignore him, I did begin to wonder whose side Romano was on and how such an outspoken individual had managed to survive Ceauşescu.

Not surprisingly, the policeman wanted to search the boat. In the strong wind *Alea* was dipping and tugging at the lines, which put the policeman off boarding, so from the safety of the quay he asked for the front hatch to be opened, which Charles did from inside. Satisfied that we were all suitably impressed by his authority, he turned about and left.

Romano came aboard for a coffee and a very interesting chat. He told us about his family's estates that had been taken away from them "by the communist gangsters." Although he longed for democracy, he summed up the reason for all his country's ills with a philosophical "Well, that's what happens when a shoemaker runs the country." He thought the revolution had been a big joke, saying the only thing that had changed was the names of the government departments.

Later on, with the prevailing wind and chop on our beam it proved too uncomfortable to stay at this berth. Leaving the crew to fend *Alea* off the jagged quay wall, I ran over to the port office to ask permission to move into the inner harbor. Although I mimed the port captain a promise that we wouldn't go into town, he was unwilling to take the responsibility of such a decision. Fortunately, after trying to telephone some higher authority several times, he was forced to accept that the buck stopped with him. The poor man sat silently thinking it over for about half a minute before giving me the OK.

Two khaki-clad guardians appeared within half an hour of our tying up in the inner dock and kept watch over us throughout the cold night. Although the morning dawned gray, it was difficult to judge the conditions outside because our berth was so sheltered. Motoring out into the outer harbor, we found a steady

15- to 20-knot northerly and so decided to leave. The port captain made out our port clearance certificate, and I was escorted back to *Alea* by a policeman who handed over our passports at the quayside.

We motored out between the harbor moles, heading southeast. Despina took the tiller while I raised the sails. The wind was a steady 15 knots, but when we cleared the last breakwater, we suddenly found ourselves in an extraordinarily rough sea, agitated out of all proportion to the strength of the wind. Erupting all about us were steep, pointed waves that didn't seem to be going anywhere but just leapt straight up and down. This explosive bouncing was on top of a short 2- to 3-meter swell that swept in from the northeast and rebounded from the harbor wall. I was still on the foredeck raising the jib when *Alea* abruptly heeled to starboard and surged rapidly forward into the air. Instinctively, I dropped to my knees and held on to the mast. With sickening suddenness we plunged down and crashed into a hissing wall of green sea, which sent a shower of spray to rattle across my back.

These conditions were no good for family sailing, so I shouted to Despina to "Go about!" She tried but found the pressure on the tiller too great. I scrambled back and reached the cockpit just as *Alea* was about to take off again. Waiting until she began to pull out of the foaming dive, we pressed the tiller over. The whole boat trembled and shuddered under the cracking sails as she staggered into the wind and waves. I gave the throttle of the outboard a tweak more. Slowly but doggedly, *Alea*'s bow began to lift and cleave back through that leaping confusion. Despina steered while I, crouching low, rushed forward to keep the jib from being flogged to pieces.

We moored back in the inner harbor and called it a rest day. Victoria and I topped up our water tank from a faucet in a nearby building site. The foreman came out and very kindly asked if there was anything else we wanted. He even offered me petrol, but because we had mostly sailed from Constantsa, all my tanks were full. When I took up his offer on bread, he refused to accept payment, and instead of the two loaves I ordered, he gave us four.

Later that day when it began to rain, another chap came over to tell Despina, in French, that his wife worked in the local meteorological office and we could be assured the weather would be clear tomorrow. And as promised, we set out next morning in bright, crisp sunshine. Although we were certainly glad to see the last of Mangalia, the simple thoughtfulness of those few people balanced the scales for us. With a friendly 10- to 15-knot nor'wester and nothing more than a 1-meter swell, we soon forgave the foibles of the Black Sea too.

Twenty-Seven
Bulgaria—and Back into the Frying Pan

11 OCTOBER

WE SAILED OUT OF MANGALIA at 9:00 A.M. and set off down the coast on a course a little east of south. The coastline was flat and fairly straight, and although there were ample prominent buildings in the area, none graced our chart. Nevertheless, there was a hearty cheer when I announced that by "dead reckoning" we had entered Bulgarian waters.

Our satisfaction at seeing Romania dissolve away in the distance was somewhat offset by apprehensions as to what lay ahead in Bulgaria. The only thing we dared hope for was that food would be more plentiful. Although Despina had worked wonders in always providing a substantial evening meal, she was having to really scrape the bottom of the barrel now. Breakfast was down to bread and jam, and lunch that day, though served under the scenic splendor of Cape Shableh, was a spartan snack of radishes and bread.

222

I had shaped a course to pass close to Cape Shableh so as to avoid a large area marked on my chart, "Entry periodically prohibited." We could slip past on the inside by hugging the coast. The dramatic increase in the height of the cliffs caused us to lose the wind and resort to the motor. Like a mouse scuttling along the skirting board, we followed that intimidatingly sheer wall of crumbling rock for three hours, to arrive at fearsome Cape Kaliakra. This timeworn landmark juts out defiantly to form the most prominent geographical feature on the western shore of the Black Sea. Here the line of cliffs hooks back to the northwest before sweeping south again to form Kavarna Bay.

As this was a very exposed part of the coast, I had felt a certain dread every time I had looked at it on the chart. However, as it was, we couldn't have picked a better day to sneak past the ogre. And just as we approached, a warm 10- to 15-knot southeasterly sprang up to give us a nice broad reach to the small harbor of Kavarna.

Another reason for my apprehension was that to reach this harbor, 5 miles distant, meant touching on another restricted area, this one marked, "Entry prohibited to foreign vessels." Fortunately, we crossed unchallenged, the only mishap being that the motor refused to start outside the harbor entrance. Continuing under sail alone, we managed to luff up gently and anchor with bow to the stone quay. A swarthy-looking fisherman willingly left the net he was mending and helped Despina with the bow line. We had made it to Bulgaria, and it certainly felt quite a milestone.

Kavarna was the sort of place we had come all this way to see: an old, picturesque fishing settlement nestled in a narrow cove. Only a few other boats were moored there, mostly small fishing smacks, but to our surprise several were local yachts that looked well maintained. When I asked a group of fishermen about a harbormaster, they indicated not to worry about such things here. They asked where we had come from, and on hearing Romania, they all shook their heads disapprovingly and gestured the thumbs-down. When the conversation moved to food, they were quick to point out that there were good restaurants here in Kavarna—"with food!"

That was exactly what we wanted to hear, and in no time we were sitting down to a delicious meal of pork chops. We thought we had landed in paradise; even the beer bottles had labels on them again and the contents tasted like the real thing. When we had eaten our fill, Despina went up to the servery to pay. We of course had no Bulgarian money and no idea of its value, so when she was presented with a bill of 17 leva, she offered the proprietor 20 deutsche marks, which he seemed very happy to accept—so much so that when Despina pointed to a large wheel of cheese she saw sitting in the kitchen, he offered to give her the whole wheel. Not seeing the significance of this gesture, she indicated that she just wanted a small slice. It wasn't until we discovered the currency exchange rate and the relative values that we realized we had paid eight times more for that meal than was asked.

The warm southerly of the day before was still with us, bringing back a touch of high summer. The crew decided to join some local people swimming and sunbathing on a nearby beach while I saw to our sick motor. Being fairly sure it was the same carburetor problem we had had in Compiègne, I wasn't too perturbed. And sure enough, after a squirt of meths up its orifice, it was as right as rain.

I had estimated five hours for our run to Varna, so noon was our departure deadline. We motor-sailed out of that idyllic little haven full of high hopes; if the rest of Bulgaria was anything like Kavarna, we would be well satisfied. The sea was flat calm, with only the occasional breeze to fill the sails. Dolphins played, but always at a distance. The phenomenon that caused the most excitement was the disturbance of large areas of the sea about us by the frantic leaping flight of small fish. They followed us for some time, until complete mayhem broke out when hundreds of gulls arrived to noisily dive on them.

We picked up a very pleasant southwest breeze that allowed us to sail up the deep bay where the city of Varna is situated. Entering the harbor, we found a yacht club right behind the main seawall. To our surprise, all the yachts there were of the large luxury type. We discovered later that the club was run by a state-owned shipping company for its employees and their friends. With committees, skippers, and crews all vetted and "democratically" elected, the club appeared to function like a leisure version of "Animal Farm," where everyone cliqued and crawled for their places. The club rules pertaining to foreign guests centered around the guests' hard currency. The rather typecast caretaker demonstrated his amazing grasp in English when he introduced himself and informed us, "A token charge of five American dollars per night is zee club's policy."

As for informing, he also told us that he had telephoned the port police, and we were to take our passports round to the police station "immediately." After a long hike we found the place, but although we were shown into a room full of policemen, the one who checked passports wasn't there.

When the "passport tyrant" finally arrived, we were impressed by his impatience and rudeness. He spoke in a snappy sort of pidgin English that was very difficult to understand. Each time we asked him to repeat what he had just said, he would quite blatantly groan and roll his eyes in exasperation. But all this we gladly forgave, for he said nothing about the boat-transit permission for which the embassy in Vienna had put us through the "hoops."

Although we found a very good vegetable market with a great variety of produce, we soon realized that Bulgaria was only a little better off than Romania. Most shops were practically empty, with the length of its queue being the measure of the practical worth of the stock within. However, we struck lucky and found a shop selling a new supply of tinned fish. When I asked why there wasn't a larger queue, I was told that it was "too expensive for most Bulgarians."

There was another essential item we couldn't find anywhere—toilet paper! Our situation was getting desperate, with us having to fall back on our last roll of disposable kitchen towels. We tried several shops without success. So on our second day in Varna we decided to ask people in the street, in the hope of locating the black-market source. I put the question to a tall and very serious looking young man. His English was very good but his reply threw me: "Toilet paper? Vhat iz that?" Fortunately, while I racked my brains for an acceptable explanation, he worked it out for himself. "Ahhh, toilet paper, I have not zeen this in zee shops for over a year now." "Well what do people use in Varna?" Despina and I chorused.

Our "savior" let us in on the local secret: "Most people uze zee shop paper." This was heavy-duty wrapping paper seen in bundles on the counter of every shop. To procure some, all you had to do was point at the pile and raise your eyebrows and the shop assistant automatically passed over two or three sheets—no questions asked. After a few of these knowing encounters, convenience, if not comfort, was assured.

Turning to more agreeable conversation, I remarked on his unusual T-shirt. It had a spectacular silk screen commemorating the London to Copenhagen Tall Ships' Race. It turned out that he had been a crew member on the Bulgarian entry, which had obviously been a great adventure for him.

In the afternoon, Victoria and I set off to try our luck "begging" for petrol. At the end of the longest queue of cars yet, we found the local filling station, and—would you believe it—there stood Varna's version of "The Imp of Calafat." Instead of "Noo benzina!" it was "Nee benzin!" I would have to go to a special filling station on the other side of town that apparently catered exclusively to "tourists and diplomats."

On passing a taxi rank, I got the idea of asking one of the drivers for petrol. I needed only to say the magic words "deutsche mark" and I had a very wily young customer prepared to do business. My opening gambit was 10 liters of petrol for 10 deutsche marks. He countered with the proviso that if I were to pay for the taxi fare to his home where he kept the petrol, he would agree. I enjoyed saying, "Nein," and added, "gute price." He obviously thought so too, for he immediately opened the door of the taxi for us. Before stepping in, I indicated I wanted to be taken back to this same taxi rank. "Ja, ja, ja"—we had a deal.

We struck another deal on the very pleasant drive out to the suburban block of flats in which he lived. This time I offered to swap a cupful of our coffee for some sugar. Although he agreed in principle, he said he would have to consult his wife, which he did by bellowing up to her on the fifth floor. I was greatly surprised when his wife came down with two 1-kilo bags of sugar; her husband seemed equally amazed when I said that one bag was ample.

With my petrol stock once again at full capacity and Victoria cradling the sugar, we were chauffeured right back to the door of the yacht club—a drive that allowed us a glimpse of a drama I had narrowly missed. Passing the filling station, we were shocked to see the "Imp of Varna" being mobbed by an angry crowd who were vandalizing her office. Curiously, our excited taxi driver pointed over at the spectacle and exclaimed, "Varna Calamity!"

Before we were to face our own "Varna Calamity," good fortune still had some favors to bestow on us. When I climbed aboard *Alea* to fetch the coffee, there, sitting in the cabin, was the "Tall Ship" fellow. He had sought *Alea* out in order to present us with two rolls of "real" toilet paper.

Without further ado, the kettle was put on so we could cement our new friendship with Vassil. Having just graduated from the Varna naval college, he was waiting for his first commission as an officer in the merchant marine. He said he was following in the footsteps of his grandfather, who had been a sea captain before the war and "had even sailed his ship to New Zealand."

We all got on so well together that we arranged to meet the following day for a stroll round his hometown. Although a storm developed during the night that sent waves crashing over the seawall, the day dawned bright and sunny. Unfortunately, our first point of interest on our tour turned out to be rather a sad shock for Vassil. This was the tall ship *Kaliakra*, which was berthed on the other side of the harbor. After admiring her from the quayside, Vassil went aboard to ask if he could show us around. When he reappeared he looked quite pale. Apparently the second mate, whom Vassil was obviously acquainted with, had drowned the night before while returning to the ship in the dark. With the *Kaliakra* now in mourning, we had to forgo our visit.

It was Sunday, October 14, and it seemed that the whole of Varna was out for a Sunday stroll. Family groups and young couples, all dressed in their best, promenaded through the spacious streets and parks. Although fashions appeared more modern here, a quaint old-world atmosphere persisted because nearly every grouping included a smartly dressed naval cadet, nicely set off with ceremonial dagger and white gloves. Vassil explained that this was their first free day after their initial six weeks at the college.

At the maritime museum, we inspected the 12-meter yacht that carried Bulgaria's first solo circumnavigator around the world, via Cuba of course. Vassil was very proud of a very basic looking torpedo boat that had disabled a Turkish battleship that had been bombarding Varna in the 1912 Balkan War. A jagged shell hole through its funnel had obviously been preserved as a trophy.

We sauntered down Lenin Boulevard, soon to be changed back to its prewar name. After forty years of one-party rule, a walk past the dilapidated buildings allotted to the newly formed opposition party for their headquarters seemed to be on everyone's itinerary. The drab interior of the cathedral was being given an extensive facelift. Vassil said that people didn't go to church before so they would not be victimized, but the previous Christmas Eve, not only the cathedral was full but the surrounding square as well. This was more than just attending church; it was defiance.

At the end of a pleasant afternoon, Vassil invited us to his parents' place for coffee. Apparently, the smallish apartment they shared with the grandmother was given as compensation for the compulsory demolition of the grandfather's two-story house, done so "The People" could build the apartment block on his land. This injustice seemed to be the family's heavy cross, which they hoped would be more fairly settled by the new government.

The time had come to pick up our own "family cross." The question of Despina's exodus to Greece couldn't be avoided any longer. I had exhausted every argument in an effort to get her to change her mind (you try telling a Greek, "Things will be better when we reach Turkey!"). Unfortunately, it all came to a head during our new habit of having our evening meal at a restaurant.

Victoria's diary reads,

After we finished the meal we started discussing a horrible subject about Mum leaving and going to Greece, because it was getting cold and she didn't like the boat. She wants both Charles and me to come with her but Dad wants Charles to stay to help him sail the boat. We all ended up crying. Mum decided that Charles, Mum, and me would leave next day.

Poor Charles was the "meat in the sandwich" and understandably didn't enjoy this role. His diary logs his views:

I wanted to stay on the boat but I also want to stay with Mum, what a difficult time it was for me. On the second night at the restaurant, Dad said to Mum that he wanted me to stay, Mum got very upset, so did I, it's not nice to be fought over! After a "friendly argument" it seemed Mum would take me to Greece. I was happy that they'd come to an agreement, I only half liked each option. The next day we packed our bags, but Dad spoke to Mum again and she asked me if I wanted to stay on the boat. I said yes because I knew Dad needed me, she said that she would stay with me. Dad said he didn't want her if she was going to be grumpy, which I thought was a bit mean! She said that she would be good.

It was a quiet *Alea* that waited for the other storm out in Kavarna Bay to abate. Although the wind had moderated, the swell was still slopping around the inside of the harbor. After I hung a car tire as a trooper on each of the mooring lines, *Alea* only dipped gently, while several other yachts broke loose due to the violent motion. The squads of rescuing club members gave passing nods of approval at *Alea*'s poise—the only gratification I received that calamitous day.

However, the next dawned with a dramatic turnabout. Early morning fog hung all around in the stillness. After getting a fair weather forecast from the harbor control, I continued on to pick up the boat papers from the port police. The long wait for the particular officer whose job it is to hand documents back put me in a sufficiently bloody-minded mood for dealing with the American dollar mooring fee. On the way back to the yacht club, I asked a crewman of a tug if he would like to change 20 deutsche marks. He gave me such a good black-market rate that it covered the total mooring fee, which of course I insisted be calculated at the official exchange rate for U.S. dollars. I had to threaten that it was that or nothing before I could get the greatly displeased caretaker finally to accept his own country's currency.

By 11:00 A.M. the fog had been dispersed by a 12- to 15-knot northwesterly, which was soon harnessed to carry us from Varna. Out past Cape Galata, we sailed down the coast in a rather confused sea. The high, steep waves caused *Alea* to pitch and roll, but nobody seemed to care at first, for the distraction and comfort of chocolate was once again aboard. We had bought this from a government-run "Free Shop," a curious corruption of a "Duty-Free Shop." It sold a very limited assortment of western consumer goods to anyone with hard currency. As there was certainly nothing free in the shop, the old neon street sign "Free Shop" seemed a cruel joke on the crowds of languishing window-shoppers.

Nevertheless, cruel fate has always played its jokes on intemperate sailors on the ocean wave. With the wind increasing to 15 to 20 knots, it wasn't long before our young tars began to complain of feeling sick, so we sat them out in the cockpit wrapped in blankets. Despina had given each of them half of the last seasickness tablet before we left, but although Victoria managed to hold on, Charles had to let go, for the first time ever.

After four hours of lively sailing we arrived at a small fishing harbor called Aspro—a Greek word meaning "white." And to leave Despina in no doubt that she was indeed getting nearer home, we found that a small Greek community still lived in the village.

A short hop round Cape Emine the next day brought us to the ancient Greek settlement of Nesebûr. Founded around 500 B.C. on a high, rocky peninsula, it looked very picturesque in the late afternoon sun. A bright jumble of sandstone and half-timbered houses seemed to peep from under a patchwork of red-tiled roofs.

Unable to enter the shallow, ancient port, we settled on what we judged to be an out-of-the-way, sheltered corner of the outer harbor. The fact that several fishing boats and launches berthed next to us after dark seemed to confirm that we had chosen the best spot.

At first light the next morning I was awakened by a sudden cacophony of men shouting and boat engines being started all around the harbor. There was such an urgency about the noise that it prompted me to get up to have a look. All the boats near us, plus another dozen or so from the other side of the pool, were all making for the harbor exit. Although I sensed there was something odd, I had no idea what it was. Five minutes later, the harbormaster arrived—middle-aged and looking every bit an old salt. But his most outstanding feature was his transport: a British "Hillman Imp." My surprise at seeing his car somewhat deflected him from his official duty. Having bought it from a destitute tourist many years ago, he was very proud of it, especially the replacement passenger seat and steering wheel, which he had got from a wrecker's yard in Ullapool in the Northwest of Scotland.

These happy memories of when he was a seaman may have saved my bacon, for I was ushered into the "Ullapool seat" and driven back to his office to view for myself the new list of harbor fees. It set out that *Alea*, being over 6 meters long and staying two nights, would cost the extraordinary fee of $80 U.S. I looked at him in disbelief and said, "These charges are ridiculous! What do the fishermen pay?" To my surprise he agreed and said: "Zhey are expected to pay the same, but of course zhey can't—zhat is vhy zhey hide from me!" He was obviously trying to be fair. He said that he had written to his head office to complain against "zhese taxes," as he termed them, but also that he wanted to keep his job. He certainly couldn't have been fairer to us, for he said that if we left early the next morning there would be no charge at all. I gave him my word.

With that delicate matter out of the way, he asked if there was anything I needed. "Yes, 5 liters of petrol." "Nee problem," replied the harbormaster, and it wasn't; all that was required was a length of plastic tubing and an accommodating Hillman Imp.

We spent the rest of the day strolling around the narrow, cobbled streets of Nesebûr. It must have been very pretty years back, but now most of the buildings had been turned into tourist-trap shops that swamp such places with their gaudy trivia. With the tourist season ended, the great majority of these were closed and boarded up, which intruded on the scene even more.

That evening I got the fishermen's side of the harbor fee story, and true enough, they all felt forced to flee the harbor in the morning and not return until after dark. The next morning we joined them in the general exodus and, picking up a gentle 10-knot westerly, set off across the Gulf of Burgas. It was a bright, clear day, and when we were out of sight of land, the children took great delight in being able to scan right round the bare horizon.

With a landfall east of Megalo Island, we carried on down the coast to the small harbor of Micurin. Again the motor refused to start, and we entered under sail. As I strained on the stern anchor, trying to berth, an army officer arrived on the stone quay demanding "Pazz-papers!"

He looked a stereotypical grim-faced Prussian Army blockhead, and it was clear we were in for trouble. After scrutinizing our passports this way and that, he asked, in German, where we were going. When I said Turkey, he immediately replied that we couldn't stay—it was "Verboten!" My attempt to ask why made him decidedly nasty, and he ordered us to leave "schnell!" Remembering our motor, I pointed to it in dismay and said, "Kaputt!" He replied, "Nein problem," and pointed to *Alea*'s sails. When I explained that I thought it unsafe to take my family sailing at night without auxiliary power, his only concession was to give me one hour to fix the motor—then "Raus," out!

Just in case we couldn't avoid being sent out, I set about fixing the motor. Luckily, I found the trouble right away: a speck of carbon was bridging the electrodes of the sparking plug. With this cleared, I decided to maintain our "lame duck" status by screwing in tight the air-bleed screw on the carburetor.

When "blockhead" returned on the deadline, I gave a few futile pulls on the starter cord and resignedly exclaimed, "Kaputt!" This hurt him, and after some incomprehensible angry muttering and a glare that said, "I'll fix you," he wheeled about and marched off purposefully. About a quarter of an hour later, we heard someone jump onto *Alea*'s deck and come scrambling over the cabin roof. A naval officer who was the spitting image of Rowan Atkinson—moles and all—came down into the cabin to tell us, in very good English, that we were being allowed to stay, but we would have to move alongside his patrol vessel in the naval dock yard. When I asked him why we were having this trouble, he just shrugged and said, "Military minds." I said I would paddle over, but first I had to go out to pick up our stern anchor. Suddenly, as if seeing what a great nuisance they were being for little purpose, he stood up and said, "Don't vorry, stay vhere you are tonight, I vill fix it!"

The sea was flat early the next morning, and a nice sailing breeze from the southeast gave us a very pleasant cruise down the last stretch of Bulgarian coast.

At 11:00 A.M. we reached the open bay that marks the border between Turkey and Bulgaria. Here for the last time we looked back on the forbidding lands of the Eastern Bloc and felt humbly grateful to all the wonderful people we had met there. We could only hope that their aspirations for the future would be realized with their emerging freedom.

Twenty-Eight
Turkey, a Land of
Milk and Honey

20 OCTOBER

WE THREW OFF THE EASTERN BLOC blues with an exuberant cheer when Charles run up the Turkish star and crescent to the starboard spreader. We were—in Turkey! On a low hill to starboard stood the first pencil-sharp minaret. From there on, the land seemed to blossom. We sailed for an hour past well-cared-for farms and cultivated fields spreading through the low, undulating terrain.

Cape Kuri, a prominent headland that shelters the small harbor of Inada, was our first Turkish waypoint. While clearing the cape by some 300 meters, we noticed that the water had become so clear we could see the bottom. Although it was a good 8 to 10 meters deep, I instinctively panicked and immediately put about to head out to sea. Despite the greater depths, it was still quite disconcerting to see huge, shadowy rocks go flitting by in the depths below.

Halfway down the huge bay, marked on our chart as Inada Roads, we entered the almost empty harbor. An officer on the bridge of a large naval vessel waved us over. We had grown to recognize this as the hallmark of a bad beginning.

The captain appeared at the rail with his second in command, who spoke very good English. He said, "Welcome to Turkey. My captain would like to see your passports and ship's papers." I had to stand on the cabin roof to hand these up. After a strange-sounding discussion in Turkish (somewhat between Japanese and French), the "S.C." apologetically translated his captain's verdict: Inada was not a port of entry, and until we had passed through customs at Istanbul, we could not go ashore.

This was a heavy blow, and I exclaimed: "We have just come from Bulgaria and have no food!" To this they conceded that they would be happy to bring us any provisions we required. This seemed highly unsatisfactory, but the S.C. was so polite about it we were completely disarmed.

We were invited aboard and served with soft drinks in the officers' mess while we compiled a list of our requirements. As there was no bank in Inada, the captain exchanged some of our deutsche marks, ordering the newspaper to be brought to us so we could check the exchange rate for Turkish lira. Then, when everything seemed organized and we were resigned to our "quarantine," the plan got turned on its head: the S.C. politely invited us to come along with him into town to help him do our shopping!

In a few minutes we were being bounced around on the floor of an army truck as it careered along the coast road to Inada. I can't remember what the town looked like at all, for all my attention was taken by the abundance of food and merchandise in the shops. We stopped in a street full of small general stores, each one so extensively stocked that the goods seemed to overflow onto the street.

What started off as a restrictive imposition by our naval captors had now turned into the most friendly VIP treatment. By a seemingly incredible turn of events, Despina, the nationalistic Greek, found herself with a Turkish naval officer and three enlisted men rushing about at her beck and call. They wouldn't let us carry the smallest item, and when a shop didn't have a particular product, a swarthy sailor was sent off, on the double, to scout out its availability elsewhere. With such naval efficiency it wasn't long before we were once again fully restocked with the bounty of civilization and rattled back to the harbor, keen to taste the delights of Turkey.

At sunset, an armed party of sailors formed on the stern of the naval vessel to lower their flag. Trying to look as marshal as he could, Charles joined in and lowered our courtesy flag in unison. He must have impressed them, for shortly afterward a large fish, called a *palamut*, was delivered to us—compliments of the captain.

Before it got dark I took the fish out onto the quay to clean it. I had no sooner started when several fishermen came out and took over the operation. I think my butchery may have offended their professional eye. One fellow appeared with a small barbecue and another summarily trampled an old fish-box to kindling. Very soon I found myself part of a cheery, firelit circle of glowing, unshaven faces. Each one added his bit of expertise, which ranged from rubbing the hot grill with half an onion to a sophisticated series of cuts along the flanks of the sizzling *palamut*.

Charles and Victoria gave a recorder recital, and when everyone agreed that the fish was done to perfection, the party broke up amid a profusion of good wishes as I reverently carried the trophy to our dining table. We turned in that night thinking that it hadn't been such a bad beginning after all.

Early the next morning I asked our naval friends for a weather report, but they said they wouldn't receive the forecast until 9:30 A.M. With the sun shining brightly from a clear blue sky and a steady 12- to 15-knot sea breeze, we agreed that the prospects looked good. I decided not to wait and thus fatefully set us up to experience just how fickle the Black Sea can be.

I set the compass ring to a course that would take us directly across the bay to the prominent Cape Serveh, where the small harbor of Midiah lay. *Alea* struck out firmly in her gait and made easy work of a long northeasterly swell. Then, just when everything seemed fine, the wind died completely.

When *Alea* nodded to a standstill, there was nothing for it but to start the motor. This caused the headsail to flog badly, so I took it down. Five minutes later the sea breeze returned, as strong and steady as before. After resetting the main, I handed over the tiller to Charles and went forward to hoist the headsail. Despina sheeted it in while I crouched by the mast and cleated the halyard. Suddenly, I was pitched forward by *Alea*'s violent jibing and heeling over under a strong gust. I landed on all fours with my head lowermost and desperately tried to crawl backward up the tilting cabintop. I heard Charles calling me and looked over to see him pinned against the stern locker, with the main sheet ropes caught across his shoulders. He was still grimly hanging on to the tiller, so I yelled for him to let it go. At the same time Despina released the mainsheet from its jamming cleat. Instantly, *Alea* sat upright again.

I scrambled back into the cockpit and gave poor Charles a piece of my mind for not concentrating on the compass course and allowing the jibe. He was a bit shaken but defended himself by saying he had been on course when the sails flew over. Sure enough, the wind was now coming from the land—it had gone round 180° and gusted in a matter of seconds.

With the panic over, I turned *Alea* on course again and set the sails to the now strengthening southwesterly that sent us bowling along. Small, choppy waves began to slap up the side of the hull and fling their spray back astern. Another strong gust struck; *Alea* heeled over and sped away, struggling to break free from the blow. Something crashed down below. I eased the main and let the bow come round a little until we felt comfortable again. Obviously, something peculiar was happening to the weather, although the only blemish in the otherwise clear blue sky was a dull gray cloud bank just emerging above the northern horizon. I decided it was time we headed nearer to the shelter of the coast.

The wind grew suddenly cold and several more gusts swept over us. The crew disappeared inside after the first dollop of water came over the cabintop. Before the last washboard was slid in place, Despina handed out my wet-weather gear and I exchanged my sun hat for a scarf and tartan tourie.

The wind was getting stronger and more vicious by the minute, stirring up the same characteristics in the sea. I was surprised by the height and steepness of some of the waves that were being produced over just a 3-mile fetch. I could see them scattered about the sea, careering and barging over the top of the other trooping whitecaps. Thankfully I was able to dodge the worst of these by luffing up, which cost me my forward momentum. Increasingly, *Alea* was left to lollop through an attendant bevy of ever growing seas until we picked up speed again. I waited for my chance, and when *Alea* was skipping over a clear patch, I quickly tipped the motor down and whipped it into life. This made a great difference in the rapidly worsening situation. I was now able to maneuver almost directly into the wind, to cleave a wave to the best advantage and still plow on through the others.

The price for this was for me to get very wet. I was now in a desperate hurry to get in under the lee of the coast. It was at this moment of grim resolve that Despina removed the top washboard and handed out two squares of chocolate. I could see the children had their life jackets on but were busy drawing pictures at the table, quite oblivious to the wild elements outside.

Although the wind seemed a lot more violent as it reached 35 to 40 knots, the largest waves had disappeared from our windward side. Now the scouring wind gusts seemed to have more of a flatting effect, lopping off the tops of the waves and sending them flying in fine, stinging spray. It took us one of life's very long hours to reach the sheltered strip of water extending out some 200 meters from the shore. Here the water only rippled, in sharp contrast to the white, frothing seascape that stretched out to the far horizon.

There was no beach; scattered black rocks broke the surface under a continuous line of 8-meter-high bluffs. Rising steeply behind these were the scrub-covered foothills of an extensive mountain range that curved round parallel with the coast. Up ahead, I could see a corridor of rough water extending right into the shore, where a steep-sided gully released the funneled wind to the sea.

I dropped the sails, for they were now only a trap for every worrying downdraft. Because of the need to keep so close inshore and the rocky nature of the coast, Despina steered while I kept lookout in the bow. The water was crystal clear, and I had to signal only once or twice for Despina to helm us out from an almost hypnotic seafloor that threatened to rise up too close. It felt quite strange to sit there in the warm sunshine and cruise along that calm, narrow ribbon while roaring winds jetted above our heads.

We traveled like this for two hours until we neared Cape Serveh, where the coastline suddenly steps back more than a mile, leaving a very exposed stretch of water between the cape and the harbor of Midiah, 2 miles farther on. As the clouds were thickening in the north and creeping around the eastern horizon, we had to cross that wave-tossed bay without delay. I started to prepare for it by hanking on the storm jib and locking the centerplate fully down. To further reduce *Alea*'s heeling force, we lashed the folded dinghy along the starboard rail and lowered the dining table into its bunk position for the crew to lie on. After we had donned our safety harnesses for the first time, I went forward to raise the sails. I made sure the reefing handle, which would allow me to reduce the size of the mainsail, was at the ready. A boat handled under some sort of sail will harness and ride a storm, whereas the brute force of a motor alone can only fight it.

With the crew battened down below and the sheets beginning to drum on the deck, I nervously watched as we approached the shorn-off end of our tranquil path. Legions of stumbling, foaming waves were stampeding out from around the point. I left the storm jib to fly free but set the main in an open position with the sheet held tightly in my hand.

In a matter of seconds we left sheltered calm for bedlam. The bow nodded, dipped once more, then leapt up and forward as the wind struck the sails. The jib went wild, causing the sheets to make a terrific din as they thrashed about. *Alea* heeled over and started to twist round into the wind. I pulled on the tiller and eased the mainsheet, making the whole rigging quiver as it sprang free. *Alea* seemed to stagger, then finding her feet again, began to surge forward. The mainsail was drum tight; I jerked its sheet into the cleat, sprang forward, and hauled in the jib. Scrambling back to my perch high on the starboard coaming, I set *Alea*'s bow diagonally across the bay, toward a cluster of white buildings crowning a prominent headland.

Alea was bounding through the turmoil, splitting all asunder. I had to kill the motor because it shrieked terribly each time the propeller was lifted out of the sea. It was truly a messy murder, for even in neutral it kept roaring back to life when the propeller was revolved by our speed through the water. Large ragged lumps of water were kicked up over the weather bow to thump down on the coach roof and cockpit. In no time I felt its cold, creeping presence in spite of my waterproofs, but it couldn't dampen the exhilaration of that fantastic careering sail. It was like riding a wild charging horse. *Alea* performed magnificently.

We arrived under the lee of a high cliff, where a crush of precariously balanced half-timbered houses seemed to peer down at us. The crew reemerged a bit dazed but otherwise none the worse for their bumpy ride. Motoring round the headland, we found the not-so-sheltered harbor tucked under the cliffs on one side and surrounded by an open, silted-up river estuary on the others. It was crowded with large fishing vessels, many of them rafted together. The skipper of one fishing boat waved us over to lie alongside him, and a crowd of crewmen and children appeared to eagerly seek our mooring lines. We were astonished to discover later that these young boys, no older than Charles, were working members of the crew.

As soon as I changed out of my wet clothes, the skipper indicated for me to climb up and follow him. He led me out and over several rafts and finally ushered me into a large, bare cabin. The only furniture was a sturdy table around which sat about twelve piratical cutthroats, who enthusiastically urged me to join them. Someone gave me a small curved glass of *chai* that sat on a small chrome-embossed saucer, around which nestled three cubes of sugar and a tiny stainless-steel spoon. Everyone had one, and it looked incongruously genteel to see such a rough gang crooking their pinkies as if at the Ritz.

They were all incredibly friendly and went to great lengths to make simple gestured conversation. To my surprise, they advised me to continue on to Istanbul, along the sheltered coast, because they assured me the wind would change the next day and blow so hard that no one would be able to leave the harbor for several days. When I indicated (with volumes of mock vomit) that I'd had quite enough of the sea for one day, they all roared with laughter. The ship's cook then started passing out dishes from a servery hatch. There was bread, olives, white crumbly cheese, and salads. I was urged to go and get Despina so we could join them for lunch, which was barbecued *palamut*—it was marvelous.

We returned to *Alea* to find Charles and Victoria scrubbing down the decks with the help of their newfound friends. Soon after, three very official looking men in smart suits and carrying clipboards appeared at the deck rail above us. It was October 21, the day of Turkey's national census, and these good-humored and practiced bureaucrats had netted us in their domain. With everyone's help we stumbled through booklets of forms and completed them to their satisfaction. We saw them much later that night, still on their paper chase, being rowed, like a shipment of tailor's dummies, from one cluster of boats to another.

More fishing boats were arriving all the time to take shelter from the impending storm as well as to be in port for the census. Each vessel carried a huge crew who packed every part of the superstructure like roosting crows. Amid the roar of revving diesels, everyone seemed to be shouting, either greetings to friends on other boats or harshly clipped orders. The whole din and spectacle gave the harbor an air of vibrant, exotic bustle.

It wasn't long before we got directed to another mooring to allow these larger vessels to raft up with their compatriots. We lasted an hour there before we had to move again. This time we decided to anchor out of everyone's way in the silted-up center of the harbor pool. With the centerplate raised, we rode safely in 2 meters of water so clear we could see the sandy bottom stretching away in all directions. This aquatic scene kept changing as *Alea* hunted about on the end of the anchor-chain, buffeted by the blustery wind that whistled out of a clear, icy blue sky.

In the evening the wind died away, leaving the perfectly calm harbor to mirror the hundreds of different colored lights strung across each fishing boat. Added to this festive illumination was the bright, sparkling sweep of the village lights high above the dark-shadowed cliff. We sat out in the cockpit and had a star-spotting session with the aid of our astronomical atlas. There wasn't a breath of wind, but the stars were twinkling madly, a sure sign that the bellows were being primed.

Before turning in, I erected the boom-tent and hung out the riding light on the backstay. Taking one last look around, I noticed that the extensive cloud bank that had been lurking on the horizon all day was now rearing up above the cliff top. This menacing backdrop set off the village lights rather nicely.

At about two o'clock in the morning, I was awakened by the noise of the wind gusting through the rigging. When I stuck my head out the forward end of the boom-tent to have a look around, I found myself staring into an all-enveloping, inky black abyss. No lights, no land, no fishing boats, no harbor—just total blackness.

As I goggled around for any sign of the reality I knew should be there, I could feel a sickening thought taking hold—we had somehow drifted out to sea! My throat tightened as I felt *Alea* rapidly moving sideways in the next howling wind gust. Then, with a sudden jolt, *Alea* brought up and snubbed at the end of the anchor chain. As if in a dream, I staggered though the dim tunnel of the boom-tent and looked out astern. There, to my immense relief, was the hard, solid-looking side of a fishing boat protruding through the sheet of darkness. We were still at our anchorage, but, although relieved, I had to sit down because I was shaking all over. I found out later that Midiah had suffered a power-cut, apparently a common occurrence in Turkey.

Before crawling back to bed, I noted the wind had gone round to the northeast. Although the harbor was more sheltered from this quarter, some very violent gusts were finding their way in. At dawn the storm was at its height, with sudden heavy rain squalls that lasted only a few minutes before they were blasted away by the shrieking wind.

With yesterday's gathering of fishing boats, rafts of up to five or six vessels had grown out toward us. The crew of the one nearest to us hailed us over to tie alongside. They indicated that because the fishing fleet was stormbound, we wouldn't be disturbed there.

So began our practical adoption by the crew of *Cesur*. The skipper introduced himself as Earl and, pointing round the other twenty-odd smiling ruffians, reeled off an exotic litany of Turkish names. The only way we could communicate was by mime and my slow grasp of simple Turkish words.

One crewman seemed to think I looked lucky and handed me his football pools coupon to fill in. It took me ages to understand his instructions, which required the use of a daily newspaper, nearly every page of which had a large color photograph of a naked female. This was surprising for a moslem country whose womenfolk are prudishly hidden away. Despite the distractions, I finally managed to fill the columns to my punter's satisfaction, and I hope he won his fortune.

Later that morning Earl offered to help us buy petrol. As we walked round the edge of the muddy estuary, Charles and I judiciously maneuvered ourselves to Earl's lee when we had to pass close by a herd of very fierce looking bullocks, paternally watched over by an old man in black baggy pantaloons who cut an almost biblical pose as he leaned on his staff.

At the foot of the cliff we started to climb up a steep, zigzagging path that skirted round some ancient ruins, heavily overgrown and half buried. Earl indicated that they had been baths in Byzantine times. On the flat cliff top we passed a field where Charles excitedly drew our attention to five grazing camels, each with a carrying frame strapped to its back. I got the feeling we were entering some strange and fascinating old world and had to remind myself that we were still on the shores of Europe, not Outer Mongolia.

We entered the village by a narrow, stony path that passed through several backyards of seemingly derelict half-timbered houses. These deserted houses could be seen all through the village, ghosts from the Turco-Greek exchange of population in the 1920s. Coupled with the persistent rain, those poignant reminders gave the whole village a drab and forsaken air. With the fishing fleet in port, the narrow main street was crowded with men, all heavily muffled against the cold. This seemed to further reduce the available space, causing everyone to take on a twisted sideways gait.

Earl took us first to an ironmonger, where he bought some heavy fishing equipment, which he very trustingly left by the shop door to pick up later. Then we walked to the other end of the main street to get the petrol. We entered a small shop with an oil-soaked earthen floor that looked quite bare apart from three 50-gallon drums in the middle of the room and a few smaller cans along the walls. In a corner stood a badly tarnished brass bed with the blankets kicked back, as if the occupant had just got up.

The elderly owner looked like a Mongolian, dressed in a bulky quilted jacket and a "pixie hat" fashioned, it appeared, from a small coal sack. He used a small hand pump to fill a liter measuring jug, then poured the content into my containers. Again Charles and I moved to Earl's protective lee when it became obvious that the Pixie had no intention of removing the glowing cigarette from the side of his mouth. This time, Earl observed our cowardice and asked what we were doing. I indicated my concern, which Earl passed on to the Pixie. To reassure us that it was perfectly safe, he raised the brimming jug to his chin and began waving it under the cigarette. At this, even Earl took an involuntary step back. But despite the strong smell of petrol, no fiery genie rose from the jug, and he carried on filling our cans.

We carried the petrol back to the ironmonger's and left it there with Earl's fishing gear. Thus unencumbered, we trudged through the village to come out onto the cliff top at the end of the windswept headland. The view was stupendous. A wild expanse of slate-green sea was beating itself into a broken lather along the rocky sweep of coastline. Ranks of dusky headlands stretched far into the distant mist, each one tucked behind the other in a subtle spectrum of languishing gray. The little harbor below looked snug and safe, while *Alea* stuck out like a sore thumb among the rows of robust and functional workboats.

Seeking the shelter of the village again, we ducked back through another side street that had some sections of old marble paving stones. Rounding a bend, we were confronted by a pair of harnessed bullocks being driven frantically up the lane toward us. They were dragging a large-diameter tree trunk and being urged on by the yells and prods from two wizened old men with long poles. My first instinct was to grab Charles and bolt back the way we had come, but Earl quickly directed us to shelter in a nearby doorway.

As the agitated animals stamped and skidded past, the log jammed on the edge of a flagstone just in front of us. While the two men set about levering the log free, I was able to marvel at the rustic construction of the harness. Thick leather straps with hand-wrought metal buckles and rings exuded a potent strength. Even the heavy chain attached to the log displayed the facets left by the blacksmith's hammer when each link had been beaten into shape. We were looking on a scene that could have taken place thousands of years ago.

Earl next took us to a crowded, smoke-filled café, where the windows ran with condensation. Here, over several rounds of *chai*, Earl taught us to play *Dama*, or Turkish checkers. This is basically the same as checkers—but the pieces are moved along the squares instead of diagonally. There is also a seemingly arbitrary rule that allows a piece that reaches the other side to go leaping back and forth across the board until either there are no more opposing counters or the player's arm tires.

When we got back to *Alea*, we found Despina and Victoria scoffing their dessert from a four-course lunch that the crew of *Cesur* had brought over to them. It wasn't long before there was a tapping on the companionway hatch, and there was *Cesur*'s cook, Aziz, at the end of a human chain that passed the many dishes that formed the latecomers' tasty Turkish lunch. We socialized with our friendly neighbors the rest of that stormbound day, which culminated in a *Dama* tournament in the evening.

Next morning, although the wind appeared to be abating, it was bitterly cold and wet. After mopping up the heavy condensation, I lit my kerosene lamp to augment our small heater. This penetrating cold apparently was the last straw. Despina couldn't bear it any longer; she felt she had to leave for Greece. For her, the "holiday" had deteriorated into a very unpleasant endurance test. And all the while she endured, there was the haunting knowledge that her parents were waiting for her in Alexandroúpolis. I had dodged around the issue ever since Yugoslavia, selfishly compelling her to persist against her will. I knew not to try this time.

There was another, more profound reason for her desperately unhappy state. Although I felt we had found salvation from the Eastern Bloc by reaching Turkey, Despina only saw this as landing in the clutches of an enemy she had been taught to hate since childhood. The fact that the Turks had overwhelmed us with their friendship and generous hospitality only seemed to make things worse. It would take another sailing season among the Turks, as well as the Greeks, to undo the many years of malicious indoctrination.

Twenty-Nine
Istanbul without the Girls

UNDER THE CIRCUMSTANCES, we agreed that there were practical advantages in Despina going on ahead and preparing winter quarters in Alexandroúpolis. Victoria was to go with her. The question of Charles staying to help sail *Alea* round was no longer an issue. Charles's diary records:

> Mum wants to leave again and Victoria is going with her. She doesn't like the holiday because it is getting into winter. I am unhappy again, but it isn't as bad as Varna.

At noon the next day, we walked up to the village to await the one o'clock bus to Istanbul.

We joined a group of locals standing around the glowing woodstove at the ticket office. When the bus arrived, the young driver came in to receive an extraordinary handshaking welcome from the ticket clerk and the other waiting passengers. Beaming with good humor, the driver brought out a large, framed photograph, which everyone crowded round admiringly. When he noticed us, he came over and politely offered it to us to have a look. There was the young man standing nervously next to his new bride. We nodded our approval and managed a *chok gazelle* (very beautiful), to the great delight of the groom and his well-wishers.

This friendly diversion did a lot to ease the gloomy nature of our family parting. Then, in a whirl of haste, Despina and Victoria were aboard and waving from the back window as the bus lumbered off down the street.

They spent two nights in Istanbul and were safely in the bosom of the grandparents by the third evening. There seems to have been only one awkward moment, when Despina had to explain to the Turkish Customs how she had got into the country. Victoria's diary captures it:

> Mum said we came by yacht and that there was no customs at Midiah. Then the man asked Mum, "Why did you leave the yacht?" "Oh, . . . it was the 'little one,' she didn't like the big waves." The man said "I see" and smiled at me. When we got outside I got very cross at Mum for blaming me!

Charles and I walked back through the village to the lookout on the headland. The storm was gradually abating, but the sea looked just as wild with a very high surf. Charles's diary recounts our afternoon:

> After Mum and Victoria left, Dad and I went for a walk. I was sad that they had gone but the walk cheered me up. We climbed up a hill and into a forest. Dad and I talked about the Greek and Turkish wars. We found a nice clearing to have lunch. Dad showed me how to light a fire without matches—with a cigarette lighter! On the way back, we saw a corpse of a sea creature with sharp teeth, we thought it was a porpoise.

Soon it was time for supper, but thinking it best to delay our introduction to my cooking, we set off in search of a restaurant. The one we chose appeared to be owned by the only customer, who was halfway through his meal. This small, round gentleman invited us to sample the food from his many side dishes. When we nodded our approval he snapped his fingers and a waiter came to take our order. He then poured out a clear spirit called *raki* for me. Topped up with water it tasted much the same as Greek ouzo. When I smacked my lips in appreciation, he snapped his fingers again and I instantly had a bottle of my own.

Next morning brought little change in the weather, so we decided to catch the eight o'clock bus to Saroy, the nearest town with a bank, and officially obtain some Turkish lira. We raced up to the village and arrived at the bus stop panting heavily just as the driver was climbing into his seat.

Safely aboard, we sat back to enjoy a veritable "magic carpet" ride, even if a somewhat bumpy one. The countryside was much like the Lake District in England, but camels and nomadic dome tents by the side of the road gave it an atmosphere all its own. The bus stopped at all the small villages on the way, picking up and dropping off voluminously robed women carrying huge bundles wrapped in bedsheets, which made the bus stops resemble laundry pickup points.

When we stopped at a petrol station, I took the opportunity to go to the toilet. But after only having air put into a tire, the driver decided to move the bus out of the forecourt. Charles apparently won everyone's heart by jumping up and calling out, "Dur baba tuvalet"—stop father toilet! Whatever the connotation, it certainly had the desired effect, for when I returned, the driver and passengers were still incapacitated with laughter.

In a climate of galloping inflation, the bank couldn't deal with us until ten o'clock, when the day's exchange rate would be unveiled. With an hour to kill, we went on a tour of the town.

While we peered through the window of a china shop, a small dark man wearing a long white apron and a huge black mustache appeared like a genie from nowhere and stood smiling beside us. Charles wanted to buy his mother a Turkish tea set for her birthday, and our new friend was eager to help him. As the shop owner brought out the various boxes, the smiling "Genie" would open them for us, and, like a very happy child opening a Christmas present, he would put on a delightful display of expectation and exuberant surprise at the treasures revealed within.

Charles made his choice of four glasses and saucers, but they didn't have the stainless-steel spoons. However, this was not a "Genie" to grant half a wish. He led us next door to his tiny tea shop and, with a twinkling smile, he served us tea before sorting out and polishing four of his own spoons to present to Charles—on the house.

So with happy memories of Saroy we arrived back at the harbor to find an armed soldier standing by *Alea*. A businesslike corporal came along wanting my *passaportum* and to search *Alea*. I was expecting trouble about our having been ashore, but he didn't seem to notice the missing passport stamp. After only a token look inside, they shook my hand and left.

Charles went off to fossick around the base of the cliffs and discovered some ancient caves. Armed with a torch, we went to investigate. Most turned out to be cell-like recesses cut into the rock, with a front wall of large, dressed stones so badly eroded on the outside that they matched the texture of the cliff face, making the entrances very difficult to spot. Inside, the walls and ceilings were covered in what looked like Greek graffiti, some script being very neatly carved into the rock. There were many crucifixes, ranging in design from the very simple to elaborate Maltese types.

Our next foray into the unknown was cooking supper. The last time Charles and I had held sway in the kitchen was when Despina was away bringing Victoria into the world. Like then, it was Charles who exhibited the most confidence in such matters. But in spite of it all being conducted along the lines of a badly organized chemistry experiment, the result—spaghetti and vegetable hotchpotch, with grated cheese on top—was almost as good as Mum's.

When done, we put all the dirty dishes out in the cockpit for washing in the morning with the breakfast lot. Another liberty of the new domestic regime was keeping the kerosene heater on all night. And before turning in, we tried another refinement: suspending the kettle over the heater. It worked wonderfully: by seven o'clock the next morning it was on the point of boiling and thus ended the ordeal of washing in cold water.

Such a luxury was much appreciated, for although the sky was bright and clear, the air was still crispy cool. The sea was calm, so in the wake of the fishing fleet we headed out of Midiah. It was Friday, October 26, and in a mixed mood of missing the other half of the crew and reveling at being back at sea, we set sail for Kara Burun, 32 miles down the coast.

Not long after we made port, *Cesur* arrived to spend the night there too. We had one last evening together, and after supper Charles entertained everyone with a puppet show starring our ship's monkey, Yo-Yo. The next morning *Cesur* passed close astern and a throaty chorus bid us farewell: "Allah iz mala duk."

A light and very cold northwesterly pressed us on to the Bosporus. Approaching that famous passage between the low, twin capes of Europe's Rumeli and Asia's Anatolia was one of the highlights of the trip. As it was also the home waters of Charles's forefathers, he posed proudly with their landmarks in the background.

We could see a continual stream of merchant ships fanning out into the Black Sea, while another dispersed ark of shipping converged purposefully on the narrow opening. By steering *Alea* close along the gently rising European shore, we kept well out of their way.

Rounding Cape Rumeli, we passed the now innocuous yet fabled "Clashing Rocks" of antiquity. As the strait opened before us, we had the impression of being back on the Danube. Green, wooded hills sloped steeply up from the water's edge to peak in a gently rolling ridge that softened the almost fjordlike appearance of the twisting, deep channel. Forts and castle ruins dotted here and there attested to the long-standing strategic importance of this scenic defile.

Although we managed to elude all the fearsome-looking ships, one vessel we couldn't avoid was the yellow and red Health Inspection launch. It came bounding over and held alongside *Alea* long enough for the crewman to scribble out a "Clean Bill of Health Certificate" and point to the customs building, deep inside a large bay on the European side.

Eventually we found a vacant berth among the hundreds of small craft lining the shore. As no official came to see us that evening, I dutifully set off with my *passaportum* in the morning, but under the fiery stare of Kemal Ataturk hanging on the office wall I was issued only another "Clean Bill of Health Certificate."

My good health reassured and with the promise of a sunny day, it felt perfect for a Sunday cruise through Istanbul. We were obviously not the only ones to think so, for boatloads of day-trippers were setting out from every bay, each flying Turkey's vivid crimson national flag. It was like taking part in a festive regatta.

The breeze came in lazy drafts, but even in a sultry wind shadow *Alea* glided on, riding the 3- to 4-knot Bosporus current. To have passed through any faster would have been sacrilege. We were drifting down an enchanting riverlike vista flanked by castle towers and walls, minarets and tree-shaded villas. Onward we ghosted, under the delicately strung arc of the second suspension bridge to be built over the Bosporus Strait. The bridge is a spectacular piece of engineering vaulting high above the same spot the Persian king Darius chose in 513 B.C. for the pontoon bridge that led him to Marathon—no doubt a comparable technical achievement for the world's first superpower.

Passing beneath the next suspension bridge at Ortakoy, we decided to anchor in front of a baroque-looking mosque built right on the waterfront. This exotic corner, with a Turkish flag of gigantic proportions billowing out from the bridge above our heads, seemed the right venue for lunch.

After lunch we headed on, and the waterfront to our right took on the bearing of grand imperial splendor with the icing-sugar filigree of the marble Dolmabahce Palace. It was here, in one of the rooms overlooking the Bosporus, that Kemal Ataturk died in 1938. This is also where the last Ottoman sultan, Mehmed VI, left his ancestral seat to seek asylum aboard the British warship *Malaya* in 1922.

The skyline of the central city is dominated by a graceful combination of heaped-up arching domes and needle-sharp minarets. This amazing architectural spectacle appears to be built upon a ramshackle jumble of tightly packed metropolitan dwellings. On the southern side of the Golden Horn, a surprising number of trees are interspersed between the buildings, but the northern side is overgrown by giant lettered advertising signs. Nevertheless, Islamic classicism reigned supreme.

The rolling hills of Asia to the east appeared only slightly less populated. One enormous building, the Selimiye barracks, stands out on top of a hill like a prison block. It was there, in 1854, that Florence Nightingale laid the foundations of modern nursing, while more recently it has been the place from where the various military juntas have administered Istanbul. Nearer to us and lying well off the Asian shore was the squat Ottoman watchtower-*cum*-lighthouse of Kizkulesi. It stands barely awash upon a small reef along with an incongruous-looking bungalow that makes them both look like marooned flood victims.

We passed between this oddity and the southeasternmost tip of mainland Europe, where once "The City" stood. Variously known as Byzantium, Nea Roma, and Constantinople, the successor of Troy and Rome is now called Istanbul, an inglorious name derived from the invading Turk's corruption of a Greek signpost that helpfully directed them, "Eis tin Poli," To the City. As we made our way round that historic foreland, a somber collage of bleached, columned ruins seemed to float past in a slow, pirouetting dance. The harem towers of Topkapi Palace, followed by the minarets of St. Sophia and then the Blue Mosque, provided us with spectacular waypoints around what must be the most extraordinary historic seafront in the world.

Like time itself we passed on westward, and out on the Sea of Marmara we wound our way through a scattered fleet of anchored merchant ships. So busy is the strait that they must wait their turn to follow the course once plied by Jason and the Argonauts.

We tracked down the local marina and, for a mooring fee equivalent to 20 deutsche marks, had the pleasure of our first hot shower since Vienna.

Although the south coast of Marmara looked the more interesting, I chose to take *Alea* north about so as to be in the lee of the northerly storms that frequent this area. Thwarting my careful planning, six hours after we arrived at the small fishing harbor of Mimarsinan, a southerly struck that kept us stormbound for four days. To make up the trio of misfortunes, Charles came down with a very bad cold, and I had to buy a local gas-bottle stove because "Camping-Gaz" was unobtainable.

Between bouts of playing "Florence Nightingale" with Charles, I decided to give the outboard motor an inspection and oil change. Performing this operation with the motor in situ, I taped plastic sheet all round the drain hole to prevent any spillage into the sea. With the task carefully completed, I set off to dump the carton of waste oil. No sooner had I stepped on the quay than a fisherman rushed over and indicated that he would dispose of the oil for me. Gladly I handed it over, only to see him turn round and toss the carton high over the seawall.

When both Charles and the weather were on the mend, we headed on, and at the tiny fishing haven of Marmara-Ereglisi we left the coast and sailed southwest to the Island of Marmara. Halfway across, my hand compass went haywire, and when I tried to take a position fix using the ship's compass, I found it bewitched too. Voodoo struck again when we were within 4 miles of our goal: the wind suddenly went round to blast out of the very mountain we were heading for. It took two more hours to beat our way up to the entrance of Saraylar Bay, where the wind abruptly ceased as if a fan had been switched off.

Lying before us was a hideous mountain landscape, scarred beyond belief by countless open marble quarries. *Marmara*, Greek for *marble*, has been quarried here for the past three thousand years. The village had the thrown-up, temporary aspect of a typical mining settlement, so we didn't linger.

Taking our leave of that "marble sea," we set off the next morning for the Dardanelles. Charles was getting back to his old self and seeking longer turns at the tiller. He had taken an alarmingly long time to recover from his cold, but as fate would have it he was now set for what he was to describe later as the adventure of his life.

Thirty

Hikmed of Troy

ALL DAY THE DARK, mountainous coast of Asia seemed to be stealthily creeping up on us as we funneled our way into the Dardanelles Strait. Ahead, our narrowing path of scuffed green jade appeared to peter out where the two rocky continents met. From this perspective and in a rising 20-knot tailwind, the ancient Greeks' idea of "Clashing Rocks" coming together to crush the unwary mariner felt quite plausible. It was time to drop the main and go on under jib alone. As if on a river, the westbound ships seemed to fly past effortlessly, while the opposing traffic resolutely slogged their way against wind and current. The port of Gelibolu (Gallipoli), hove into view by the side of a large open bay. Its exposed waterfront presented a very poor harbor in the confused sea that was running. Disappointed, I surveyed a line of berthed ferries and merchantmen heaving and straining at their moorings. As I dithered where to go I caught a glimpse of a large fishing boat, which had followed us in, suddenly disappearing—into a restaurant on the quayside!

Doubling back, I found that hidden between two flanking terraces of tables and chairs was a narrow passageway leading into a small inner harbor. As I gingerly nosed *Alea* into the opening, an elderly man in a green plastic raincoat leaned out over one of the terrace guardrails and dramatically called out: "Velcome! Tonight I am going to a restaurant—to eat fish—and I invite you to join me! Ve vill eat *palamut* together!"

Wispy-white-haired, weather-beaten and stocky, this was the indomitable Hikmed—one of life's characters. At first we thought he was German, but he was a 68-year-old retired railway inspector from Istanbul. He pointed out to us his relatively new 18-foot GRP sloop, called *Hoko-Moko*, moored two berths along. My gaze was instantly arrested by two glaring features of the yacht. First, the mainsail was laced to the mast, which was just a plain aluminum pole. The other feature was an impractical-looking "self-steering aid" fixed not on the centerline but well over to the port side of the sloping transom. Of course, at that moment, I had no idea he was intent on being the first Turk to circumnavigate the world—solo!

When we got *Alea* snug, I invited him aboard but got the decisive reply: "No, ve must hurry—come—for my television program vill soon begin." At the mention of television, Charles was also "reeving" to go, so we were led round the harbor to a small back-street café that had a large television perched high up in a corner. Waiting for him were two young men who resembled a sort of Turkish version of Abbott and Costello. Apparently, Hikmed had met them earlier that afternoon and had invited them to eat *palamut* as well.

A round of *chai* was ordered for our merry band as we settled down to watch "Hikmed's" program, which turned out to be an American soap opera called "The Young and the Restless." The only entertainment I could extract was from the hilarious way the Turkish had been dubbed in, and how Hikmed *shushed* even people at other tables who forgot that this was "his program."

Fortunately, after just ten minutes of this "riveting epic" we experienced our second Turkish power cut. Hikmed took it surprisingly well as we stumbled back through the blacked-out streets to the restaurant, where *palamut* was served by candlelight. The evening was made all the more memorable by our eccentric host's outlining his rather disquieting plans to sail round the world. It transpired that he was being sponsored by a newspaper, which was obviously going to get a good story no matter what. Putting aside my own misgivings, I toasted him the best of luck.

Hikmed joined us for breakfast the following morning and offered to accompany us on our next leg to Çanakkale. *Hoko-Moko* cast off first and headed out through the harbor exit. *Alea* followed ten minutes later.

The sky was overcast and a 20- to 25-knot northeasterly was blowing right down the channel. I momentarily considered turning back, but seeing *Hoko-Moko* motoring bravely on, I decided to follow my leader. Charles steered while I raised the working jib, and under that one sail we soon caught up. But within half an hour of our setting out, the wind began to gust and I had to quickly change down to the storm jib. Although we began to draw ahead of *Hoko-Moko*, *Alea* was by no means the fastest vessel in our small fleet. Hikmed carried an inflated air mattress lashed to the deck, which, he had explained, "doubled as a tender–*cum*–life raft." Suddenly, it went somersaulting past us to port.

Glancing back over my shoulder, I was appalled to see *Hoko-Moko*, some distance back, broached over on her starboard side. Hikmed was hanging across the coach roof with one arm around the mast and trying to yank down the partly raised mainsail with the other. I let fly the jib, but as I made to start the motor, Hikmed began waving emphatically for us to continue on. He gave up on the tangled sail, crawled back to the cockpit, and started motoring across to the Asiatic side of the strait. I assumed he would fix his sail in the shelter of one of the bays and then follow on.

The weather was obviously deteriorating again, but by pressing on quickly, I hoped to reach the shelter of the Dardanelles' Narrows. This is a sharp Z bend that squeezes and twists the waterway round past the harbor town of Çanakkale. It was here, in 480 B.C., that the Persian king Xerxes, son of Darius, had to build two bridges before he could cross for his appointments at Thermopylae and Salamis. Apparently, the first bridge was destroyed in a storm, for which he ordered all the building supervisors beheaded. Being an evenhanded sort of a judge, he sentenced the waters of the Dardanelles to three hundred strokes of the lash for its part in the affair.

Alexander the Great had no problems when using the same crossing point in the "return bout" of 332 B.C. And like him, our luck was in too. Just after the first bend, we turned into a sheltered open reach backed by steep, wooded hills, which were dominated by the image of a giant Trojan spearman laid out in painted stones. Alongside, in huge white script, is a rendering from a thought of Ataturk on the cost of the land in human lives.

With the sting now taken from the wind, we raised the main-sail and went bounding off on an exhilarating beam-reach right to Çanakkale Roads. Çanakkale looked quite a large town with a phalanx of modern apartment blocks lining the embayed water-front. We moored bow-to in a small harbor at about three o'clock and spent the rest of the afternoon with Customs. As Çanakkale and Istanbul are the only ports of entry in northwestern Turkey, it puzzled the bureaucrats how they were to check us out when in fact we hadn't actually checked in. Inevitably, we got passed from one person to another until the buck stopped with one pragmatic pasha who simply handed back my passport and said, "Ve vill say you never came to Turkey."

When it started getting dark and there was still no sign of Hikmed, I decided to inform the coast guard. Of course, no sooner had I raised the alarm than Hikmed arrived—towed in by a fishing boat. Sadly, he had managed to untangle his wayward sail, only to have the end of the mainsheet foul the propeller of his 4-horsepower outboard motor. (This was to require a com-bined effort the following day to unshackle the taut mainsheet from the boom just to raise the motor.) But for the moment he seemed quite undaunted by his ordeal, for the first thing he said after checking the time was, "Ah, good, I vill see my program!" Charles and I had just started preparing supper, so we invited him to come back and join us. "Vhat is it you cook?" was the reply. "Sausages!" And like a true-life Popeye he announced: "No, no, tonight I eat spinach!

For the next two stormbound days, we followed "Hikmed's rule" and accompanied him to a restaurant for our evening meal. On the first night we did this, I insisted on picking up the bill. In true Hikmed fashion, he insisted on checking the waiter's arith-metic—there was an error that, when corrected, meant that I had to pay 6,000 lira more!

The 1915 Gallipoli Campaign seemed to be the main industry of Çanakkale, with countless agencies and taxi drivers offering "good price" tours of the battlefields. The campaign to enlist us began when we were approached in the street by a young Turk with a heavy Australian accent: "G'day mate!" On discovering we were from New Zealand, he invited us to view a documentary on Gallipoli that evening—"and bring a friend."

Hikmed found the documentary very interesting too but caused a bit of a disturbance halfway through, when he thought there was something wrong with the soft drink he was served. This was from the same Hikmed who had to have a drink from every faucet and fountain we passed in order, as he so quaintly put it, "to make my stomach strong against mice." (It turned out he actually meant *germs*.) At the end of our evening's varied entertainment, we barely managed to escape our hosts' hard sell. Even after explaining we would be leaving in the morning, they decided a visit to the ruins of Troy was more our "glass of tea."

Alas for them, we had already made plans concerning ancient Troy. Hikmed knew of a small, unmarked *liman*—harbor—just inside the Dardanelles and within walking distance of the ruins. This sounded ideal for me, not only for visiting Troy, but also as a convenient haven from which I could get a feel for the Aegean before venturing out on it.

As the significance of his last brush with the Dardanelles started to sink in, Hikmed was beginning to see some of the shortcomings of *Hoko-Moko* for a circumnavigation. Being a man of decisive action, he resolved to leave it moored at Çanakkale and return to Istanbul to see his sponsors. However, before heading back he planned to make a detour to see an old friend who lived in a village near Troy. I proposed he come with us aboard *Alea* so he could make his visit and pilot us to the secret "Trojan" harbor.

Our departure the next morning, Saturday, November 10, turned out to be the opening act in a gala performance of the Spectacular and Bizarre. Hikmed locked up *Hoko-Moko* and came aboard *Alea* with his stern anchor, on which he had attached an extra long line (using the curious "Ventchi knot"). But when I fell back to pick up my stern anchor, he threw his overboard while there were still coils of slack line and chain to pay out. To top this, when I made to drop him back aboard *Hoko-Moko* to tighten in the line, he was adamant that it should be left as it was. I kept my own counsel and set *Alea*'s bow for the harbor exit.

There was quite a bit of blue sky showing now, although it was still cool, with a 15- to 20-knot northeasterly funneling down the strait. The view down the Dardanelles looked full of promise. Flanked on either side by steep rugged mountains, the strait curved round to the southwest, fjordlike, to reveal a small section of blue horizon—the Aegean. With only the working jib raised and Hikmed at the tiller, we headed out into midchannel to ride the 3- to 4-knot following current. The surface of the water was turbulent and choppy, but *Alea* rolled over it resolutely.

Off to our left the channel opened up in a wide sweeping bay, where I called excitedly for Charles and Hikmed to look at a school of large porpoises jumping. They were leaping so high into the air that they appeared to lose control of their vertical flight and ungracefully crashed back into the sea with enormous splashes.

Hikmed was clearly enjoying his sail in *Alea*, so much so that he began having eyes for her. He suddenly asked if I would sell her to him. I told him I would be glad to, if only he could wait until September the following year. But of course he wanted her now.

Having come to an impasse on the future, we sought diversion in the past. Ranged along the shoreline like broken milestones stood the battered remains of the strait's naval forts—the handiwork of the Allied battleships that had tried to force their way through to Istanbul in 1915. In Çanakkale we had visited the little mine-laying vessel *Nousret*, which put paid to this "grand strategy" by making a timely sortie that claimed six battleships in one disastrous day. Well, disastrous for some, for Hikmed waxed lyrical on his country's heroic defense against the invader. As if taking its cue from Hikmed's patriotism, the gigantic Turkish war memorial that towers over the tip of the Gallipoli Peninsula, hove into view. Designed somewhat like a table with massive, elongated, square legs, the monument impresses with its colossal proportions.

Nearing our destination on the Asiatic shore, we closed with the land, which was beginning to flatten on both sides into low dune-type hills. The wind began to increase, raising a considerable sea that punched heavily on our port quarter before rolling on underneath. This boisterous keel-heaving behavior of the waves seemed to unnerve Hikmed, for when we finally arrived outside the narrow, surf-tossed harbor entrance, he was having qualms about assailing ancient Troy through such a small port.

I started the motor and, while some 150 meters offshore, turned into the wind so as to drop the sails. But when I offered the tiller to Hikmed, he didn't seem to understand my intentions. With an expression almost of terror he recoiled away from me and, pointing at the breakwater, called out: "The rocks! I fear them!"

Charles took over to keep us luffed while I saw to the sails. Then, with everything and everyone hankered down, I set tilt for the gap. Catching the crest of a hissing, surging wave, we shot through. One moment we were pitching and rolling on the open sea and the next we were served up in the crystal-clear calm of Kum Kale Liman.

When we had changed course to head inshore, I had chosen as a leading mark an odd blue smudge on a hillside, which lay in the general area where Hikmed thought the harbor was. When the harbor breakwater miraculously appeared directly below this now extensive blue-pinkish bloom, I quite innocently marveled at my lucky choice of heading. Now safely inside the harbor, I gawked in astonishment at my hillside beacon: thousands upon thousands of discarded supermarket plastic shopping bags.

Predominantly blue, they formed a 3-meter-thick margin down either side of the harbor pool. It stretched out beyond the water like a carpet, up the gently sloping beach and up through the low scrub, decorating every branch and twig like a tugging, billowing avalanche in reverse.

I ran *Alea* into a vacant berth in a row of some twenty small fishing boats moored with bow toward the breakwater. There was no fear of hitting the loose boulders at the water's edge, for the thick cushion of plastic bags brought us to a soft, squelching halt. Charles and Hikmed climbed ashore with the bow lines and made them fast around some large stones. Hikmed was still feeling rather stressed, which resulted in another "Hik-up" as Charles's diary recalls:

When he doesn't understand something he shouts: "I understand nothing!" He is also a bit deaf. When we arrived at the small harbour and Hik and I got out, Dad asked me to lower one of the ropes. Hik said "Pardon?" Dad told him: "I was speaking to Charles." Hik shouted back: "Charles?—Vhat is Charles?!—I understand nothing!" Dad and I laughed our heads off!

Laughter almost got the better of Charles in our next escapade. As we set off to walk to Troy, we found about a dozen fishermen attempting to launch a fishing vessel, stern first, from a corner of the harbor beach. As it was all being done with muscle power, we gladly volunteered our combined brawn. But our contribution was undermined the instant we made to join the hard-pressed gang. To reach them, we had to wade through this ankle-deep mass of sodden and partially inflated plastic bags, which at each step set off a cannonade of the most raucous farts. If this novel accompaniment wasn't enough, the sight of Hikmed daintily tiptoeing across in his shoes while holding his trouser legs high at the knees set Charles and me off with the giggles. No one else seemed to take any notice of the clamor of their tread, and the blank puzzled looks we got only added to our mirth.

The *pièce de résistance* came when we all had to lift and push the boat together. With a line of fishermen ranged along either side of the hull, we were given the task of pushing at the bow. Now, Turkey is a land where one can see all manner of baggy pants, worn by women as well as men. But when Turkish fishermen tuck their pants into the tops of their gum boots, the billowing, flexing result is truly titanic. Being confronted by a row of these lively pantaloons when I bent my shoulder to the bow was hard enough, but when they began to flex to the quick, urgent staggering of their owners, all seemingly synchronized to the thunderous fusillade from below, I was rendered useless. Almost blind with tears and clutching my chest for fear of a coronary, I had to leave the scene. Charles was already running back up the beach howling with laughter and desperately fumbling at the fly of his pants as he darted behind a solitary storage shed.

Beset by Hikmed's questioning looks, we didn't recover our composure until we had climbed high up the rough winding road that led over the bluffs and inland. It was decidedly cooler, with the fresh northerly sweeping in across from the Gallipoli

Peninsula. Out on the Aegean, whitecaps ruffled the blue, right up to the misty shadow of the Gökçe Island lying to the northwest.

The countryside above the bluffs was a high, rolling plateau, carefully divided into small square fields. All the crops had been gathered in, leaving the land looking scoured, which somehow evoked the millennia through which man has tilled this ground. It was quite apparent that he has been littering it for just as long, for broken bits of pottery and marble lay everywhere.

This archaeological "I spy" took on greater proportions when we ambled into the small village of Kum Kale, 2 kilometers from the coast. There, huge, ancient marble blocks and column stones were built into the stonework of the village houses and their garden walls. Despite this sprinkling of classical architecture, Kum Kale didn't have a restaurant. Hikmed made inquiries, then led us to the local butcher's shop. The jolly butcher, wearing a frilly lace skullcap, spread out a newspaper on his counter and served us a sort of hamburger cooked in a toaster. Dessert was grapes and feta cheese, and in spite of the gory decor, it was compliments to the chef.

We set off to walk the last 2 kilometers to Troy, but no sooner had we left the village than a truck driver offered us a lift right to the site.

Apparently, many people get a bit of a disappointment with Troy, because it doesn't square with the exaggerated splendors of Homer's *Iliad*. But whether the beautiful Helen was just a euphemism for the area, Hellespont, and the wooden horse just a fanciful report of the use of a siege tower, I found walking round those ancient walls a fantastic experience. Even the fact that the excavations have been badly done gave the site a special pioneering atmosphere, as if we had just unearthed the jumble of ruins ourselves. Topping it off is that panoramic view out over the plain of Troy from the top of the citadel. This must be hard to beat, just for the spiritual imagery it evokes.

I asked Hikmed: "From what direction do you think the Greeks came?" He replied rather thoughtfully, "Who can tell?" Then his face darkened as if his next words tasted foul: "The Greeks have come many times after this—every time killing and burning our land!" He went on to justify this three-thousand-year-old grudge with his theory that because the words "Trojan" and "Turk" sound "similar," his people could well be the original displaced inhabitants of Troy. Well, if Homer can get away with adding a bit of color to a story, why not Hikmed?

And so it was time to take our leave of ancient Troy and, of course, of Hikmed, who had found someone to give him a lift to his friend's village. He had certainly lightened our stormbound days in Çanakkale and added another dimension to our visit to Troy. With a rather sad "*Guley-guley*," we wished him well with his dream and promised to keep a lookout for him when he and *Hoko-Moko* made their landfall in New Zealand.

Thirty-One
The Road to Yenikoy

11 NOVEMBER

SUNDAY, NOVEMBER 11, brought a bustle of activity to the tiny harbor as the local fishermen readied their boats for sea. We decided to follow their example and make an early start ourselves. Although it was just seven o'clock, it was already warm enough to have breakfast out in the cockpit.

We had no sooner sat down when we were distracted by the heavy sound of an old bus groaning its way down the steep road to the harbor. It came to a halt not far from us, and a crowd of fishermen got off, then, to our great surprise, out stepped Hikmed.

As he walked round, he jovially called out in greeting: "Am I in time for my special breakfast?" (cornflakes, apparently quite a novelty in Turkey). He had been hitchhiking since five o'clock to bring us an invitation from his friends to visit them, with the option of staying the night at their home. The chance of meeting a Turkish family at home was too good to miss, so with toothbrushes and pajamas packed, we set off on foot for the village of Yenikoy, 16 kilometers away on the Aegean coast.

When we reached Kum Kale, Hikmed decided that the hamburger meat we had tasted the day before would make a fine gift for his friends.

With the newspaper-wrapped gift under his arm, Hikmed approached a large group of men standing outside the shop and asked about buses to Yenikoy. They were unanimous: there weren't any—"everyone just walks." However, it was a different story when he asked the best route to take. Instantly, the small crowd seemed to fall apart as bodies turned and arms raised to point every which way. Seeing this, accompanied by a smattering of cuffed ears and dislodged caps, everyone spontaneously burst out laughing.

After a lot of good-humored debate, it was finally agreed that we were to head down the main street, then, once clear of the village—ask someone else!

We were still in the main street when a large tractor towing a trailer stopped to offer us a lift. The trailer appeared to contain some work crew's lunch. There were two large aluminum urns and several baskets of food, all wrapped individually in spotless white napkins, which contrasted starkly with the rough decking of the trailer. Although there was plenty of room on the trailer, Hikmed ushered us up onto the tractor, to perch on the giant mudguards on either side of the driver. It felt precariously high but allowed us a marvelous view.

With the driver glancing round at every opportunity to shout questions at Hikmed, we roared off at seemingly breakneck speed. The road snaked round and over a stretch of hillocks before dipping down a steep bluff to the flat delta of the northern Trojan plain. Having left my stomach somewhere back on the bluff, I imagined this was what a battle-shocked Trojan charioteer felt like, but by the exhilarated expression on Charles's face, I could tell that he, for one, was enjoying every minute of it.

At last our "grand prix" driver pulled in at his turnoff. He invited us into the nearby field to pick some huge tomatoes for refreshment. Before we went munching down the road he showed us a heavy gold coin he had found while plowing his fields. On one side, a tiny charioteer cut a heroic pose in a timeless salute to proud finder and covetous hopefuls.

After walking some distance, in which the road crossed many branches of the reed-fringed Menderes (Homer's Scamander), we became unsure of the way. Hikmed was very reluctant to ask directions from the scattered groups of women working in the fields: "There is no man," he would say. Growing impatient, I decided to force the issue when we came upon a multicolored row of six or eight voluminous backsides, all pointing skyward.

I stepped nearer and, clearing my throat, diplomatically said: "Merhaba," hello. Simultaneously, each bale of clothing grew taller and took on a dumpy pear shape. With a deft tuck of their head scarves, all faces were instantly hidden. I asked: "Yenikoy— nereda?"—where? They stood stock still and silent, staring intently at the "roving male."

Of course, Hikmed was obliged to come to my rescue and asked for the directions in "real" Turkish. In response, the assembly of mute swaddled heads turned slowly to their right. We followed their gaze to see a man come walking through the field toward us. He greeted us cheerfully and put us on the right track. When the last word of their male spokesman was uttered, the women, like a practiced troupe at the *Folies Bergère*, did a quick about-face and, with a jerky jackknifing action, gave us a dismissive bottoms-up.

We walked through a small wood and came out at a road junction with an enormous man-made conical hill that served as a traffic island—and local cemetery. All over this steep, 10-meter-high mound, tall, slender marble gravestones stuck out from the long yellow grass at all angles. Each one was covered with snaking Arabic script carved deep into the white marble. The inside of the carved script had been newly painted with bloodred paint that had dripped and run, giving it a spine-chilling aspect.

To add to the grisly scene, Hikmed suddenly took off on a frantic stumbling run, yelling and waving his arm above his head. As he disappeared to the left of the mound we got a glimpse of a tractor, towing two trailers, pass behind to the right. The realization that Hikmed was trying to head it off to cadge a lift spurred us into hectic pursuit.

With a friendly smile, our next rustic chauffeur waved us aboard. This time we sat comfortably upon a stack of empty fruit crates in the first trailer, while fifteen to twenty tightly swathed women scrutinized us from the second. One middle-aged woman momentarily pulled back the end of her scarf, as if opening a little cupboard door, and gave Charles a bright maternal smile. But when I smiled in acknowledgment, the door was instantly snapped shut.

In spite of these cultural sensitivities, the ride was sheer magic. The road began to climb gently out of the delta, allowing us to look out over the patchwork-quilted array of small fields to the enigmatic remains of Troy.

We were traveling south along the landward side of a long finger of raised land that separated the delta on our left from the sea. I could imagine that in the days of Troy, this may well have been a seaward spit, and the delta area a large sheltered bay reaching in almost to the city itself. As I swayed to the motion of the farm train, I could almost see those ships of old riding to their anchors in that phantom bay.

After another seemingly gender-estranged farewell, we caught our last chariot ride on a stampeding tractor that whisked us right into Yenikoy. Derelict houses flanked the rough, unsealed roads. Apparently, the village was in the process of being abandoned for the second time this century. Hikmed explained that it had been a Greek settlement up until the 1923 expulsions, and now "The young people want new houses—outside the village."

As we walked up a side street, we came upon a young girl chopping kindling on a large-diameter column capital, which had a beautiful leaf motif carved around it. Judging by its chipped top, it must have been used as a chopping block for generations.

Hikmed stopped outside an old two-story house and announced, "My friends live here!" We entered a very neat and tidy backyard, the floor surface of which was of rock-hard trampled earth, swept spotlessly clean. Low outhouses were built along one side of the stone perimeter wall, and a row of six beehives ranged along another. In a corner squatted a dome-shaped stone baking oven, whitewashed yet blackened by recent use. By the gate stood several huge terra-cotta water jars, which brought to mind the story of Ali Baba.

There was no one at home, from which Hikmed deduced, "They must be building—the son's house." So off we traipsed to the building site, which was just outside the village in a magnificent location overlooking the sea. Indeed, all the family were there, and they welcomed us as if we were long lost friends. There was "the son" (to use Hikmed's introduction), a black-mustached fisherman; his wife, "the daughter-in-law," who, although wearing the same type of floral caftan and pantaloons as the farm women, had her head uncovered and was surprisingly normal and friendly; and their six-year-old son, "the little one," who clung securely to his mother's pantaloons. Then there was "the grandmother," who wore the tightly bound head scarf but did not hide her smiling, moon-shaped face. She was very much taken with Charles and made a big fuss over him, especially after he answered some of her questions in Turkish. Her husband, "the grandfather," was a powerfully built man and possibly younger than Hikmed.

They were just finishing off the walls, which were constructed of a rough-hewn sandstone. The son, obviously proud of his "dream home," invited me to have a look around. The grandfather had made such a neat job of the stonework that I asked through Hikmed if any of the stonework was to be left exposed. "Hayir!," no, it was all to be plastered. Then, looking down below the floor level, I was horrified to see a long section of marble cornice built into the foundation. It had the same leaf motif carved along it as the column capital "chopping block" we had seen earlier. When I pointed it out to Hikmed, he shrugged and said, "It is sad, but these people don't understand such things. To them it is just a building stone."

This is probably how most ancient monuments disappeared. We had seen it at Hadrian's Wall in England—nearly every farmhouse in the area is built from it. I made a feeble attempt to save the stone by saying that it would look nice built into their lounge walls and left so that people could see it. But I could tell by the humoring smiles, universally reserved for foreigners and their funny ways, that the "Trojan treasure" was going to be displayed just where it was.

As it was now early afternoon and Hikmed had presented his treasure of the hamburger meat, we all trooped back to the village for lunch. This was truly a scene straight out of the Arabian Nights, although the twentieth-century twist of the omnipresent television might well have flawed such a fantasy had it not provided the requisite Turkish music and belly dancers.

We all sat down on the thickly carpeted floor around a raised metal tray that formed a low dining table. It was novel to discover that here in Turkey, the tablecloth is laid on the floor and the table then placed on top. This allows the diners to tuck their legs under the tablecloth and use it like a huge communal napkin. As we all ate with our fingers, I noticed that the grandmother's were covered in a thick brown shellac-type dye. I thought this was the result of staining from some food-preserving process but found out later that it's the traditional way of showing her married status.

After the meal, Hikmed took us to see the fishing-boat harbor. From the top of the coastal bluff, we could see that it was really just an open anchorage in front of a narrow strip of sandy beach. At the start of the steep access road, a signpost with an English translation underneath read, "Trojan Harbour." This was very hard to believe, because the coastline was so straight and exposed. But Hikmed pointed out that the anchorage was protected by three distinct sandbars we could see running parallel to the coast and some 50 meters apart. True enough, although a heavy swell was breaking on the outer bar, the fishing boats anchored inside the inner one were hardly moving.

I noticed a prominent rocky point 2 kilometers farther south. Now *that* looked a more likely place for the Trojans to build a harbor. As Hikmed thought so too, we decided to walk there for a closer look.

On our way along the cliff top, my eye was attracted by an unusual egg shape sticking out of the earth in a shallow drainage ditch. Prizing it out, I found it was a small glass bottle, like a medicine phial, with a conical bottom and a neck formed by decorative spirals. The surface of the glass had that dusty, well-worn texture like the glass one finds washed up on the beach. We had seen similarly shaped bottles in England at a museum display on Roman Britain.

Charles did even better when we reached the headland, where he found a solitary watermelon in a reaped field. This was shared out as we sat with our legs over the cliff's edge and surveyed an enchanting view. Although the present-day shoreline was only slightly embayed, the expanse of flat ground showed that it had once been a deep bay.

While we sat there imagining bronze-helmeted spearmen leaping ashore, the sun's waxen glow pierced the far mist on the horizon, to set behind the island of Bozcaada (Homer's Tenethos). It was too late to go down and fossick around, but I vowed I would return here the next year. Little did I know the trauma this pledge was to cause, when *Alea* was destined to make too close an inspection.

We made our way back, beckoned by the mullah's haunting call from Yenikoy's high minaret. Hikmed led us to the village teahouse, where we found the grandfather relaxing after his day's work—just like a pub back home, but instead of swilling beer, these men were sipping tea.

Back at the house, we enjoyed another marvelous banquet and took part in a pleasant chat to pass the evening. In spite of the exotic surroundings, I was taken by the normality of it all—this was just a family scene in which they all appeared to be very happy with their lot.

Because we had to catch a bus that would take us back as far as Troy at 7:00 A.M., we went to bed quite early. To my disappointment our beds were quite conventional, although this was compensated by our being awakened in the morning by the calling of the *mullah*, who sounded as if he was just outside the window.

A group of talkative Turks congregated around our table at the teahouse while we waited for the bus. Then suddenly a man popped his head round the door and yelled something that sent everyone scurrying after him. The bus had arrived, and amidst this hectic scramble Charles and I took our leave of the grandfather and missed Hikmed altogether. Just as we made to follow him into the bus, we got directed away to a large mechanical "digger" truck parked nearby. It appeared that only the truck was going to Troy. In a trice the bus was taking off down the street and that was the last we saw of Hikmed; yesterday's farewell would have to suffice.

There was only room for Charles in the truck's cab, squeezed between the driver and another chap. I climbed up on the back with two other men and froze while we rattled and jolted back to Troy through the chill early morning air. We were dropped off just outside the site, where the truck and the men are employed in the continuing archaeological excavations. While I beat some warmth back into my limbs, Charles cheerfully called, "Allah iz mala duk," to his two bosom pals waving gleefully from the cab.

We followed the now familiar road back to Kum Kale. There were no more lifts, which was fortunate, for I felt a last stroll through that remarkable countryside made a fitting end to our visit to Yenikoy. And by the time we got back aboard *Alea*, the sky was clear and the sun warm; everything was just right for venturing out on the Aegean.

Thirty-Two

Gallipoli: In the Wake of Heroes

BEFORE SETTING SAIL I climbed up on the cabintop and, looking north across the strait, took a compass sight on the Turkish war memorial. And what a sight it was: boldly conspicuous beyond the great blue sweep of the Dardanelles, austere and ominous above the long dark shadow of the Gallipoli peninsula— unreal against the backcloth of a cloudless blue sky. Useful too, for it gave me the position line for Kum Kale Liman on my chart: 142° true.

As we neared the low foreland of Cape Hellas, the rusting skeleton ribs of several wrecks from the 1915 Gallipoli Campaign could be seen awash. One was perhaps the tragic *River Clyde*, an ill-conceived landing craft with an incredible draft of over 3 meters. This fatal oversight meant that when the vessel was run aground, it was still well out from "V" beach. Of the fifteen hundred brave men who tried to get ashore, only four hundred made it.

With the wind astern and the strong Dardanelles current, we ghosted past all the main Allied landing beaches. The white stone monoliths of the British Commonwealth and French monuments stood out on the headland, stark testimony to the wasting of human life. Charles excitedly pointed back to the gleaming white naval fort on the Asiatic side of the strait, no doubt performing its present guard duty on the same site from which Trojan eyes watched for the foreign invader, for men have always fought for control of this strategic waterway.

I ran *Alea* out into the sparkling blue Aegean, with its islands in hazy outline far to the south. Then, well past the cape, I turned north on a straight heading to Kaba Tepe, our next port of call, 12 miles distant. With mixed feelings I trimmed the sails, for with the rounding of Cape Hellas, I sensed the satisfaction of beginning the final stage of our trip, as well as a touch of regret at the nearness of its inevitable end.

To starboard were the crumbling cliffs of "Y" beach, the landing that was least opposed by the Turks—perhaps because they thought it was impossible to land there, or knew the invader would stay only one night. Next morning, it is thought, an army request for ships to take off some wounded was somehow mistaken as an order to evacuate everyone. Sadly, when the commanding officer woke up, he found that his fighting force had been literally "taken out" by his own Ambulance Corps: "Y?" No one really knows. . . .

As we sailed further up the coast, the land started to rise and buckle into increasingly rugged terrain. This barrier seemed to redirect the wind to blow dead against us. Now with sails curved tight, *Alea* made long exhilarating tacks out to sea, toward the huge, forbidden island of Gökçe, then slanting in again toward the rocky shore of Gallipoli, we could inspect close-up the deep craggy gorges that gouged inland.

Despite this zigzagging course we made good progress, and it wasn't long before the prominent white monuments from the landings at Anzac Cove came into view. Set high up on the dark, brooding mountains, these gleaming lone sentinels acted as leading marks to guide us to the brand-new harbor of Kaba Tepe, 2 miles south of the cove.

The harbor was deserted. Freshly painted yellow bollards and lamp standards made an eerie guard of honor around the vacant quays. We had got only halfway across the harbor pool when a solitary man appeared, running along the quayside toward us with his arms waving wildly in the air.

No sooner had *Alea* touched alongside where directed, than I was completely nonplussed. First by our dictatorial guide, who abruptly introduced himself as the "postmaster" and ordered me to follow him "quickly" to report to the port authorities. And then by a crowd of men who suddenly appeared from everywhere to swamp me with vying proposals for a guided tour of the battlefields. Even the impatient "postmaster" offered his motorcycle for hire as he ushered me through the pushy crowd.

In the very plush domain of the harbormaster sat an overweight, snappy executive type who got straight down to business.

"How many nights you stay?"

I replied, "Two."

He suddenly sprawled himself across his desk at me and, thrusting the one-finger salute under my nose, said, "Right—you pay now—one U.S. dollar for every gross ton of your ship."

"Fair enough," I shrugged, but when I told him that *Alea* weighed two tons, he asked to see the ship's papers.

Then, without the slightest qualm, he decreed: "You must pay now—five U.S. dollars for every night you stay."

I tried to protest, but it only got me a brusque "Anchor out on the rocks then!"

With the taste of humble pie still in my mouth, I stoked back to *Alea*. But all strife was forgotten when I stepped aboard to find that Charles had prepared lunch. Things further improved when we discovered a small fleet of fishermen moored round in a hidden side dock.

It was when I took my chart over to ask one of these fishermen about harbors farther up the coast that I had my last fateful encounter with the harbormaster of Kaba Tepe. Surprisingly, the fisherman didn't know of any other harbors, but just then the harbormaster came walking past and the fisherman called him over to help. I watched the supercilious way he drew two circles on the chart, one on the north side of the Gallipoli peninsular at Ece, and one around the coastal town of Enez, near the border with Greece. No doubt sensing my poor opinion of him, he tapped the pencil on Enez and said, "Here at the port of Enez you find no harbormaster, only fishermen and soldiers." On hearing "soldiers" I asked if I would be allowed there. "Of course!" And like a fool, I believed him.

The position of these harbors suited my purpose, for it would allow me to set a fairly accurate time of arrival at Alexandroúpolis. So with a grand finale in mind, I telephoned Despina (not as easy as it sounds, even in a new Turkish post office) and made my pledge for 3:00 P.M., Friday, 16 November—in four days' time. She of course was skeptical but nevertheless promised to be there. Her news was a bit more pragmatic: she had found herself a job teaching, as well as a flat for us all.

After Victoria and Charles had completed this family exchange, it was straight back to our "Boys' Own" adventure in Kaba Tepe. Or more appropriately "Alice in Wonderland," for when we returned to *Alea* we found "The Walrus" waiting for us on the quay. This was a chubby, red-faced, elderly man with a white bushy mustache and an infectious twinkling smile. He introduced himself as "Kapatan" and pointed out his own boat, a sponge diver's launch called *Poseidon*. Over a glass of *raki*, he was very amused to hear about my dealings with the harbormaster. To my chagrin, he explained that they could only charge mooring fees for the outer harbor, which was why no one moored there.

Then, perhaps as a consolation for my having been duped, "The Walrus" insisted we "Green Oysters" have supper at his house. This turned out to be a veritable museum of artifacts and curios from all over the world, each one having an exotic tale that traced his long career as a deep-sea diver. We had a marvelous evening "Talking of many things—Why the sea is boiling hot— And whether pigs have wings."

Early next morning, Charles and I set off on our own tour of the battlefields by shank's mare. Climbing up a steep bank behind the side dock, we entered a fairly open pine forest. A shaded path followed the back parapet of a scrub-choked trench, which ran along the edge of the cliff top. This commanded a sweeping view of the Aegean and the rocky foreshore below.

The land ahead began to dip, allowing us to look out over a narrow valley that swept down from the far mountains to end abruptly in a broad, open bay. This was the place the Anzacs (Australian and New Zealand Army Corps) were supposed to have been put ashore, but instead they were landed just round the next point. Some historians believe this to be one of the main causes for the campaign's initial failure. Although controversy still rages over the landing at the wrong beach, it would appear that someone did get it right, for there, run up on the beach, lay the forlorn, corroding skeleton of a wreck, half buried at the water's edge.

It drew us like a magnet as we hurried down through the thick scrub to the shore. The sea washed gently in around the heavily encrusted ribs. Only the riveted steel plates below the water still survived. At the front an old-fashioned vertical stem stuck up from the sand, much like the early naval picket boats.

Looking up the beach, I noticed a small, dry creek bed that would have provided the only natural cover for troops moving inland. Crouching low we crept along the narrow watercourse and found it littered with bits of badly corroded cartridge shells and ferrous metal objects rusted beyond recognition. In one corner a distorted lead .303 bullet lay grimly culpable among some broken fragments of bone.

Returning to the beach, we continued on until we came to a Turkish army garrison, still watching this strategic coast. Until twenty years ago this isolated area had been a forbidden military zone, which has made it the best-preserved battleground in Europe.

At the northern corner of the bay, we crossed the small promontory (Hell Spit) that shelters Anzac Cove from the south. I was struck by the narrowness of the beach and the steepness of the eroding embankment. Latter-day concrete pillboxes lay defunct on the beach, attesting to the extent of the erosion.

Glancing up at the overhanging edge of the embankment, my heart leapt as my eyes fixed on a bleached white spherical shape protruding from the earth—the unmistakable round of a human skull! We scrambled up the steep, 5- to 6-meter bank. Charles was going to give up but I chivied him on, telling him to think of the Anzacs having to do it while being shot at. Up he went!

By lying down on the grassy lip and hanging our arms and shoulders over the side, we managed to remove the skull along with some other bones. A sinister, ragged wound showed through the temple, as if a bullet had just skimmed past his head. There was no way of telling if the victim was an Anzac or a Turk, but it was clear the grave needed proper investigation before it was lost to the sea. Leaving the bones exposed, we piled up some large stones as a marker, with the hope of informing someone in authority later.

In November 1915, the troops had suffered terribly from the bad weather, whereas we were getting warm sunshine. We decided to take advantage of this and resolved to reenact the Anzac landing and capture Chunuk Bair, the highest point on the coastal range and the main objective of the "Diggers."

Our first stop was at the impressive Anzac Cove Memorial and cemetery, near the mouth of "Shrapnel Valley." While we were looking for the grave of Jack Simpson (the man with the donkey), a Range Rover pulled up outside and a smartly dressed young man entered the cemetery. He superficially inspected a few graves before confronting us.

Over a pouting bottom lip drooled a refined Australian accent: "Where are you heading?"

I thought he was about to offer us a lift, so replied: "Chunuk Bair."

Then, casting a suspicious look at our rucksack, he asked more pointedly, "And how do you propose getting there?"

To my reply of "straight up," he revealed that he was employed by the War Graves Commission, and that it was their policy to discourage people from wandering around the Çanakkale National Park. To this end he recited a litany of such nasties as breaking legs, snakes, unexploded bombs, damage to flora and fauna, erosion, and last but not least—our getting lost and his being called out to look for us.

Now, it was obvious that the commission had done a marvelous job with the cemeteries, but I believed the park should be open to people who made the effort to experience the battlefield as it was—and is. Here was just another attempt to monopolize another historic place for the packaged coach-tour fraternity. We could see already that roads were being bulldozed in over the flora and fauna—for them!

It was plain that the biggest threat to our mission was this officious killjoy. And what was needed was a diversion (in the finest military tradition of course). So while he scurried off to officially inspect the human remains by the beach, we advanced with vigor up Shrapnel Valley.

Trying to remember my army cadet field craft, we cut up the steep valley side to reach a flattish plateau (Plugges Plateau). This gave us a fantastic view along the sweeping coast to Suvla Bay and inland to the contorted interior. A confusion of steep cliffs and eroded gullies rose up to the far ridges, where the monument at Quinn's Post stood out bright in the sun, marking the eventual front line. Confronted with such a desolate scene, my only thought was: "How on earth did they manage to get so far!"

We walked along a surprisingly well-preserved trench dug round the edge of the plateau, intending to carry on up to the high ground beyond (Russell's Top). But we were stopped in our tracks by a sudden precipice that dropped into a rock-strewn canyon. Bridged by only a thin wall of sandy rock (Razor's Edge), it was too dangerous to cross. So doubling back, we cut down into Shrapnel Valley again. Apparently the leading Anzacs, confronted with the very same problem, had done likewise and surprised, with deadly effect, a large body of Turks moving down the valley.

On our way up the other side, we passed through a large gully (Rest Gully) and found several dugouts with caved-in roofs of rusting corrugated iron. All around was broken litter from the army supplies—tin cans and bizarre heavy fired-clay pots, which looked very much out of place on a battlefield.

By the time we reached the top, the sun was getting low in the west. Dark, creeping shadows put an eerie cast on every silent crag and ravine. Clearly, we needed to quicken our pace.

Russell's Top is a gently rising, long broad hill. This made the going easier, apart from our struggle crossing the many collapsed trenches that went at all angles. Suddenly, Charles stopped by a small hollow in the hillside. Seeing him cocking his head this way and that in puzzlement, I called on him to hurry but was brought up sharply myself on hearing him reply, "I think there is someone here."

Traced out in the earth by a succession of shaded colors was the outline of a body lying in a fetal position. The ends of his arms and legs faded into the surrounding dust. Small crumbling pieces of bone were ranged along the sad image. Corroded brass fasteners, a belt buckle and a shirt collar stud, were all that was left of his uniform. Quickly, we raised a tripod of branches nearby as a marker, then pressed on to our next objective—the "Nek."

With the sun setting red behind us, we arrived in a blaze of bloodstained light on that infamous broad ridge of exposed moorland known as the "Nek." It was here that a horrific event took place (so dramatically portrayed in the final scenes of that memorable Australian film *Gallipoli*.) In an operation gone wrong from the start, four waves of incredibly brave men were needlessly sent to certain death.

The enormity of their sacrifice is overwhelming in the serene atmosphere that Turkish gardeners have created in the tree-fringed cemetery. I'll never forget the mixture of emotions I felt as I watched Charles reading aloud the inscriptions on the headstones. In the stillness of the gathering dusk, that youthful roll call sounded a most poignant yet fitting wake.

It seemed fitting too that, like the Anzacs we were following, we found the goal of Chunuk Bair, so tantalizingly near, just beyond our reach. With darkness approaching, we would have to leave it for another day.

Skirting round the side of a small hill (Baby 700), we reached the sealed road that runs south down the middle of "no man's land." As we walked we could look into the shadowy remains of both the Anzac trenches on our right and the Turkish on our left; they were that close. Charles was still full of energy and kept darting from one side into the other.

It was dark by the time we reached the other celebrated killing ground, Lone Pine. It certainly has plenty of company now, for a well-established forest crowds in at either side of the steep and twisting road. At the entrance to the large cemetery, we had the good fortune to meet a "lone Australian" from Wollongong standing in the shadows. He was waiting for a taxi that picked him up at the end of each day he spent on the battlefields, researching for a book he was writing on the campaign.

Not only did he generously offer us a lift back, but as if to crown our day, he gave us an authoritative history lesson on the route we had chosen, which by luck had followed near enough the way taken by the advancing troops on that fateful first day.

Kapatan came down to see us off in the morning, and we promised to visit him again the next season. Our next port of call was just 15 miles away, giving us plenty of time for a leisurely sail along the coast. Ghosting in around the shore of Anzac Cove was strangely satisfying. We looked up the dark, brooding chasm of Shrapnel Valley and traced our route of yesterday across that wild scene. Farther along the land flattened out, but our gaze was always drawn back to those quiet mountains that seemed to change shape by the minute. From this perspective we could see the full extent of the battleground, each notorious feature tagged by a vivid white cemetery.

As we followed the curving coast round to the northwest, the offshore breeze hauled round to the north and freshened to 15 to 20 knots. This was fine until we cleared the southern point of Suvla Bay; then, heeled hard over, *Alea* had to make long slanting tacks across that desolate bay to reach the lee of the northern rocky point.

This is the bay where the Allies landed, three months after the initial invasion, in a very promising bid to break the stalemate. But again, poor leadership produced another "Y" beach–type fiasco. This time, after landing unopposed, the commanding officer deemed his troops needed to rest. An incredible twenty-six hours later, the first single company was tentatively ordered to advance inland. Needless to say, the Turkish commanders made better use of the time given to them, and the "rest" is now history.

For our part, we anchored for lunch by the rusting hulks of two naval wrecks and let our imaginations run free. Then, setting daydreams aside, I turned my mind to the last leg of the day's run. The northerly was still blowing on the other side of the point, with only the occasional draft disturbing our shelter. With increasing high clouds, I decided to replace the genoa with the working jib and lock down the centerplate. Then, with sails a-ripple, we motored along past the wild rock jumble of Suvla Point. It looked bleak and lonely, which made the white cut stone war memorial erected near the end look the most forlorn I've ever seen. Another feature that made a particular impression on me was the seemingly insignificant light beacon perched precariously on top of the last crowning rock slab. Did I somehow know that it was soon to become the object of my most ardent prayers?

With a sudden crack of the sails, *Alea* heeled and went romping out over a lumpy sea. Sufficiently clear of the breaking shoals that lie off the northern point, I put about and got a good heading straight up the Gulf of Saros. From the point the coastal range grew steadily higher, with dark, sheer cliffs rising straight from the sea. After an hour we hauled past an isolated coven of black rocks, gnashing in a flurry of white froth almost a mile out from the foot of the cliffs.

Soon after, the wind began to veer to the northeast, forcing *Alea* to "dig in" and start clawing her way up in long zigzagging tacks. After another hour of this I began anxiously looking for the harbor behind every headland, each growing progressively more shadowy and dim in the failing light. I took consolation in the brisk way *Alea* was handling the steadily increasing wind and waves. Charles was reading down below, oblivious to his surroundings, although he now had to hold his book up to the cabin light.

Near the end of a seaward tack, I glanced over at a headland to judge the moment to go about, and out from behind it appeared a large fishing boat. Thank God—the harbor at last! The vessel turned and raced off down the coast, passing between us and an outlying reef. I put *Alea* about and we seemed to fly on over the breaking waves that swept right into the large, gloomy bay.

With Charles on deck as lookout, we skirted round the steep, dusky headland, expecting the harbor breakwater to appear at any moment. The indistinct shapes of houses came into view, then the dark hulks of several fishing boats, all drawn high up on a foaming shingle beach. I was mortified—there was no harbor and no shelter. A group of men, all in dim silhouette, stepped out onto the foreshore and watched us approach. I started the motor and, luffing round into the wind, made a pass as near to the shore as I dared. "Liman?" I called, to which most gave a "sharp round the corner" hand signal, then the shaking of the arm in the air that indicates "it's a long way back."

They of course meant Suvla Bay. This was grim, but we had no choice—we would have to go back, and the sooner the better, before the weather deteriorated further. I waved to the ghostlike figures on the beach and headed for the open sea. *Alea* went bounding along as we were now on a far better point of sailing. One of my main fears was getting past the areas of offshore rocks. They had looked forbidding enough in daylight, but in the growing darkness they took on an almost predatory nature.

Once out past the headland I set *Alea* to the northwest for sea room and called Charles up to take the tiller while I charted a proper course. To my surprise, he appeared in the companionway looking like a veteran seaman—even wearing his life jacket. It was the first time he had put it on without prompting; obviously the situation was having an effect on him.

Quickly, I ducked below and did the needful. In twenty minutes' time we could chance turning to the southwest to pick up the beacon light on Suvla Point. Charles's call—"Dad! I can't hold the tiller!"—sent me dashing up the companionway steps. He was stretched out horizontally athwart the cockpit with the tiller in a desperate embrace, his woolen hat tipped over one eye. I checked the compass; still on course—that's my boy!

I was soon having trouble myself, not with the tiller but seeing the compass to steer by. Our world had shrunk to the confines of a wild, tossing deck, vaguely discernible in the dim loom of the navigation lights. I cursed myself for being so slack in not rigging up a light over the compass. This was all the more galling because I had bought all the necessary bits and pieces for a compass light less than a week ago in Çanakkale. Nevertheless, I soon discovered that I could steer the course fairly well by judging the wind direction on the side of my face. This required only occasional checks with the torch, which allowed me to retain some vestige of night vision.

When the twenty minutes were up, I felt very uneasy about changing onto the new course in the dark and waited another five before casting the die. I pulled the tiller over, and *Alea* swept round in the blackness and instantly took on a quieter, rolling motion. With the wind almost directly astern, I squared out the sails and settled on course. Then almost immediately I got into a right pickle.

Trying the same "wind on cheek" steering technique, I discovered I was no use at it on a straight run. Suddenly, the boom came crashing over and *Alea* heeled violently to starboard. Frantically, I shone the torch on the compass again—we were heading straight inshore. Quickly, I helmed *Alea* around until she jibed back on course. It may have been the shock or the fact that I'd had the torch on too long, but when I switched it off again, I was completely blind and disoriented. Suddenly I found myself sprawling on the floor of the cockpit as *Alea* jibed again. Charles managed to dim the torch sufficiently with his handkerchief that some of my night vision returned—enough at least to see the white flash of the breaking waves out on the heaving blackness.

Apart from the occasional flicker of lightning to the north, we saw nothing else—no moon, stars, or even clouds. Then, seemingly hours later, the Suvla Point flashing red beacon mercifully appeared off our port bow. I held on course until its demon firefly bursts were abeam. Then, keeping it square off, I slowly tracked *Alea* around to port in a large clearance circle. Again it seemed like hours that we watched that jumping spark as *Alea* tossed and rolled. Then suddenly the bright white loom of a light appeared, highlighting the black silhouette of a steep rocky cape no more than 200 meters away. Almost at the same time the wind completely dropped, forcing us to continue round under motor. There before us was a fishing boat, so brightly floodlit that it appeared to be floating in midair. Loud, quaking Turkish music echoed out toward us as we glided over the millpond calm of the bay.

We spent a quiet night on both anchors shackled in line. This "overkill," deemed imperative in the unease of darkness, seemed quite unnecessary when we awoke next morning to find ourselves in a small sheltered cove just under Suvla Point.

It wasn't long before we were taking our leave of that point for a second time. It was also farewell to Gallipoli and all her ghosts. Yet in spite of all its disquieting surprises, my sentiments were the same as Charles's: I wouldn't have missed it for the world.

Thirty-Three
A Welcome in the Dock

WE CROSSED THE GULF OF SAROS with a gentle easterly drawing on the sails. By the time Gökçe and the last high peaks of Gallipoli had disappeared astern, the low, featureless Thracian coast lay to starboard. To the west, the bright autumn sun was setting behind the Greek island of Samothrace, highlighting that colossal mountain peak in a stupendous halo of radiating shafts of light. It was under this fateful aurora that we sailed into the so-called "port" of Enez to find yet another empty harbor.

However, this one was unfinished. The quaysides were a wasteland of bulldozed red earth dappled with extensive rain puddles, presumably the result of the distant lightning we had observed the night before.

We moored bow-to the quay, hitching our warps to reinforcing rods protruding from the harbor wall. While Charles completed this, I tightened in the stern anchor warp so that our bow stood off about 2 meters from the quay. With darkness falling fast, we retired below to prepare our bachelors' supper.

Just as Charles dropped the last of the ingredients into the wok, we felt the boat move rapidly forward and strike the quay with a jarring *thump!* Instinctively I dived to save the wok and the freestanding gas-bottle stove from toppling over. Charles shot up the companionway, and as I followed I caught the anxiety in his subdued voice: "Dad . . . it's soldiers!"

I was horrified to see, in the dazzling glare of several vehicles' headlights, twelve to fifteen heavily armed soldiers grouped along the quay. Five or six were pulling on our mooring lines as though in a dogged tug-of-war, while another leveled a large machine gun at us, the ammunition belt of which hung in heavy coils about his body.

A surprisingly young-looking officer, with a drawn pistol, began shouting at me in English, "Get out!—Come out!" over and over again, even as I stepped down onto the quay. Then he changed his tune to German, saying that something was *verboten* and that he wanted my *pazz-paper*.

I gestured that our passports were in the boat, at which he started shooing me back aboard. I climbed back over the bow rail and in quick succession six army-issue mud-caked boots crashed aboard—one demolishing my port navigation light again.

I tried to protest, but the officer impatiently waved me on. Hurriedly, I undid the boom-tent to save it from damage but was too slow in removing the cockpit seat cushions, which instantly received several yeti-sized, muddy footprints.

The officer examined my New Zealand passport briskly, then, waving it in the air, he said, "Commandant!" and began to order us both out again. "Why?" I asked, and to my consternation he replied, "You sleep soldier's house tonight!" I protested, but he was unmoved. I cited the safety of my boat, to which he countered, "Ve guard!" "We haven't eaten!"—"Ve feed!" There was no way out.

We were herded off toward the blinding stare of an army jeep. It had a canvas top that allowed entry to the back seats only by climbing over the front ones. Just in the few steps it took to reach the door, our feet got heavy with clinging wet mud. Seeing Charles hesitate as he realized the mess he would make of the passenger seat, I said: "Don't worry about it, son—we'll give them some of their own medicine." There was no need to tell him twice, and I made sure I dithered sufficiently on the upholstery too.

One of the soldiers followed and squeezed in on the far side of Charles, while the officer plunked himself down in the passenger seat. Purposefully the jeep began to jolt over the wasteland and up a rough country road.

Utterly frustrated at being detained like this, I tried to recall how Enez had been recommended to me by the harbormaster of Kaba Tepe. I might have known his "advice" for this harbor would be as disastrous as it had been for last night's anchorage.

While I sat dejected, the officer, thinking it was now time for some polite chitchat, twisted round in his seat and surveyed his prisoners with a smug, patronizing smile. Knowing it was more prudent to start with Charles, he began asking him all the usual questions you would put to a youngster. Charles answered politely and tentatively at first, then, warming to the friendly attention, threw in some of his Turkish. This of course greatly impressed them, which brought the guard and the driver into the now jovial conversation.

This was too much for me, so rounding on poor Charles, I blew my top: "Keep quiet! Don't you realize these people are taking us away against our will!" At this the officer turned and faced the front, but the guard burst out laughing and, putting his arm around Charles's shoulder, gave him a consolatory hug. I instantly snatched hold of his cuff and threw his arm back, whereupon a stony silence prevailed for the rest of the journey.

Ten minutes later we stopped in the forecourt of an imposing stone barracks where armed soldiers stood on guard. As the officer led us down a long, brightly lit corridor, I noticed with satisfaction that his backside was quite wet with red mud.

He ushered us into a small office and left us with two very jovial NCOs. They took an instant shine to Charles and began fussing over some mud that had splashed on his pants. After trying to brush it off, they gestured that they wanted to take him some other place to wash it off. I found it impossible to maintain my truculence in the face of this almost gushy concern and agreed but indicated that I would come too. Like excited children, the two NCOs bore Charles off down the corridor as if he were some great trophy.

They took him in past a large common room, where he was introduced to the off-duty assembly of television viewers. When he was asked to say something to them in Turkish, he looked round at me rather sheepishly. I had to give in, much to the amusement of our still-attendant guard.

After his linguistic performance, six more instant fans joined the retinue through to a kitchen, where his royal person was cleaned up to everyone's satisfaction. The return procession went via a canteen, where he was invited to chose a chocolate sweet from a rack of confectionary, then given one more for good measure.

Back in the office we were rejoined by our officer, who had meantime changed his pants, and I suspect also had a peep at his English phrase book, for he trotted out a very priggish, "Vould you like some tea?" This was brought to us on the double by a young soldier who showed almost white-faced animal fear at the task. On entering the room, he rushed forward to place the tray on the desk before jumping back to take up the most exaggerated, sinew-stressing posture of attention I have ever seen.

He gave an encore of this performance when he returned with the promised "Ve feed" banquet—a plateful of cold beans in oil and dry bread. It tasted as bad as it sounds, but by this time we were both very hungry. The sophistication of having our tea served in large tumblers was due to our officer having heard that the British use "gross" cups (in the "big" sense).

Then it was our officer's turn to do a stint of the tea-boy's rigor mortis when a middle-aged man, dressed in civilian clothes and resembling a bespectacled family doctor, swept into the room. He looked me over warily while our officer rattled off to him in Turkish. "Sprechen Sie Deutsch?" he asked me, and when I answered no, he pulled a face.

After a brief discussion, they brought in another nervous young soldier to act as our interpreter. Flushed with acute embarrassment and some hesitation as to what to do with his rifle, the soldier explained to me in pidgin English that I had entered a military harbor in a restricted border zone and that I was suspected of spying.

It soon became apparent that what fired their suspicion was our Greek destination. The "Doc" asked so many questions about why I hadn't gone straight there from Gallipoli that even to me, the excuse of arranging a "grand entrance" to my wife's hometown for tomorrow seemed rather weak.

Next, he wanted to see the boat papers, which required us all to be transported back to the harbor. This time Memhet, the interpreter, sat in the back with us. Although sympathetic, he was at pains to let me know that he could do little to help because of his lowly rank. His solemn mood prompted me to ask him what was likely to happen, to which he replied apologetically, "You go to . . . aaah . . . special house . . . how you say . . . law house? . . . a Jug?"

"What!? You don't mean jail!?—prison!?"

My panic clearly unnerved him, and he rummaged out a small phrase book from his pocket. After several "thumbing throughs" he brightened, "Aaah! . . . Yes! . . . A Jug!" I checked where his finger was on the page—a sodding judge.

This news was a shock, for our situation was obviously a lot more serious than I had imagined. The rest of the journey passed in a dazed haze, until I was brought to my senses when we jolted to a halt in front of *Alea*.

Backed up beside her was a truck, with a diving compressor operating in the back. Someone was standing up on the cab shining a searchlight down on a man feeding a thick hose and line over the edge of the quay. A masked diver was submerged just off the boat's stern. The eerie glow from his torch illuminating the depths made the whole scene look like something from a science fiction film. I was dumbfounded; what on earth could they be looking for? I felt the stomach-sinking dread that they might confiscate our boat, so close to its goal.

After all we had been through, our trip had taken on a persona of its own. In the blinking of an eye, I could see it all, a kaleidoscope of past memories and future dreams tinged now by the sharp hollow of regret for failing it. What on earth had possessed me to turn in here? How stupid of me! I might have guessed these people would be hypersensitive about their border area. I had really done it this time.

The two sentries dragged *Alea*'s bow in so that we could board. The combination of oily beans and chocolate Charles had been given back at the army barracks were beginning to have their "surprise effect" on him. So while he rushed off to the head, the Doc started searching the cabin. I showed him the boat papers, but he was more interested in the children's scrapbooks and diaries. In fact, it was very odd how he scrutinized any piece of paper with writing on it, especially after implying that he couldn't speak English.

While he flicked through our library, we could hear the diver moving about under the hull and tapping on the keel. I looked in on Charles and asked how he was. He was clearly feeling better, for on hearing the diver, he said with a mischievous grin, "It's a pity that the sea toilet wasn't connected, as I could give him a nasty flush!"

Later, with our pockets stuffed full of toilet paper and the Doc apparently satisfied, we trooped off ashore. Thankfully, I saw the diver shaking his head to the Doc—he hadn't found anything incriminating.

After seeing the extremes they were going to in order to check me out, I thought it was time I started being a little more diplomatic. So, as we entered the foyer back at the barracks, I stopped by an old photograph on the wall and asked, "Is this Ataturk?" Immediately there were proud smiles all round and the Doc grew quite animated, telling us, through our interpreter Memhet, when and where the photograph was taken. Then to my surprise we were ushered up another corridor that led to a heavy oak-paneled door. As it was locked, orders were screamed from one end of the building to the other until one harassed soldier came running with the keys.

It was a huge boardroom, all plushly decorated with flags and heavy, polished furniture. The Doc proudly showed us a large painting of Ataturk hanging on the wall. To my horror, just next to the picture was a huge map of the border area. It was covered with little pin flags, presumably showing the disposition of their defenses. I thought, Typical—they think me a spy, so they show me this.

I quickly averted my eyes and in order to show how impressed I was, I said to Memhet, "Wonderful—what a great soldier he was!" But instead of translating it for the Doc, Memhet replied to me, "Just another dictator!" I couldn't believe my ears, for if the Doc did in fact understand English, poor Memhet would be in deep trouble. Apparently to say anything disparaging about

Ataturk is still against the law in Turkey. The Doc looked quite deadpan, so I blurted out, "Ataturk—vunderbar! vunderbar!" which got him nodding and smiling again.

With Memhet's indiscretion seemingly undetected, it was back to the office for the typing up of the Doc's report—in triplicate—and it took forever.

Just as Charles's eyelids were beginning to droop, a very short, stocky man marched in, causing all the soldiers to jump to their feet. He looked a very mean sergeant major type and seemed most put out when the officer asked him to allocate beds for us. Ranting and raving, he stormed out of the office, to return a short time later to rattle out a few orders. Memhet was snapped forward to explain that we would be taken back to *Alea* for the night. I checked my watch—it was almost midnight.

I didn't get to thank Memhet for his help, because as we got into the jeep the officer ordered him away and we never saw him again. When we stopped on the quay the officer indicated that he would pick us up again tomorrow morning. There was no point in trying to ask, "What for?" Besides, at that moment reaching our bunks seemed infinitely more important.

The next morning, Friday, November 16, I got up early and scrubbed the mud from *Alea*'s decks. As compensation for polluting their environment, I fed the fish the congealed contents of our abandoned wok. At 8:30 A.M., the officer arrived to drive us back to Enez.

Everything looked so different in the bright light of day. Entering the town, we passed the ruin of a Norman-type castle that certainly looked in keeping with the dilapidated, almost medieval appearance of the town. The only thing I recognized from the previous night was the facade of the barracks, as we swept to a halt outside its main entrance.

We were shown into the spacious office of the district commander, who was standing behind his desk as if he had just risen from bed. My first impression was of a middle-aged man with a seedy complexion and decidedly overweight. His uniform was made of the same coarse battle-dress material as the others, but his was terribly crumpled and his shirttail was hanging out. In broken English he welcomed us affably, shaking my hand, and showed us to leather-upholstered chairs in front of his desk.

He then started shouting at the officer who was standing at attention by the door. Not quite the full-blown rigor mortis, for he kept nervously shifting his weight from one foot to the other as if trying desperately not to wet himself. In very short shift he was sent running from the room with a very loud flea in his ear.

The commander now slumped down at his desk and peered at us as if through the fog of a massive hangover. His mouth formed as if to speak, then sighed away. I smiled encouragingly, and he brightened as though he had found what he was looking for, "Ahh—tea?" Our refreshment was brought with the usual martial haste. We drank in partial silence, for now the commander had remembered his hangover and started making soft groaning noises and rubbing his hands over his face in the roughest manner imaginable.

We sat like this for some time and I sensed he was waiting for something. To pass the time I tried to assess his age and to my surprise it dawned on me that this aging man was probably no more than thirty. Sensing my scrutiny he suddenly focused on me and asked if I was married. I jumped at the opportunity to explain that my wife and daughter would be waiting for me this afternoon, and that if I was to be on time, I would need to leave quite soon. He didn't seem to understand and replied that he had recently got married, adding that we should come and visit them both at their home in Çanakkale.

I thanked him, and silence descended again. After a pause, a young soldier appeared to act as interpreter. Now the commander asked the oddest questions: Which country did we like best—Greece or Turkey? Which had the best soldiers? And when he discovered that I hoped to teach English in Greece, he offered me a job teaching his troops in Enez. To this I said, "I'll ask my wife."

Our rigid interpreter could have certainly done with a few lessons. For every second question, he had to ask the commander's permission to refer to a dictionary he kept in his breast pocket. Each time the correct word was found he would laboriously fasten his "little gem" away, ready for the next time.

This chat session came to an end when the officer returned with the typewritten report. The commander said that this was a statement that I had "entered a forbidden military zone," and passed me the pen to sign. Before committing myself, I asked when we would be allowed to leave, to which I got the reply that we had to go first to another building, for a mere formality, then we could leave. I signed!

We were then left to wait for ages in a side office near the entrance hall. I grew impatient, and every time I heard footsteps in the hallway I would go out into the adjoining corridors in the hope of seeing someone I could appeal to. But all I got was shrugs from the uncomprehending passersby.

One of these "lobbying" excursions led me past a large window that looked out onto the back parade yard. Not 10 meters away was a squad of some twenty soldiers drawn up in that incredibly rigid attention stance. The little sergeant major from the previous night was slowly moving along the front rank and having an "individual word" with each soldier. This entailed grasping the head of the soldier between his hands, then, while shouting, drawing his hands back along the sides of their cheeks in order to pucker and distort his face. He would end this pep talk by suddenly throwing his hands wide apart and bringing them sharply together again on the soldier's face, as if clashing a pair of cymbals. Then, leaving one very red and smarting face, he moved on to the next rigid and very white one. An officer was in attendance, but he contorted his own face as he kept walking away in short circles in an effort to control himself from open laughter.

Then it was back to the hallway for more infernal waiting. One consolation was that Charles seemed to be bearing up; at least he had brought a book to read. I could only sit by the window and sulk. A rising easterly was swaying the trees outside. If we were to keep our appointment at Alexandroúpolis, that wind needed to be filling *Alea*'s sails—now!

Finally at 1:30 the officer appeared and motioned for us to follow him. We walked a short distance down the street to what I took to be the town hall. Here an official typed up our "file" and stapled it into a new, pink cardboard folder that sported a set of blue ribbons as fastenings. Then, holding it aloft like a banner, he led our small procession into a courtroom.

The judge, a fatherly, middle-aged man wearing a black gown over a smart suit, came over and shook our hands—"Welcome! Welcome!" Unfortunately, by this stage I was feeling pretty downcast and very resentful, so I failed to recognize this friendly gesture for what it was. More stunned by it, I let the judge lead us to the dock, where he introduced me to a small, sad-looking man already seated behind the dock. He was the local schoolteacher and was to act as interpreter.

The judge, piously clasping his hands, started the proceedings off, "Vould you like some tea?" This was the "last straw"—exasperated, I refused the offer and told him we were being held against our will and that all we wanted was to leave—as quickly as possible! The judge was sympathetic and solicitously remarked, "It is the army way—they don't understand tourists," and again tried to coax me into having a glass of tea. But I was adamant—I wanted away!

Seeing that I was inconsolable, they decided to rush through the proceedings. The schoolteacher asked, "Why did you come here?" I explained again, even suggesting they telephone the harbormaster at Kaba Tepe to confirm my story. This the schoolteacher translated for the typist. I then added that if they didn't want people entering their harbor, they should put up a sign at the entrance forbidding it. The judge thought that this was such a good idea he translated it himself. When this was typed in, the judge was given the transcript to sign, and apparently that was it. He came over and shook my hand again, saying he was sorry for all the trouble.

After thanking the schoolteacher, I found myself with Charles outside the town hall, presumably a free man. I was just gathering my thoughts as to what to do next when the officer appeared at the top of the entrance steps with my passport. I smiled with relief and put my hand out to receive it, but he indicated that he would only give it back at the harbor. This suited us, for it meant he proposed giving us a lift.

It was three o'clock now, so the girls would be already waiting. Even with the favorable easterly, it would take us at least two hours to reach Alexandroúpolis. The jeep stopped in front of *Alea* for the last time and our equally thankful captor handed me the passport. What a wonderful feeling it was to walk away from him and climb aboard the sanctuary of *Alea*.

While Charles steered us round one circuit of the pool, I raised the sails. Then, without a backward glance, we literally bolted out thought the exit. A blustery 15- to 20-knot easterly was stirring up whitecaps close inshore, but it backed to the northeast and moderated once we had cleared the Turkish coast.

I held *Alea* firmly to the compass course, laid to the east of Alexandroúpolis. This was to avoid wasting time making up against the wind if we took on too much leeway to the west. But I needn't have worried, for the wind was fair and *Alea* true. Soon the angular jumble of Alexandroupolis lay off to port. To add to the moment, several brightly painted Greek fishing boats altered course to come over and give us a friendly "Kahlee-spehrah," good afternoon.

As we neared the harbor, we could just make out two small figures standing right on the end of the breakwater by the port entrance light, waving wildly. Despite the slackening breeze *Alea* rushed on, as if also swept up in the enthusiasm of the home-stretch. Charles dashed below, to reappear a second later with "Yo-Yo," the ship's monkey, much to Victoria's delight. There was a lot of shouting to and fro, which only stopped when a challenge was given as to who would be first round to the inner dock.

In the shelter of the outer harbor, I turned *Alea* into the wind and went forward to drop the sails for the last time. I felt so proud of her—she had certainly seen us through. And there, positively beaming at the tiller, was my boy, who had truly seen me through—I couldn't help but grin too. In the gathering dusk, my hero steered us through into the inner harbor, where willing hands waited to catch the mooring lines. It was 6:30 P.M., and the girls had been waiting since 2:00. After a lot of delicious hugs and kisses, we hastily packed our sleeping bags and set off to Customs. With Despina being a local girl, the only formality was a round of hearty handshakes and a chorus of "Kalossorisaté," welcome. Then it was off to the in-laws' for more hugs and kisses.

So there it was—hardly a textbook voyage, but after 3,000 nautical miles we had finally made it to Greece and the awaiting Aegean. Yet in the glorious hubbub of our family's reunion, I couldn't decide whether I was now on the threshold of my dream or just awakening from one. And when the proper time came for dreaming, at the end of that incredible day, it was very much like the way the whole adventure had begun: on the floor of a bare, empty flat, but this time with the prospect of furniture gathering in the morn.

and farther down the track

With the last full stop struck in our tale, I must concede that eight years have slipped under my keel since our odyssey to Greece. To everyone's surprise, we are all still together. Whether this is due to our trip or in spite of it seems to be the question on people's minds. We were never in any doubt: a habit of "time-out" *with* your family is hard to break.

The following year I managed to coax Despina back aboard for our planned cruise around the Aegean. And despite the odd moment of nautical or matrimonial mishap, we completed the voyage with a smile and a nice tan. In fact, three years later she even volunteered to crew the first leg of *Alea*'s return to England, but of course that's all another story.

So, when Charles reached high school age, it was back to the real world and the grindstone. Unsealing the room in which we had stored our furniture was like entering a pharaoh's tomb and finding it full of old friends. Settling into our home again after living together for much of three years in a space no bigger than our hallway, I felt the isolation on finding myself alone in a room. But this was more than compensated when I lay in bed on a stormy night, safe in the knowledge that no anchor need be checked.

People ask: Why did we do it? What did we gain most? This is never easy to answer. On one level we wanted to see old friends, family, and places. On another, we wanted to have more time together as a family, to enjoy our children at a very special age. In this busy world of ours the enjoyment of parenthood as well as childhood is being increasingly undermined. The family, bombarded by so many external pressures, is becoming just a stressful time-and-motion exercise. By the time adolescence raises its many heads, the die is cast. There is no going back, and parenting inevitably gets harder. While our children were still young, we adopted a different lifestyle, made time available, and actively sought to tip the balance in our favor.

On the more practical side of our children's development, we were worried about how they would fare returning to school after such a long absence. It was soon apparent that it was not a question of what they had missed in the past three years, but what on earth their schoolmates had being doing. Within the first term Charles and Victoria shot to the top of the class, and there they remained with glowing reports for the rest of their school careers. Charles is twenty now and studying ancient Greek and economics at Canterbury University. Little Victoria is eighteen and taller than both her parents. She has set her sights on becoming an architect and, with the same resourceful industry she has always shown, is beavering away to this end at Canterbury.

What of the future? Well, who can say. Until Charles and Victoria are ready to cast off to follow their own stars, I guess Despina and I will be on "anchor watch" for some time yet. Perhaps *Alea* is waiting somewhere to take us on another of life's sideshows. Keep a weather eye peeled for us.

Les Horn
"Avonneuk"
Christchurch

about the author

Les Horn was born in Aberdeen, Scotland, in 1948, the son of a village blacksmith. His education commenced when he left school, at the age of fifteen, and is still progressing, he says. After a five-year carpentry apprenticeship he moved to London and became an architectural draftsman. There he met his future sailing companion Despina in 1970 and was so taken by her he married her twice. Emigration to New Zealand saw him learning to sail and graduating from Christchurch Teachers' College with distinction in 1977. Following an eleven-year career as a high school teacher, he retired to pursue his love of the outdoors and storytelling. Les and Despina Horn live in a quiet corner of Christchurch with their children Charles and Victoria.

Despina under the symbol of London.

Istanbul's answer to Cape Canaveral.

A peaceful anchorage on a flood lake in Romania.

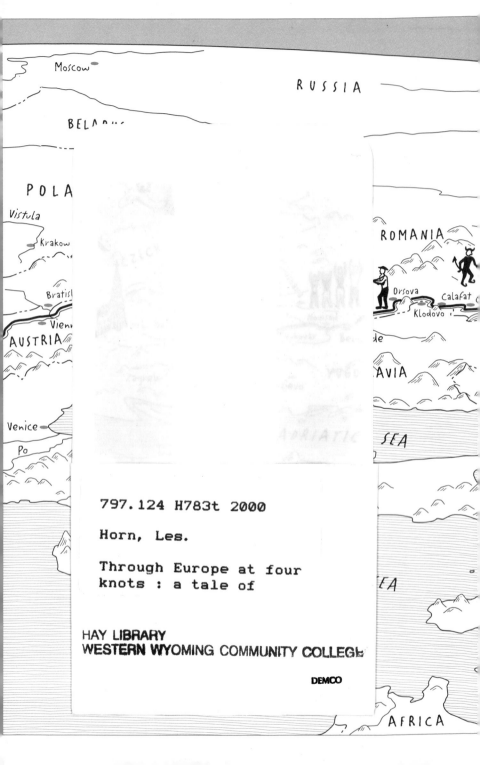

797.124 H783t 2000

Horn, Les.

Through Europe at four
knots : a tale of

HAY LIBRARY
WESTERN WYOMING COMMUNITY COLLEGE

DEMCO